Psychological Processes
in Pattern Recognition

This is the first volume in a series entitled

ACADEMIC PRESS SERIES IN COGNITION AND PERCEPTION

Under the Editorship of E. C. Carterette and M. P. Friedman, *University of California, Los Angeles*

PSYCHOLOGICAL PROCESSES
IN PATTERN RECOGNITION

Stephen K. Reed

Department of Psychology
Case Western Reserve University
Cleveland, Ohio

ACADEMIC PRESS   New York and London   1973
A Subsidiary of Harcourt Brace Jovanovich, Publishers

ACADEMIC PRESS, INC.
111 Fifth Avenue, New York, New York 10003

United Kingdom Edition published by
ACADEMIC PRESS, INC. (LONDON) LTD.
24/28 Oval Road, London NW1

Library of Congress Cataloging in Publication Data

Reed, Stephen K
        Psychological processes in pattern recognition.

        (Cognition and perception)
        Bibliography: p.
                1.   Human information processing.   2.   Pattern
perception.   I.   Title.   [DNLM: 1.   Form perception.
2.   Models: Psychological. WW103 R326p 1973]
BF455.R34   152.1'423   72-13620
ISBN 0−12−585350−5

To Karen

Contents

vii

Preface

Zusne (1970), in his book on form perception, suggests that research on the psychological aspects of pattern recognition is so extensive that entire books are needed to focus on particular aspects of the problem. This is reflected in recent books by Gibson (1969) on perceptual learning, Dodwell (1970) on the physiological aspects of pattern recognition, and Moray (1969) on attention. The present book continues in this tradition by focusing on information-processing models of pattern recognition. The emphasis is on visual pattern recognition, but I hope that many of the issues raised will be relevant to a more general theory of pattern recognition. My own theoretical bias is toward formal models, and various examples of these are included. However, in most cases, I have tried to describe the models verbally, so there are few equations in the book.

The book is intended primarily for graduate students and psychologists interested in the problems of pattern recognition and human information processing. For people who are unfamiliar with this theoretical approach, I would recommend Lindsay and Norman's (1972) *Human Information Processing* at an introductory level, Norman's (1969) *Mem-*

ory and Attention at an intermediate level, and Neisser's (1967) *Cognitive Psychology* at an advanced level.

I would like to thank my editors, Professors Morton P. Friedman and Edward C. Carterette for their critical reading of the manuscript and for their many useful suggestions. Lloyd Nakatani read selected chapters. Karen Reed, Janet Hawkins, and Sharon Laurenti typed the manuscript. I completed the first draft as a postdoctoral fellow of the National Institute of Mental Health (NIMH) at the University of Sussex, Brighton, England. I am grateful to Professor N. S. Sutherland for sponsoring this fellowship. United States NIMH grant MH-21115 enabled me to complete the manuscript in its final form.

Acknowledgments

Figure 1.1. From: Shriffrin, R. M., and Atkinson, R. C. Storage and retrieval processes in long-term memory. *Psychological Review,* 1969, **76**, 179–193. Fig. 1. Copyright 1969 by the American Psychological Association and reproduced by permission.

Figures 2.1 and 2.3. From: *Principles of Perceptual Learning and Development,* by Eleanor J. Gibson. Figs. 5–5 and 8–4. Copyright © 1969. By permission of Appleton-Century-Crofts, Educational Division, Meredith Corporation.

Figure 2.2. From: Gibson, J. J., and Gibson, E. Perceptual learning; Differentiation or enrichment. *Psychological Review,* 1955, **62**, 32–41. Fig. 1. Copyright 1955 by the American Psychological Association and reproduced by permission.

Figure 2.4. From: Pick, A. Improvement of visual and tactual form discrimination. *Journal of Experimental Psychology,* 1965, **69**, 331–339. Fig. 1. Copyright 1965 by the American Psychological Association and reproduced by permission.

Figure 2.5. Reprinted with permission from B. J. Fellows, *The discrimination process and development,* Fig. 14.1. Copyright 1968, Pergamon Press, Ltd.

Figures 2.6 and 2.7. From: Vurpillot, E. The development of scanning strategies and their relation to visual differentiation. *Journal of Experimental Child Psychology,* 1968, 6, 622–650. Figs. 1 and 5.

Figure 2.8. From: Saltz, E., and Sigel, I. Concept Overdiscrimination in Children. *Journal of Experimental Psychology,* 1967, 73, 7–8. Fig. 2. Copyright 1967 by the American Psychological Association and reproduced by permission.

Figure 2.9. From:- Attneave, F. Transfer of experience with a class schema to identification learning of patterns and shapes. *Journal of Experimental Psychology,* 1957, **54**, 81–88. Fig. 2. Copyright 1957 by the American Psychological Association and reproduced by permission.

Figure 2.10. From: Franks, J. J., and Bransford, J. D. Abstraction of visual patterns. *Journal of Experimental Psychology,* 1971, **90**, 65–74. Fig. 1. Copyright 1971 by the American Psychological Association and reproduced by permission.

Figure 2.11. From: Posner, M. I., Goldsmith, R. and Welton, K. E. Perceived distance and the classification of distorted patterns. *Journal of Experimental Psychology,* 1967, **73**, 28–38. Fig. 1. Copyright 1967 by the American Psychological Association and reproduced by permission.

Figures 3.1 and 3.2. From: Asso, D., and Wyke, M. Visual discrimination and verbal comprehension of spatial relations by young children. *British Journal of Psychology,* 1970, **61**, 99-107. Figs. 1 and 2.

Figure 3.3. From: Narasimhan, R., and Reddy, V. S. N. A generative model for handprinted English letters and its computer implementation. *ICC Bulletin,* 1967, **6**, 275–287. Fig. 1.

Figures 3.4 and 3.5. From: Guzmán, A. Decomposition of a visual scene into three-dimensional bodies. In A. Grasselli (Ed.), *Automatic interpretation and classification of images.* New York: Academic Press, 1969.

Figure 3.6. From: Sutherland, N. S. Object recognition. In E. C. Carterette and M. P. Friedman (Eds.), *Handbook of Perception,* Vol. 3. New York: Academic Press, 1973.

Figure 4.1. Reprinted with permission of author and publisher: Nickerson, R. S. "Same"–"different" response times with multi-attribute stimulus differences. *Perceptual and Motor Skills,* 1967, **24**, 543–554. Fig. 1.

Figure 4.2. From: Bradshaw, J. L., and Wallace, G. Models for the processing and identification of faces. *Perception and Psychophysics,* 1971, **9**, 443–448. Fig. 1.

Figure 4.3. From: Sternberg, S. Two operations in character recognition: Some evidence from reaction time measurements. *Perception and Psychophysics,* 1967, **2**, 45–53. Fig. 4.

Figure 4.4. From: Juola, J. F., Fischler, I., Wood, C. T., and Atkinson, R. C. Recognition time for information stored in long-term memory. *Perception and Psychophysics,* 1971, **10**, 8–14. Fig. 4.

Figure 4.5. Selfridge, O. G. Pandemonium: A paradigm for learning: In *The mechanization of thought processes.* London: Her Majesty's Stationery Office, 1959. Fig. 3.

Figure 4.6. Reprinted with permission of author and publisher: Neisser, U., Novick, R., and Lazar, R. Searching for ten targets simultaneously. *Perceptual and Motor Skills,* 1963, **17**, 955–961.

Figure 4.7. From: Rabbitt, P. M. Learning to ignore irrelevant information. *American Journal of Psychology,* 1967, **80**, 1–13. Fig. 1.

Figure 4.8. From: Posner, M. I., and Mitchell, R. F. Chronometric analysis of classification. *Psychological Review,* 1967, **74**, 392–409. Fig. 2. Copyright 1967 by the American Psychological Association and reproduced by permission.

Figure 5.1. From: Jackson, R. H., and Dick, A. O. Visual summation and its relation to processing and memory. *Perception and Psychophysics,* 1969, **6**, 13–15. Fig. 1.

Figures 5.2 and 5.3. Eriksen, C. W., and Collins, J. F. Sensory traces versus the psychological moment in the temporal organization of form. *Journal of Experimental Psychology,* 1968, **77**, 376–382. Figs. 1 and 2. Copyright 1968 by the American Psychological Association and reproduced by permission.

Figures 5.5 and 5.6. From: Sperling, G. Successive approximations to a model for short-term memory. *Acta Psychologica,* 1967, **27**, 285–292. Figs. 3 and 4.

Figures 5.7, 5.8 and 5.9. Rumelhart, D. E. A multicomponent theory of perception of briefly exposed visual displays. *Journal of Mathematical Psychology,* 1970, **7**, 191–218. Figs. 1, 4, and 7.

Figure 6.1. From: Nickerson, R. S. The use of binary-classification tasks in the study of human information processing. In S. Kornblum (Ed.), *Attention and performance,* IV. New York: Academic Press, 1973.

Figure 6.2. Posner, M. I., Boies, S. J., Eichelman, W. H., and Taylor, R. L. Retention of visual and name codes of single letters. *Journal of Experimental Psychology Monograph,* 1969, **80**, 1–13. Fig. 1. Copyright 1969 by the American Psychological Association and reproduced by permission.

Figure 6.3. Cohen, G. Some evidence for parallel comparisons in a letter recognition task. *Quarterly Journal of Experimental Psychology,* 1969, **21**, 272–279. Fig. 1.

Figure 6.4. Tversky, B. Pictorial and verbal encoding in a short-term memory task. *Perception and Psychophysics,* 1969, **6**, 225–233. Fig. 1.

Figure 6.5. Fagan, J. F. Infant's recognition memory for faces. *Journal of Experimental Child Psychology,* 1972. **14**, 453–472. Fig. 1.

Figure 6.6. Cohen, R. L., and Granstrom, K. The role of verbalizing in the memorizing of conventional figures. *Journal of Verbal Learning and Verbal Behavior,* 1968, **7**, 380–383. Fig. 1.

Figures 6.7, 6.8 and 6.9. Cohen, R. L., and Granstrom, K. Interpolated task and mode of recall as variables in STM for visual figures. *Journal of Verbal Learning and Verbal Behavior,* 1968, **7**, 653–658. Figs. 1 and 23.

Figure 6.10. Shepard, R. N., and Chipman, S. Second-order isomorphism and internal representations: Shapes of states, *Cognitive Psychology,* 1970, **1**, 1–17. Fig. 1.

Figures 6.11 and 6.12. Bahrick, H. P., Clark, S., and Bahrick, P. Generalization gradients as indicants of learning and retention of a recognition task. *Journal of Experimental Psychology,* 1967, **75**, 464–471. Figs. 1 and 2. Copyright 1967 by the American Psychological Association and reproduced by permission.

Figure 6.13. Dallett, K., and Wilcox, S. Remembering pictures vs. remembering descriptions. *Psychonomic Science,* 1968, **11**, 139–140. Fig. 2.

Figure 7.1. Norman, D. A., and Rumelhart, D. E. A system for perception and memory. In D. A. Norman (Ed.), *Models of human memory.* New York: Academic Press, 1970.

Figure 7.2. Reed, S. K. Pattern recognition and categorization. *Cognitive Psychology*, 1972, 3, 382–408. Fig. 1.

Figure 7.3. Friedman, M. P., Reed, S. K., and Carterette, E. C. Feature saliency and recognition memory for schematic faces. *Perception and Psychophysics*, 1971, **10**, 47–50. Fig. 2.

Figures 7.4 and 7.5. From: Goldstein, A. G., and Mackenberg, E. Recognition of human faces from isolated facial features: A developmental study. *Perception and Psychophysics*, 1971, **6**, 149–150. Figs. 1 and 2.

Figure 7.7. Shepard, R. N., and Metzler, J. Mental rotation of three dimensional objects. *Science*, 1971, **171**, 701–703. Fig. 1. Copyright 1971 by the American Association for the Advancement of Science.

Figure 7.8. Royer, F. Spatial orientational and figural information in free recall of visual figures. *Journal of Experimental Psychology*. 1971, **91**, 326–332. Fig. 1. Copyright 1971 by the American Psychological Association and reproduced by permission.

Figure 8.2. Reprinted with permission of author and publisher: Lee, W. Choosing among confusably distributed stimuli with specified likelihood ratios. *Perceptual and Motor Skills*, 1963, **16**, 445–467. Fig. 2.

Figure 8.3. Lee, W., and Janke, M. Categorizing externally distributed stimulus samples for three continua. *Journal of Experimental Psychology*, 1964, **68**, 376–382. Fig. 1. Copyright 1964 by the American Psychological Association and reproduced by permission.

Figures 9.2 and 9.3. Carroll, J. D., and Chang, J. J. Reanalysis of some color data of Helm's by INDSCAL procedure for individual differences multidimensional scaling. *Proceedings of the APA*, 78th Annual Convention, 1970. Figs. 1 and 3. Copyright 1970 by the American Psychological Association and reproduced by permission.

Figure 9.4. From: Reed, S. K. Pattern recognition and categorization. *Cognitive Psychology*, 1972, 3, 382–407. Fig. 2.

Figure 9.5. From: Goldstein, A. J., Harmon, L. D., and Lesk, A. B. Man machine interaction in human face identification. *Bell System Technical Journal*, 1972, **51**, 399–497. Fig. 2.

Figure 10.1. From: Biederman, I. Perceiving real-world scenes. *Science*, 1972, **177**, 77–79. Cover photo. Copyright 1972 by the American Association for the Advancement of Science.

Figure 10.2. Aderman, D., and Smith, E. E. Expectancy as a determinant of functional units in perceptual recognition. *Cognitive Psychology*, 1971, **2**, 117–129. Fig. 1.

Figure 11.1. From: Nakatani, L. H. Confusion-choice matrix for multidimensional psychophysics. *Journal of Mathematical Psychology*, 1972, 9, 104–127. Fig. 2.

Figure 11.2. Rumelhart, D. E. A multicomponent theory of confusion among briefly exposed alphabetic characters. Technical Report 22, University of California, San Diego, 1971.

I | Introduction

Man's ability to acquire knowledge has been a popular topic of discussion throughout history. The area of modern psychology that is particularly concerned with the acquisition of knowledge is cognitive psychology, which has been defined as referring "to all processes by which the sensory input is transformed, reduced, elaborated, stored, recovered, and used [Neisser, 1967, p. 4]." There are several important implications of Neisser's definition. First, cognition begins with a person's contact with the external world; that is to say that the physical world is somehow internally represented within the person. Second, this internal representation is not a passive registration of our physical surroundings, but an active transformation that may involve either reduction or elaboration.

Information-Processing Models

The acquisition, storage, retrieval, and utilization of information involves a number of separate stages, the first stage being the initial encoding of the physical stimulus. How the physical stimulus is initially encoded and represented psychologically is the primary problem of pattern recognition and the main focus of this book. Equating pattern recognition with the first stage of cognitive activity does not imply that recognition is independent of subsequent stages. The continuity of different levels of processing is one of the primary assumptions of information-processing models.

> Sensation, perception, memory, and thought must be considered on a continuum of cognitive activity. They are mutually interdependent and cannot be separated except by arbitrary rules of momentary expediency. Further, to understand how these processes function and interact, they should be subjected to an information-processing analysis, rather than be viewed as static structural systems. Such an analysis makes it clear that a proper explication of thought processes must begin with perceptual behavior, just as thought cannot prosper in the absence of stimulation. Equally as important, it is not possible to understand perception, especially recognition, identification, and perceptual memory, without understanding the whole range of cognitive activity [Haber, 1969, p. 1].

There are three basic assumptions of information-processing models according to Haber's formulation. The first assumption is that perception is not immediate, but involves a number of stages, each of which requires some finite amount of time. Information-processing models attempt to specify the operations which occur from the onset of the stimulus to the response of the observer. Usually a block design is used to represent the different stages of processing and the blocks connected to suggest the order in which the operations are performed. Haber's second assumption is that there are limitations in the processing capacities of the various stages. When people are not able to perform adequately on a task, the psychologists' task is to identify where the limitations occur. A third assumption is related to the continuity of sensation, perception, memory, and thought. Information-processing models assume that perception cannot be isolated from memory, since recoding and retention of information occurs at all stages of information processing.

The emphasis on the continuity of the various stages of processing has resulted in theories encompassing and interrelating a number of different stages. One example is the theory of human memory proposed by Atkinson and Shiffrin (1968). Figure 1.1 shows an outline of their system. Atkinson and Shiffrin distinguished between the permanent structural components of the system and the control processes or strategies selected according to the options of the subject. The major structural components are the sensory register, the short-term store, and the long-term store. The sensory register is a very temporary memory store that holds sensory in-

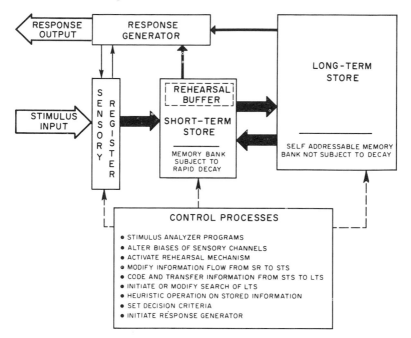

Figure 1.1. An information-processing model of human memory. [After Shiffrin and Atkinson (1969).]

formation while it is initially being recognized and transferred to the short-term store. The short-term store can hold nonattended information for up to 30 seconds. It serves a number of useful functions, such as holding new information before it is transferred into the long-term store or acting as a working memory for information activated from the long-term store. The long-term store is assumed to be a permanent repository of information, although failure to retrieve information from it may result in forgetting. The interrelationship of the permanent structural components, particularly as influenced by the control processes or strategies of the subject (S), is an important part of Atkinson and Shiffrin's theory.

The interdependence among different stages of information processing makes it difficult to organize such a book. My goal is to present a summary of the major contributions made by information-processing models to our understanding of human pattern recognition. These contributions are related to a number of different topics, and each chapter focuses upon a particular topic. However, the experiments presented in each chapter usually involve more than a single issue. I will try to relate the material in the different chapters, but would also like to invite the reader to consider how the different topics might be integrated into a more complete model.

Content and Organization

The book is organized into five sections: Representation, Temporal Effects, Memory Codes, Perceptual Classification, and Response Selection. The first two chapters are concerned with the general issue of *representation*. What do we mean by a pattern and how do we represent or describe a pattern? The word "pattern" usually refers to a configuration consisting of several elements that somehow belong together (Zusne, 1970). Patterns consist of various elements which we can call features, attributes, cues, dimensions, or components. These words will be used interchangeably.

In some cases, it is possible to describe or represent a pattern by simply listing its attributes. For example, we might describe a face by describing its attributes as short hair, wide eyes, concave nose, and receding chin. Or we might describe a person by saying that he is 35 years old, earns $10,000 a year, has two children, and attended three years of college. In other cases, a listing of attributes provides an insufficient description of a pattern. We could not distinguish between the letters **T** and **L** if their attributes were listed only as one horizontal line and one vertical line. It is also necessary to know how the lines are joined together, for example, the letter **L** consists of a vertical line joined at its bottom to the left end of a horizontal line.

Chapter II is organized according to Eleanor Gibson's (1969) analysis of the cognitive processes related to perceptual learning. Gibson proposes that the discovery of features precedes the formation of permanent representations. After the child discovers the features and relations that distinguish one object from another, he can combine this knowledge to form a concrete image of the object and later an abstract concept. Chapter II begins with a discussion of feature theories and gives examples of how they have been applied to speech recognition, perceptual learning of visual patterns, and animal discrimination learning. The formation of concrete images is studied within the framework of a transfer discrimination experiment in which either the standard pattern or the features are changed in the transfer task. The extent to which a concrete image is utilized can be evaluated by using the same standard in both tasks. The idea of an abstract image is similar to the concept of a "prototype" in schema theory. Schema theory proposes that observers can create an image to represent a class of patterns. The created image may never have been actually seen, but may represent the central tendency of the patterns in the class.

Chapter III emphasizes the importance of relations and structure. As noted earlier, many patterns cannot be described very adequately by a list of features. Structural theories are more complex than feature theories because, in addition to a set of features, we must specify a set of relations, and a set of rules describing the patterns in terms of the features and relations. Structural theories are less developed than feature theories, but their additional complexity is necessary to overcome the descriptive limitations of feature theories.

Chapters IV and V are concerned with *temporal effects* or processing speed. Many information-processing theories have been constructed from a data base consisting of reaction times. A major issue is the number of processing operations that can be performed simultaneously. "Serial" processing means that only a single operation can occur at any moment in time whereas "parallel" processing means that two or more operations can occur simultaneously. Let us imagine that we are asked to scan an array of letters looking for the letters **K** and **R**. If we assume that pattern recognition involves comparing patterns in the array to some internal representation of the letters **K** and **R** there are at least three operations that would increase our scanning rate if the operations could be carried out in parallel. The first operation is feature identification and the issue is whether the features of a letter are identified simultaneously or serially. Second, we can ask whether more than one letter in the array can be processed at a time. Do we scan a single letter at a time or can we extract features from several letters simultaneously? Finally, do we serially test whether a letter matches our description of a **K** or an **R** or can we make the two attempted matches in parallel? These issues are examined in Chapter IV and to some extent in Chapter V.

Chapter V has two purposes. First, the chapter continues the discussion of serial versus parallel processing. Temporal processing remains a central issue but the response measure changes from reaction time to the amount recognized during a brief tachistoscopic exposure. Second, various properties of iconic memory are examined. Iconic memory may be likened to a visual afterimage, which persists after a brief exposure and extends the effective duration of the visual display.

Since information is held in iconic memory for less than 1 second, the subject must form a more permanent *memory code* in order to retain the information in short-term memory (STM) or long-term memory (LTM). The memory code may be the name of the pattern, a verbal description of the pattern, or a visual image. In Chapter VI, we review the evidence for the existence of these different types of memory codes. Several experimental studies suggest the conclusion that a verbal code is utilized in tasks requiring the reproduction or recall of patterns whereas a visual code is utilized in tasks requiring the recognition of patterns. Evidence for visual images is presented along with a discussion of their characteristics.

Chapter VII continues the discussion of memory codes, but emphasizes the structure, rather than the modality, of the code. A multicomponent model of memory assumes that patterns are stored in memory in the form of a list of feature values. This assumption leads to further questions about the memory for the individual components. Is the rate of forgetting the same for all components and is the memory for one component independent of the memory for the other components? An example of a multicomponent model is a phonemic model which assumes that speech can be analyzed into phonemes, the basic sounds of a language. The limitations of multicomponent models are discussed in the final section. An alternative approach, a network model, captures the complex relationships that exist among items but like the structural models of Chapter III, is more complex and is just beginning to be tested by psychologists.

The next two chapters contrast two different approaches to the problem of *perceptual classification*. One of the tasks of pattern recognition is to account for our ability to treat different exemplars of a pattern as belonging to a common category. We respond "dog" to a wide variety of dogs which vary greatly in physical appearance, and we can easily classify dogs that we have never seen before. One approach to the classification problem is based upon the probability of a category, given a particular feature value. For example, let us say that we are trying to classify a person as a boy or a girl and all we know is that the person is 5 feet tall, has long hair, blue eyes, and is wearing pants. Each attribute may differ in its degree of informativeness. If we take a survey, we may find from our sample that the probability of a person being a girl is .90 for being 5 feet tall, .75 for having long hair, .50 for having blue eyes, and .20 for wearing pants. Chapter VIII shows alternative ways of using these probabilities to arrive at a classification decision. An alternative to the probability models are the distance models discussed in Chapter IX.

It seems that intuitively we generally classify an object into a category because the object is more similar to the members of that category than to the members of other categories. Chapter IX shows how the concept of similarity can be specified more precisely. The basic idea is that the greater the similarity between two patterns, the less should be the distance between the patterns when they are represented as points in a multidimensional space. Distance models assume that each pattern is represented as a list of features and each feature varies along a continuous scale called a dimension. For example, let the coordinates (x_1, y_1) represent the values of two features of one pattern and the coordinates (x_2, y_2) represent the values of two features of a second pattern. Each pattern can be represented as a point in a two-dimensional space, and the length of the straight line connecting the two points is one possible measure of the distance between the two patterns. Several alternative ways of calculating distance are discussed, and the measures are used to predict how people make classifications.

Chapter X differs from the previous chapters by considering what factors besides the information in the stimulus pattern determine the observer's response. The S's prior biases and additional information supplied by the experimenter can both influence *response selection*. If the observer is given prior information about a stimulus, he can sometimes utilize this information to choose an optimal coding strategy. Several examples are discussed to illustrate how changing a coding strategy can result in improved perception. One common type of set is the effect of context. Sometimes we are able to read poor handwriting only because we can utilize the rest of the sentence to guess an illegible word. It is also easier to identify an object when it appears in a familiar context of related objects. A second important determinant of which response is selected is response bias. Common words are more accurately reported than uncommon words, presumably because observers are more likely to choose the more common word if the perceptual information is consistent with several words.

In order to predict which errors occur in a recognition experiment, we have to know the response biases of the observer and the similarities that exist among the items in the stimulus set. In Chapter XI, we compare alternative models that attempt to predict the probability that the observer will give a particular response for each stimulus in the stimulus set. The models propose that when only partial information is known about a stimulus, the observer chooses his response from the subset of stimuli that are consistent with the perceived stimulus information. The stimuli in the subset are determined by their similarity to the stimulus that actually occurred. The final section of Chapter XI contrasts the recognition models with an analysis-by-synthesis model which postulates that the identification of the parts of a stimulus is dependent upon actively matching the perceived stimulus information to rules describing the stimuli in the stimulus set.

Chapter XII attempts to integrate the major issues discussed in the previous chapters.

Part 1 | REPRESENTATION

II | Features, Templates, and Schemata

Eleanor Gibson (1963) suggested in a review of perceptual learning that a distinction could be made between theories of perceptual learning based on a template-matching process, and those based on the detection of features. She pointed out that programs for pattern recognition by machines are also divided into these two types. This thesis was elaborated by Neisser (1967). The two main theoretical approaches to the problem of pattern recognition, according to Neisser, are *template matching*, in which each new input is compared to a standard and *feature analysis*, in which the presence of particular parts of a pattern is decisive. The most common conceptualization of a template, and the one discussed by Neisser, involves measuring the degree of overlap between the templates and the patterns to be recognized. Such a recognition procedure is usually quickly dismissed because of its limitations whenever there are many possible instances of the same pattern (see Neisser, 1967, pp. 61–65). For example, many instances of the letter **A** may overlap only minimally with a template of an **A**.

A possible salvation for the template theory as applied to psychology experiments is that many pattern-recognition experiments do not use more than one instance of a pattern—the letter **A** may always occur in the same type font. In such situations, a template match may be a very efficient strategy when comparing two patterns. Another possible candidate for the name "template" is the abstract images or prototypes which we consider in the final section of this chapter. If a prototype pattern were abstracted to represent a class of patterns, one possible classification strategy would be to classify a pattern by comparing its similarity to the prototype pattern representing each class. In both cases, however, we can raise the question of whether the internal representation of these patterns is in the form of the features making up the pattern or in the form of some unanalyzed holistic template.

A very useful conceptualization of this problem was provided by Gibson (1969) in her discussion of the various stages of perceptual learning and how these stages form part of a cognitive hierarchy (Figure 2.1).

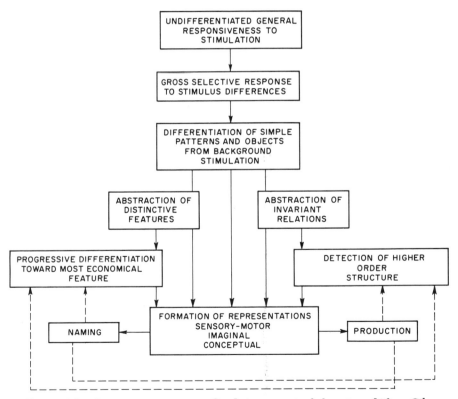

Figure 2.1. Cognitive processes utilized in perceptual learning. [After Gibson (1969).]

According to her formulation, the early stages of perceptual learning involve the discovery of distinctive features and invariant relations. The child utilizes these features and relations to form a more permanent representation of patterns. The more permanent representation may take the form of a concrete image which is necessary for attaching verbal labels or producing a drawing of the pattern. Finally, the common features of a class of patterns may be abstracted to form a class concept or an abstract image.

This chapter is organized into three sections based upon Gibson's formulation. The first section describes feature theories, the second is concerned with concrete images, and the third considers abstract images. I will use the term *concrete image* to refer to the internal representation of a pattern which was physically present in the environment. For example, if someone showed you a chair and asked you to remember what that chair looked like, your memory for that particular chair would be a concrete image. The experimental literature most relevant to this usage of the term are the studies on feature versus prototype learning, which are reviewed in the second section of this chapter. I will not use the word "prototype," however, when discussing these studies because the word has been more frequently used to describe the abstract images discussed as a part of schema theory. By an *abstract image,* I mean an internal representation of a pattern created by someone to represent a class of patterns. An abstract image is like the concrete image in that it is an internal representation of a particular pattern, but that pattern may never have physically existed and it should be representative of a class of patterns.

I am deliberately using a neutral term such as "internal representation" so as to avoid a committment to a particular type of image. An image may be simply a list of features or it may have a more complex structure. It may be either visual or verbal. These issues will be discussed in subsequent chapters. I am assuming, however, that the formation of an image depends upon the prior discovery of features and attributes and is therefore not an unanalyzed template. Although this view places images within the context of Gibson's cognitive hierarchy, my particular interpretation of the terms "concrete image" and "abstract image" may differ from her intended usage of these terms. Various examples of features are presented in the next section.

Features

Three classic papers (Jakobson, Fant, & Halle, 1952; Gibson & Gibson, 1955; Sutherland, 1959) were published in the 1950s in support of the concept of features. Jakobson, Fant, and Halle (1952) proposed that distinctive features could be used to represent the differences between phonemes, the basic sounds of a language. They suggested that phonemes are distinguished from one another on the basis of certain distinctive features which form the ultimate entities of a language, since no one of them can be broken down into smaller linguistic units. These distinctive features consist of 12 binary oppositions such as consonantal/nonconsonantal and nasal/oral. Jakobson, Fant, and Halle (1961) argue that the whole development of acoustic investigation of speech sounds has been toward a more selective portrayal of sound stimuli. The wave trace contains too much information and means must be provided for selecting essential information. On the other hand, the extremely limited set of distinctive features underlying a language, the restrictions on their actual combinations into bundles and sequences, and finally, a high amount of redundancy, lighten the information processing load imposed upon the listener.

A second paper of major influence in support of a feature theory was on the feature differentiation theory of perceptual learning proposed by the Gibsons (Gibson & Gibson, 1955; see also J. J. Gibson, 1966). The Gibsons rejected theories based on association or organization in which the development of perception is one of supplementing, interpreting, or organizing. As an alternative, they proposed that percepts change over time by progressive elaboration of qualities, features, and dimensions of variation. Perceptual learning consists of responding to variables of physical stimulation not previously responded to so that perception becomes richer in differential responses, not in images. Human observers learn to detect the values and meanings of things, putting them into categories and subcategories, by learning to attend to the invariant stimulus information.

The experimental paradigm often used by the Gibsons requires children to select from a set of patterns those patterns which exactly match a standard pattern. An illustration of the procedure is shown in Figure 2.2 in which the stimuli consisted of nonsense forms differing along three dimensions of variation (Gibson & Gibson, 1955). The standard is shown in the center, and the remaining items differ from the standard in the number of coils, horizontal stretching or compression, and right–left reversal. Subjects in the experiment were shown the standard item for 5 seconds and were told that some items in a pack of cards would be exactly like the one shown. The subjects then saw the series of cards, one at a time, and indicated which cards exactly matched the standard. For adults, the number of undifferentiated items identified as matching the standard was small (mean $= 3$) and only a few repetitions of the

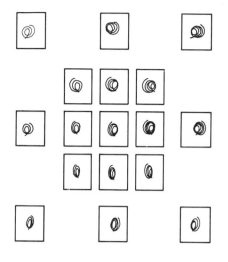

Figure 2.2. Nonsense items differing in three dimensions of variation. [After Gibson & Gibson (1955).]

series were needed before only the standard item was chosen. However, a group of younger children, between 6 and 8 years old, identified nearly all the scribbles as matching the standard. Although the number of un-differentiated items was greatly reduced on successive repetitions of the series, the majority of children did not reach the criterion of choosing only the standard. Results obtained from a group of older children were intermediate between these two extremes. The Gibsons interpreted the findings as supporting the differentiation theory in which children learn to identify an object by being able to identify the differences between it and other objects.

An early attempt to extend the concept of distinctive features to reading was made by E. Gibson and her associates. Gibson, Osser, Shiff, and Smith (1963) postulated two sets of critical features in letters and tested the lists by examining confusion errors made by 4-year-old children. Features included horizontal, vertical, and oblique straight lines; curves which were closed, open vertically, or open horizontally; and number of strokes. Relational properties were also considered. Figure 2.3 shows the complete set of distinctive features and how they were used to represent letters. The writers proposed that certain distinctive features which differentiate objects of the world are transferred to letter discrimination. Other specified features, previously not critical but needed to differentiate letters, are detected after school age when letters are encountered.

A further test of how the concept of distinctive features might be applied to letters was made by Gibson, Schapiro, and Yonas (1968). Two sets of nine letters each were chosen for a test based on the amount of time required to decide whether two simultaneously presented letters

Features	A	E	F	H	I	L	T	K	M	N	V	W	X	Y	Z	B	C	D	G	J	O	P	R	Q	S	U
Straight																										
horizontal	+	+	+	+		+	+								+											
vertical		+	+	+	+	+	+	+	+	+																
diagonal								+	+	+	+	+	+	+	+											
diagonal								+		+	+	+	+	+	+											
Curve																										
closed																+		+			+	+	+	+		
open vertically																	+		+	+						
open horizontally																			+	+						+
Intersection	+	+	+	+				+					+			+						+	+	+		
Redundancy																										
cyclic change		+	+						+		+	+				+		+			+					
symmetry	+	+	+	+	+		+		+		+	+	+	+		+	+	+			+				+	+
Discontinuity																										
vertical	+			+	+									+								+	+			
horizontal		+	+																							

Figure 2.3. Chart of distinctive features for a set of graphemes. [After Gibson (1969).]

16

were the same or different. Seven-year-old children and adults served as Ss. The experimenters predicted that the time needed to respond that two letters were different would depend upon what distinctive features were shared by the two letters. The amount of time needed to respond "different" did vary widely for different pairs of letters. For example, adults required, on the average, 458 msec to respond that (GW) were different, compared to 571 msec to respond that (PR) were different letters. Reaction times of the children were much longer, but also showed a wide range in latencies among different pairs. In order to test whether the range in latencies could be accounted for by the concept of distinctive features, the data were subjected to a cluster analysis. The analysis revealed that certain features were important in determining what letters were grouped together: curve versus straight line; diagonality; vertical line versus horizontal lines; intersection; and closed versus open. Although distinctive features had an important influence on "different" judgments, their effect on "same" judgments was much less. "Same" judgments took less time than "different" judgments and "same" judgments for some pairs were reliably shorter than judgments for other pairs. The investigators concluded that in some cases, a decision of "same" was based upon a direct perception of replication, without an analysis of distinctive features. We shall return to this issue when discussing the speed of matching operations in Chapter IV.

A third important paper on features was written by N. S. Sutherland in 1959. He proposed a theory of animal discrimination learning which had more of a physiological emphasis than did previous theories. Sutherland rejected theories based on adaptive neural networks in favor of a theory incorporating a limited number of stimulus analyzing mechanisms. The first type of model, based upon the neural network theories of Hebb (1949), Uttley (1956), and Ashby (1952), postulated intially random connections that become modified by learning. Such theories assume a very general analyzing system which is capable in principle of categorizing stimuli in all possible ways. Sutherland argued that such an approach was limited in its application to behavioral studies in that it could not account for data suggesting innate classifications, nor would it be easy to make predictions about what animals will actually do when confronted with various patterns.

The alternative approach, put forward by Deutsch (1955), Dodwell (1957), and Sutherland (1957), assumes specific analyzing mechanisms that can categorize stimuli in only a limited number of ways. Sutherland postulated a model containing: (1) a number of different analyzing mechanisms; (2) a control center which determines which of these mechanisms shall be "switched in" on any given occasion and in what sequence they shall be switched in; (3) a further mechanism for selecting the response to be attached to the ouput from the analyzing mechanisms. Sutherland argued that the existence of specific analyzing mechanisms would not only be economical in terms of the number of nerve cells required, but would account for many experimental findings. Competition for specific analyzing mechanisms would explain why human beings function as limited information channels, why neurological findings suggest peripheral blocking of incoming stimuli, and why animals learn not only to attach a response to a stimulus but which analyzing mechanism to use.

Although the concept of features remains important in pattern recognition theories, recent theories have stressed additional processing which occurs after feature learning. Sutherland (1968) outlined the main characteristics of a more complex theory which we will consider in the next chapter. Gibson (1969) primarily stressed feature learning but placed feature learning as an intermediate stage within the framework of a more complete cognitive hierarchy (Figure 2.1). In the next section we contrast feature learning with the formation of a concrete image.

Concrete Images

I have used the term "concrete image" to refer to an internal representation of a pattern that was perceived, rather than created. Once a complete representation of a pattern is formed, a subject should be able to discriminate that pattern from other patterns. But the ability to make this discrimination may also depend upon what features are varied to form the different patterns. This idea was tested in a well-known study by Pick (1965).

Sixty kindergarten children served as Ss in a task that required them to find those patterns which exactly matched a standard from a set of patterns containing transformations of the standard. There were six standards and six transformations (Figure 2.4) although only three standards (A, B, C, or D, E, F) and three transformations (1, 2, 3, or 4, 5, 6) were used during a single task. Group E1 reflected the extent to which learning of the standards had occurred during training. This group received the same standards as in training, but three new transformations of these standards served as distracting stimuli. If the children had formed an adequate representation of the standards in the pretraining task it would be an easy task for them to locate the standards among the distracting stimuli. Group E2 reflected the extent to which distinctive feature learning had occurred during training. This group received three new stan-

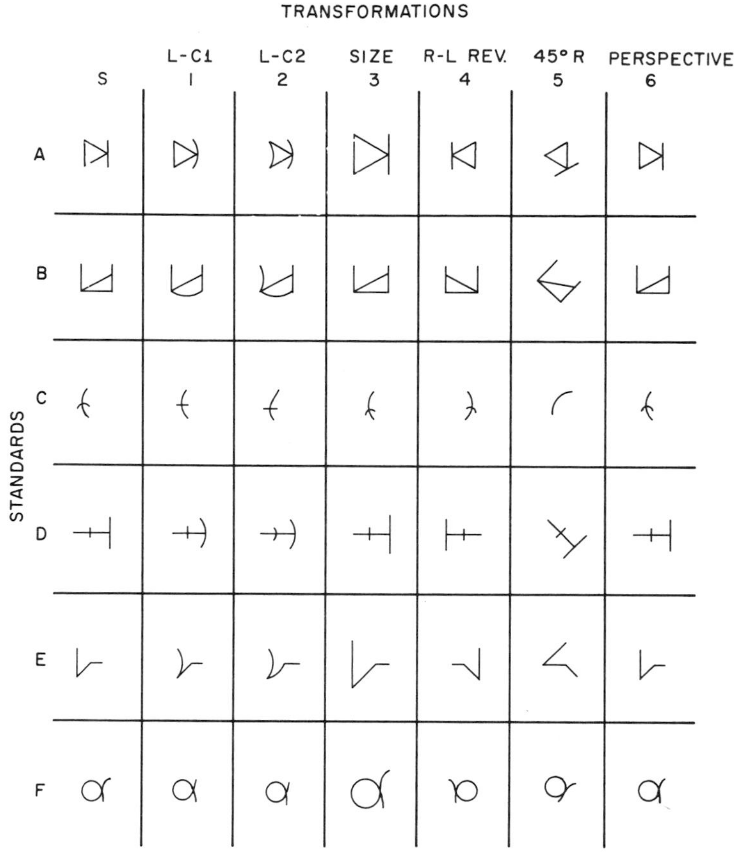

TRANSFORMATIONS

| | S | L-C1
1 | L-C2
2 | SIZE
3 | R-L REV.
4 | 45°R
5 | PERSPECTIVE
6 |

STANDARDS: A, B, C, D, E, F

Figure 2.4. Standards and transformations of letter-like stimuli. [After Pick (1965).]

dards but the same three types of transformations served as distracting stimuli. If the children had learned to discriminate between the different transformations (distinctive features), the transfer task would be easy since the same transformations were used in both tasks. With simultaneous presentation, results for both visual and tactual forms supported the distinctive features hypothesis in that Group E2 made significantly less confusion errors in transfer. With successive presentation of the tactual forms, there was no difference suggesting that forming a representation of the standard is more important when comparisons cannot be made simultaneously.

However, according to Caldwell and Hall (1970), the Pick study did not provide a fair test of the two theories because more information was given to the distinctive features group regarding the experimenter's concept of "same" and "different." For example, a child in the standard group who had trained on transformations 1, 2, and 3 may not know that a rotation of a pattern should be called a "different" pattern on the transfer task even though he may be able to discriminate the differently rotated patterns. Caldwell and Hall therefore changed the grouping of the transformations so that 1, 3, and 4 would be used on one task and 2, 5, and 6 would be used on the other task (see Figure 2.4). As a result of the new grouping, both the feature (E2) and standard (E1) groups should learn during the training task that line-to-curve changes make a difference (from 1 or 2), size transformations make a difference (from 3 or 6), and rotational transformations make a difference (from 4 or 5). When equal information was given to the two groups, no significant differences were obtained between standard or feature pretraining. Caldwell and Hall concluded that distinctive features and representation learning were not opposing types of learning, since the formation of a representation was nothing more than storing enough distinctive features.

A third experiment (Aiken, 1969) used the basic experimental paradigm of the Pick study, but changed certain aspects of the design. The stimuli were auditory patterns which varied in frequency, amplitude, duration, and direction. Four standards were used in the experiment, but only two standards and two features varied during the training task and during the transfer task. The "standard" group was given the same standards, but new features, on the transfer task and the "features" group was given the same features, but new standards, on the transfer task. A control group transferred to both new standards and new features. The task required that Ss (Navy recruits) learn to discriminate between a standard signal and a comparison signal which followed the standard by 1.5 seconds. The mean number of errors on the transfer task was 7.75 for the control group, 5.94 for the feature group, and 4.56 for the standard group. Both experimental groups differed significantly from the control group indicating both learning of specific features and learning of the standard. But, in contrast to Pick's (1965) results, the "standard" group made significantly fewer errors than the "features" group.

The issue raised by the Pick study is an important one, but the results have been inconsistent. One experiment found feature learning superior; another experiment found no difference between feature and standard learning; and a third experiment found standard learning superior. A fundamental question raised by experiments on discrimination learning is what exactly goes wrong when a child fails to make a discrimination. The answer to such a question depends upon the extent to which we can identify the operations utilized in discriminating between two stimuli.

A detailed specification of the operations involved in a matching-to-sample task has been proposed by Fellows (1968). Figure 2.5 specifies the sequence of operations involved in a task requiring Ss to choose the bottom window which contains a pattern identical to the pattern in the top window. Each bottom window of the apparatus contains a choice stimulus but only one choice stimulus matches the sample stimulus in the top window (see Figure 2.5a). The model assumes that only one window can be perceived during a single fixation and that a subject has learned to match in an efficient manner by looking at only one of the bottom windows. Whether the model is correct in all its details is not our present concern. What is illustrated by Fellows's approach is the type of detailed analysis which is necessary to discover the source of errors. If a child makes a discrimination error, is it the result of a failure in orienting, processing the stimulus, comparing the two stimuli, or in the response strategy?

When very complex stimuli are used, it may be necessary for Ss to repeat the operations shown in the model for the separate parts or features of a stimulus. An example of a complex pattern requiring a number of comparisons are the houses shown in Figure 2.6. These stimuli were used in an experiment by Vurpillot (1968) designed to explore the development of scanning strategies and their relation to visual differentiation. Children were instructed to look carefully at the pictures of two houses in order to decide whether they were the same or not. The experimenter was able to determine the location, duration, and sequence of eye fixations by filming the corneal reflections of the stimuli. An ideal scanning strategy would be to compare successively, corresponding pairs of windows along a general direction to keep in mind the areas which have already been examined. Improvement in performance with increasing age was primarily the result of a more systematic use of the ideal scanning strategy. Older children not only made more paired comparisons, but the number of paired comparisons was related to the number of actual differences between the two houses. The effect of the younger children making fewer paired comparisons was that they readily accepted many houses as being the same when they actually differed. On the other hand, Ss' low criteria for judging two houses the same resulted in a high accuracy for judging identical houses and more than 90% of the judgments of identical houses were correct at age 5. Figure 2.7 shows how well the children performed on houses differing on one window (P1), three windows (P3), five windows (P5), and identical houses.

In addition to the comparison and scanning operations, Vurpillot emphasizes the child's criteria of "same" or "different" as having an important influence on judgments. Very young children may have either

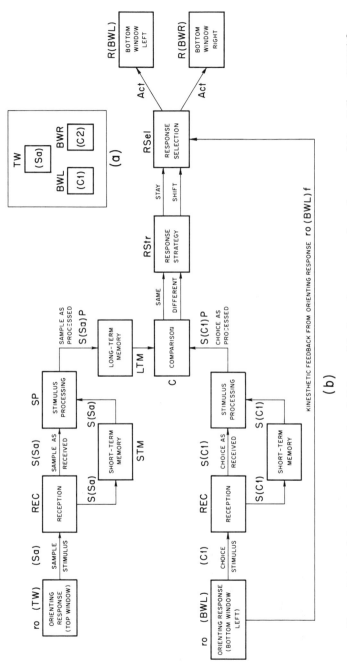

Figure 2.5. (a) Stimulus display panel and (b) a model of matching-to-sample performance. [After Fellows (1968).]

Figure 2.6. Houses used to study eye movements in perceptual matching. [After Vurpillot (1968).]

Figure 2.7. Percentage of correct answers as a function of age and stimulus. Group I, mean age 3.11 years; Group II, mean age 5.0 years; Group III, mean age 6.6 years; Group IV, mean age 8.9 years. △: identical pairs; □: different pairs P5; ○: different pairs P3; ▽: different Pairs P1. See text for description of stimuli. [After Vurpillot (1968).]

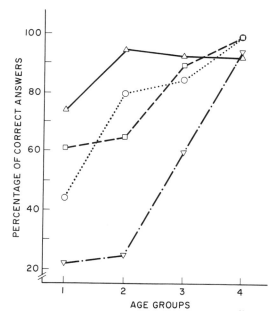

no criteria of what "same" means or they may have an inadequate criteria
such as judging two houses the same if only some of the windows match.
It should be noted that in most discrimination tasks only one type of an
error can occur—an overgeneralization error resulting from a failure to
discriminate between two different stimuli. If pattern recognition is
treated as a categorization problem in which there are more than one
possible instances of a pattern, a second type of error is possible—an
overdiscrimination error resulting from a failure to classify two instances
of a pattern as being the same pattern. In this case, Ss would have to
adopt a criteria so as to avoid both overgeneralization and overdiscrimination errors. Whether children would be more likely to overgeneralize
or overdiscriminate, was the problem investigated in an interesting study
by Saltz and Sigel (1967). Subjects compared pictures of boys to a
standard, judging whether the pictures were of the same boy or a different boy. Pictures of the same boy differed slightly in head position or
facial expression and Ss were informed of these differences. Saltz and
Sigel found that younger Ss had overly narrow concepts and tended
primarily to overdiscriminate. While this tendency usually led to a poorer
performance by the younger Ss, 6-year-olds actually did better than
adults in one condition by correctly judging the difference between two
very similar pictures of different boys (Figure 2.8).

The model proposed by Fellows (1968) is useful because it suggests
that even when the standard can be represented as a list of features (as

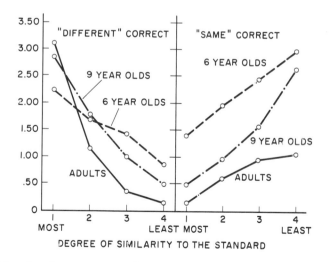

Figure 2.8. Overdiscrimination and overgeneralization errors at different age levels
as a function of similarity between instance and standard. [After Saltz & Sigel (1967).]

suggested by Caldwell and Hall, 1970), there is likely to be an emphasis on different operations depending upon whether the features or the standards are changed on the transfer task. When the features are changed, the child may have to learn to attend to the new features, code their values, and compare the two patterns along new dimensions of variation. If the values along these dimensions are difficult to discriminate, the child may not be able to discriminate two different values even after making the comparison. The advantage of feature learning is that we learn to attend to the relevant dimensions and learn to discriminate different values along these dimensions, providing practice in the orienting and comparison operations of Figure 2.5.

The advantage of retaining the same standard is that it provides the opportunity to learn the particular values for each dimension of the standard. This facilitates the stimulus processing stage of the model and may result in storing the feature values of the standard in long-term memory. Learning the particular values of the standard is particularly important when comparisons are made sequentially. Pick (1965) found that feature learning was superior for all conditions except the sequential comparison of tactual forms and Aiken (1969) found that learning the standard was superior for the sequential comparison of tones. There are two different ways in which sequential presentation can influence learning the standard. The most obvious, of course, is that in comparing two stimuli during the transfer task, a representation of the first stimulus must be stored in memory until the second stimulus is presented. This part of the task would be facilitated if the first stimulus were always a standard that had been previously learned during the training task. But it is important that the values of all dimensions of the standard are learned and not only the dimensions which varied during training, since new dimensions vary on the transfer task. It seems more likely that all dimensions of the standard would be learned if the training task also involved sequential presentation. The separate effects of sequential presentation during training and transfer could be studied by using sequential presentation in one task and simultaneous presentation in the other task.

The establishment of a criterion for deciding "same" or "different" is related to the response strategy stage of Fellows's model. The problem of how the child establishes such a criterion was a central issue in the studies by Caldwell and Hall (1970), Vurpillot (1968), and Saltz and Sigel (1967). Caldwell and Hall showed how the selection of a criterion applied to the Pick paradigm. Further research is necessary to show, in more detail, how the other stages of discrimination learning apply to this paradigm.

Schema Theory

The experiments that we have reviewed so far have been primarily investigations of discrimination learning—learning to distinguish one pattern from another. An equally important part of perceptual learning is generalization learning—learning to group discriminable patterns as being equivalent. Even a single object can often appear differently, as was illustrated by the study of Saltz and Sigel (1967), which required Ss to decide whether two different pictures were really of the same boy.

One theory of generalization learning is called *schema theory*. Schema theory—based on the idea of cognitive structures that organize systems of stored information—entered into psychology primarily through the writings of Bartlett (1932).

> "Schema" refers to an active organization of past reactions, or of past experiences, which must always be supposed to be operating in any well-adapted organic response. That is, whenever there is any order or regularity of behavior, a particular response is possible only because it is related to other similar responses which have been serially organized, yet which operate, not simply as individual members coming one after another, but as a unitary mass [Bartlett, 1932, p. 201].

The idea has been reintroduced into psychology primarily by researchers working within the general framework of information theory. Information theory not only emphasizes that a stimulus is related to a larger class of stimuli and is not an isolated entity, but provides a measure of the redundancy or variability of stimuli within this class. A statement of a modern variant of schema theory was given by Evans (1967). A *schema* is "a set of rules which would serve as instructions for producing in essential aspects a population prototype and object typical of the population." *Schematic redundancy* is a measure of the "extent to which individual members of the population adhere to *schema rules*." A *schema family* is "a population of objects, all of which can be efficiently described by the same schema rules." The theory proposes that humans abstract and use redundant aspects of the environment to reduce information processing and storage requirements. Reduction in memory storage requirements could be achieved by encoding stimuli having a common prototype in the form of prototype plus correction.

Since abstraction is an important concept of schema theory, I would like to relate it to an abstract image in the following way. Whenever an internal representation of the central tendency of a category of patterns is created by the subject, the created pattern is an abstract image. In some cases, the prototype is presented in the experiment and if the S merely formed an internal representation of the pattern, it would not be an abstract image. However, if the subject recognized the prototype as the central tendency, this would suggest that the subject had previously created an abstract image of the central tendency. Regardless of whether the prototype is supplied by the experimenter or created by the subject, it can serve as a useful reference for discriminating among the patterns within a category, learning which patterns belong to a category, or classfying new patterns into the appropriate category.

The question of whether familiarization with the prototype would aid later identification learning was investigated by Attneave (1957). Ten prototype shapes were constructed by plotting points with random co-ordinates and then connecting the points with the shortest possible closed contour. The ten shapes used as prototypes are shown in the upper two rows of Figure 2.9. Two sets of eight variations were constructed for each prototype by moving slightly one-third of the dots. In the first set, the same dots were varied throughout the whole set, whereas, in the second set, the points to be moved were randomly selected for each member of the set. A sample set of variations is shown in the lower two rows of Figure 2.9. Subjects were assigned to one of the prototype subgroups and were required to learn a paired-associate response to each of the eight variations. Experimental Ss received pretraining which consisted of eight reproduction trials with the relevant prototype. Control Ss received the same pretraining, but with an unrelated shape.

Figure 2.9. Ten shapes used as prototypes are shown in the upper two rows; a sample set of variations is shown in the two lower rows. [After Attneave (1957).]

The results indicated that experimental Ss, who had received prior familiarization with the central prototype, made less errors on the paired-associates task than control Ss. However, the effect was much greater when the same parts of the transfer shapes were varied. The experiment suggested a number of important theoretical implications, which were discussed by Attneave. The finding that pretraining on the prototype was more beneficial when the same parts were varied suggests that Ss can use their knowledge of the prototype to determine where to look for distinguishing characteristics. A close relationship must therefore exist between prototype formation and "stimulus predifferentiation" as studied by the Gibsons. Attneave suggested that Ss pretrained on a class of stimuli are likely to learn at least three characteristics of the class: (a) its central tendency; (b) how its members may differ from one another, that is, on what dimensions; and (c) its dispersion, that is, how much its members may differ from one another along several dimensions of variability.

The finding that Ss can abstract a prototype pattern to represent the central tendency of patterns was nicely demonstrated in an experiment by Franks and Bransford (1971). Their research was directed at the idea of a generative memory composed of relational concepts consisting of vocabulary symbols and rules for combining the symbols. The stimuli consisted of well-structured arrays of geometrical forms which were varied by applying systematic transformations to a prototype (base) pattern (Figure 2.10). Transformations included reversing the left and right half of a configuration, deleting a figure, substituting one figure for another, etc. The experimental procedure consisted of an acquisition phase and a recognition phase. During acquisition, Ss were exposed to transformations of the prototype, but were not told that they would later be given a recognition test. After acquisition, Ss were given a series of patterns in order to obtain confidence ratings regarding which patterns they had previously seen. The highest confidence rating was given to the prototype pattern defined as the pattern having the least transformational distance from the set of acquisition patterns. Subjects were most confident of having seen the prototype pattern, even when it was not presented during acquisition. The greater the transformational distance from the prototype, the lower was the recognition rating given to a pattern. Furthermore, there appeared to be almost no memory for specific instances, since previously seen configurations did not receive higher ratings than new configurations. The predictions supported a prototype model when the frequency of the individual cues was controlled, so the results could not be due to the number of times Ss saw the various components making up a configuration.

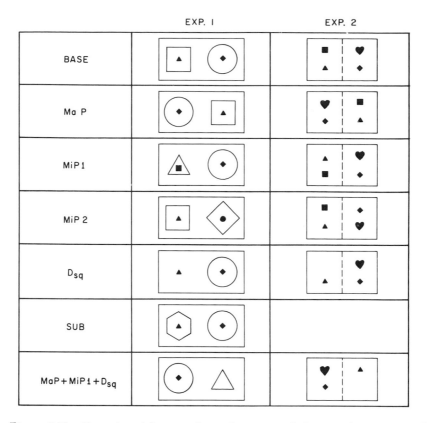

Figure 2.10. Examples of bases and transformations. [After Franks & Bransford (1971).]

The findings obtained by Franks and Bransford have several important implications. First, they support Attneave's suggestion that when Ss are presented with a class of patterns, they learn something about the central tendency of a class. However, unlike Attneave's findings in which prior familiarization with the prototype facilitated discrimination learning, the emphasis in their experiment is clearly on generalization. Whether or not Ss classified a pattern as previously seen depended upon its similarity to the prototype. A prototype can therefore be useful for both discrimination and generalization learning. One way in which the prototype can be used in generalization learning is as a basis for classifying patterns into different categories. If Ss could abstract a prototype to represent each category, they could classify or learn new patterns by comparing the similarity of the new patterns to the category prototypes.

Posner and Keele (1968) designed an experiment to test whether the abstraction of a prototype would aid Ss in classifying patterns into one of four categories. In such a task, both generalization and discrimination are involved—generalization among patterns belonging to the same category and discrimination between patterns belonging to different categories. Prototype patterns consisting of a triangle, the letters **M** and **F**, and a random pattern were made from nine dots within a 30 × 30 matrix. Distortions of each prototype were constructed at each of three different levels of variability. Figure 2.11 shows the degree of distortion for the different levels of variability. The level 1 distortion is a low variability pattern; the level 5 distortion is a moderate variability pattern; and the level 7.7 distortion is a high variability pattern. Subjects learned a list of 12 patterns, three from each prototype. Group 1 Ss learned a list of low variability distortions and Group 5 Ss learned a list of moderate variability distortions. Both groups were then transferred to a list of high variability distortions. Posner and Keele were interested in testing the hypothesis that Group 1 Ss would do better on transfer, since their training on low variability patterns made the category prototypes more obvious. However, Group 5 Ss made fewer errors on the transfer task, indicating the greater variation of patterns during original learning was more beneficial when Ss were transferred to a task consisting of highly variable patterns.

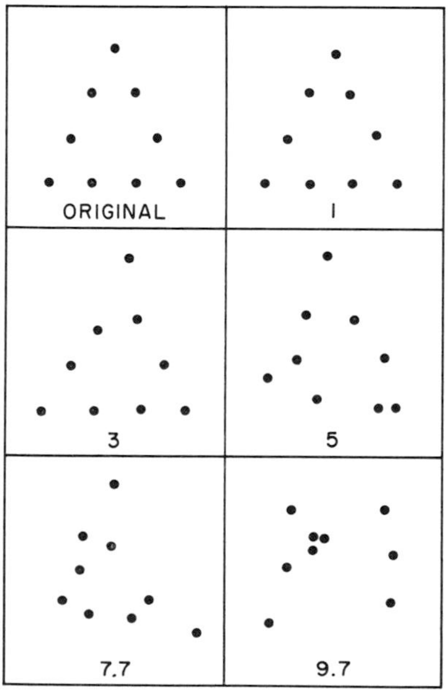

Figure 2.11. Original and five levels of distortion for set of triangles. [After Posner & Keele (1968).]

This finding was confirmed in a pattern recognition experiment in which another sample of Group 1 and Group 5 Ss classified 24 high variability distortions into one of the four categories that they had learned during an initial learning task. Once again, Group 5 Ss did better on transfer. Although these results primarily emphasize that the variability of the individual patterns is an important factor, there was some indication that Ss were learning information about the prototype even for the highly variable patterns. In a third experiment, after learning three high variability distortion patterns per category, Ss made fewer errors in classifying the prototypes than in classifying other patterns that were equally distant from the categories.

All these studies emphasize the importance of a particular pattern that is representative of a class of patterns because it is the central tendency of that class. Although the question of whether a noncentral standard could be effectively utilized was raised by Attneave (1957) some years ago, it is only recently that this issue has been systematically explored. According to Rosch (1973), the reason why the central tendency has been emphasized is that many of the studies in schema theory have used artificially defined categories. In contrast, some stimuli of "real" categories (concepts designable by words) are also better exemplars of the concept than others, but such stimuli may not be the central tendency. For example, some colors are considered better exemplars of that color than others, such as a "pure" blue versus an "off" blue. Rosch refers to these focal points as "natural prototypes" since they do not necessarily have to be the central tendency of the category. Such focal points exist prior to naming in that they should also be important points of reference for Ss who do not have names for the stimuli.

Rosch tested the importance of central and noncentral focal points by presenting a classification task to the Dani tribe of New Guinea. Only Dani who used two basic color terms (corresponding to dark and light) participated in the experiment. The task required learning a correct category response for each of 24 stimuli. There were three stimuli in each of the eight categories, chosen so as to correspond to the eight basic chromatic color terms. One group of Ss learned categories in which the natural prototype was in a central position, such as "pure" blue surrounded by blues of two Munsell steps to either side. Another group learned categories in which the natural prototype was on one end of the category—a "pure" blue and blues two and four Munsell steps longer in wavelength. Rosch found that (a) the natural prototypes were learned more rapidly than other colors even when they were peripheral members of categories, but (b) the Dani made fewer errors in learning all the colors when the natural prototype was the central member of the category. Essentially the same results were obtained using geometric forms as stimuli. The natural prototypes were a circle, square, and triangle, and transformations of these forms were the other members of a category.

These results, along with the experiments on schema theory, suggest that some patterns are particularly representative of a class of patterns and can serve as a focal point for that class. Insofar as a prototype may be thought of as a type of template, these results also support a template theory. But a prototype is not an unanalyzed template in which the amount of overlap is used to judge its similarity to other patterns. Instead, a prototype consists of features, and when it represents the central tendency, is determined by the mean value of each feature when the mean is calculated from all the patterns in the category. The similarity of the prototype to other patterns can be based on a distance metric and the distance metric may also depend upon feature values. This issue will be discussed in greater detail in the chapter on distance models. Our current objective is to evaluate alternative theories of representation and we will continue in this direction in the next chapter by considering the structural properties of patterns.

Summary

A useful conceptualization of the stages involved in perceptual learning was provided by Eleanor Gibson. Successively, these are: the discovery of distinctive features, the construction of a concrete image from these features, and the formation of an abstract image. Jakobson, Fant, and Halle proposed that distinctive features could be used to represent the basic sounds of a language. According to their theory, phonemes are discriminated by their values on twelve binary dimensions. The feature differentiation theory proposed by the Gibsons emphasized that perceptual learning occurs by the discovery and discrimination of stimulus features and not by the attachment of associations. Lines of different orientations, various types of curves, horizontal and vertical discontinuity, and symmetry are examples of features which the child must learn in order to discriminate the letters of the alphabet. Sutherland also argued for a feature theory, in opposition to theories that postulate modification of a randomly organized neural network. He assumed that animals discriminated patterns on the basis of a few specific analyzing mechanisms. These few mechanisms would not only require fewer nerve cells than modification of neural networks, but would account for more experimental findings.

A difficult problem concerns how features are combined to form a concrete image of an object. In a transfer task involving discrimination learning of letter-like forms, Pick found that pretraining on features was superior to pretraining on a standard, at least when Ss did not have to remember the standard. Since more recent experiments have not always suggested the same conclusions, it is necessary to study in more detail how different types of pretraining influence the operations used in discrimination learning. These operations include learning to attend to the relevant features, discriminate different values of these features, remember the values of relevant features, remember the values of irrelevant features, and establish a criterion of what constitutes a difference.

Another aspect of perceptual learning which has received much less attention than discrimination learning is the process of generalization learning. Generalization learning is important in that it is often necessary to treat different exemplars of a pattern as belonging to the same category. One theory of how people make classifications assumes that they form an abstract image or prototype to represent the central tendency of a category. The prototype can be used as a reference pattern to facilitate both discrimination and generalization learning. Attneave demonstrated that Ss pretrained on reproducing the prototype of a category were better able to discriminate the patterns within that category, particularly when the patterns always differed on the same features. Franks and Bransford showed that people can abstract a prototype from a class of patterns and that the prototype is important in generalization. In a study by Posner and Keele, Ss classified patterns into one of four categories, a task involving both generalization and discrimination. Evidence for prototype formation was again obtained, although the results primarily emphasized how success in classifying patterns is influenced by the variability of the patterns composing a category. Although the previous studies equated the prototype with the central tendency of a category, Rosch has presented evidence which suggests that there are natural prototypes which serve as points of reference even when they are a peripheral member of a category.

III | Structural Descriptions

The type of representation emphasized in the previous chapter was a feature list, which described the feature values for each pattern. In some cases, a feature representation is sufficient for adequately describing complex patterns. Scientists at Bell Laboratories, for example, have written a computer program which, using a small list of features (see p. 183), can choose the correct face from among 255 alternatives. In other cases, a feature list is less capable of describing a pattern, even when structural characteristics are included in the list. The feature list proposed by Gibson for letters of the alphabet (Figure 2.3, p. 16) included not only the parts or lines composing the letter, but also more global attributes such as the intersection of lines or symmetry of the pattern. Although these global attributes tell us something about the structure of a pattern, they are not sufficient to represent the patterns completely.

There are several characteristics of a feature list that we can use to test for its adequacy as a model of discrimination learning. First, the list should be capable of discriminating between different letters so that two different letters cannot have the same set of features. Second, the list should be able to account for errors so that confusions should be made between patterns that have almost the same set of features. A feature list like the one proposed by Gibson may satisfy both of these criteria and yet not provide a complete description of a pattern. It may not allow discrimination between letters and nonletters or between letters and rotated letters. For example, does the feature list for the letter **A** distinguish between a normal and inverted **A**? If we can make discriminations that the feature list cannot, the feature list does not completely describe our internal representation of a pattern.

Another reason for questioning the appropriateness of a feature list is our intuitions about how we would describe these patterns. If asked to describe the letter **A**, we might say something like "The letter **A** consists of a negative oblique line joined at the top to a positive oblique line, and a horizontal line connects the midpoints of the two oblique lines." A structural description of this type specifies the features which are part of the letter, the relations among the features (in this case, the relation "join" or "connect"), and a rule describing how the features are related. Our objective in this chapter is to examine the issues related to structural descriptions, particularly as applied to line patterns such as letters or overlapping geometric forms. The first section describes some examples of perceptual development and the learning of spatial relations. The next section contains a brief discussion of the development of structural models in artificial intelligence in order to illustrate the main characteristics of these models. The final section describes some initial attempts of psychologists to incorporate structural models into theories of human pattern recognition.

Spatial Relations and Development

A question previously raised during our discussion of features and templates (Chapter II) was whether the formation of a concrete image involves anything more than learning the distinctive features of the pattern. Activities such as integrating parts into wholes, reorganizing a pattern, learning spatial relationships, and sequential organization in drawing are important aspects of perceptual learning. Some of these activities have been investigated by Elkind (1969), as part of his studies on the development of figurative perception. Influenced by the work of Piaget, Elkind made the distinction between molecular and molar perceptual processes. Molecular processes involve responding to individual elements, whereas molar processes involve perceptual activities such as exploration, schematization, referencing, reorganization, and anticipation.

Schematization is used here to refer to the integration of parts into unified wholes such that neither the parts nor the whole lose their unique identity. Reorganization is the ability to perceive variations in a static configuration, such as occurs during figure–ground reversal. Elkind concluded from his studies that the growth of figurative perception is characterized by a change from a process which is relatively passive and static to one which is relatively active and dynamic. The child becomes less dependent on the Gestalt properties of stimuli, and is better able to reverse figure and ground, integrate parts and wholes, and scan more complexly. The development of such skills always involves cognitive as well as perceptual factors.

A perceptual task which requires the integration of parts into wholes and reorganization of parts is the embedded figures task. The illustration on page 149 shows an example of an embedded figures task in which the figures 2A–2E are embedded in pattern 2. Although this task has been often used by psychologists and related to developmental issues, intelligence, personality variables, and mental retardation, it is surprising that the characteristics of the figures themselves have seldom been studied. The best discussion of the stimulus properties which make embedded figures hard to find is contained in Gottschaldt's (1926) original report. Gottschaldt listed the following factors as contributing to the difficulty of finding a figure (F) embedded in a more complex pattern (P).

(1) Continuation of the contour lines of F to form contour lines of P.
(2) Division of F in P in a manner unlike the mode of possible division implied by F itself.
(3) Enlarging the assymmetrical parts of F into symmetrical parts of P.
(4) Embedding F in P such that a formerly emphasized part of F becomes unemphasized.

In order to obtain more information on what stimulus characteristics cause poor performance in young children, Ghent (1956) presented both an embedded figures task and an overlapping figures task to young children. Since significantly more errors were made on the embedded figures, Ghent concluded that the basic problem was specifying why lines are organized into particular groupings and why the ease of selecting particular groupings changes with age. She suggested that figures are difficult when contours are shared rather than intersect, and that younger children have difficulty in seeing lines simultaneously belonging to more than one figure.

A study by Reed and Angaran (1972) was designed to investigate further which stimulus variables correlate with the difficulty of finding an embedded figure and how these variables are related to mental development. Four groups of children were used. The mentally retarded (MR) group consisted of children with a mean IQ of 60; the lower elementary group (LE) consisted of normal children 6–7 years old; the middle elementary group (ME) consisted of children 8–10 years old; and the upper elementary group (UE) consisted of children 10–12 years old. All Ss were given the same series of 16 embedded figures and were asked to find a smaller form embedded in a larger form. The term "pattern" will be used to refer to the larger form, the term "figure" to the smaller form, and the term "ground" to refer to that part of the pattern excluding the figure. In order to test for the importance of different stimulus variables it was hypothesized that the difficulty in finding the figure would be determined by (1) figure complexity, (2) ground complexity, (3) pattern complexity, (4) analysis complexity defined as the amount by which the combined complexity of the parts (figure and ground) exceeds the complexity of the whole pattern, (5) the number of *shared contours* between figure and ground, and (6) the number of *overlapping lines,* overlapping the figure.

The results indicated that the complexity of the figure, the complexity of the complete pattern, and the number of overlapping lines resulted in nonsignificant, though positive correlations with the difficulty in finding the figure. The number of shared contours, the complexity of the ground, and analysis complexity resulted in significant, positive correlations with the difficulty of finding an embedded figure. The stimulus variables which were significant had their greatest effect on children low on the scale of mental development. Analysis complexity, for example, correlated .71 with response times for group MR, .62 with group LE, .61 with group ME, and .57 with group UE. The number of shared contours correlated .79 with group MR, .68 with group LE, and .55 with ME, and .49 with group UE. The generality of these results is at present limited because only a limited number af patterns were used for testing. The results do support, however, Ghent's suggestion that the number of shared contours is an important variable and Elkind's conclusion that young children are more bound by the Gestalt properties of a pattern, making it difficult for them to reorganize a pattern.

Another issue relevant to perceptual development is the child's ability to respond to spatial relations. Asso and Wyke (1970) compared the ability of children to discriminate visually between different spatial relations with their comprehension of verbal instructions regarding the same relations. Three sets of stimuli were used which varied in complexity of the relationship between a circle and one or more lines (Figure 3.1). The visual discrimination task required the child to match a standard to one

SET 1

SET 2

SET 3

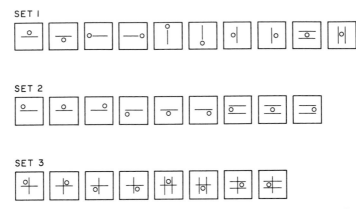

Figure 3.1. Cards used in testing children's ability to respond to spatial relations. [After Asso and Wyke (1970).]

of the cards in a set. The verbal comprehension task required the child to point to a card which matched a verbal description given by the experimenter. Both visual discrimination and verbal comprehension improved with age, although verbal comprehension showed the more dramatic improvement over the age range tested (Figure 3.2). A low correlation between individual performances on the two types of tasks suggested that performance on the two tasks requires two distinct abilities.

In comparison to research on pattern perception, there have been relatively few studies on the production or copying of patterns. This area of research has received renewed interest, however, and was the subject of a symposium reported in the *Ontario Journal of Educational Research* (Spring, 1968). The topic of the symposium focused on the question of why children learn to copy a geometric form much later than they learn to discriminate between various forms. One suggestion (Maccoby, 1968) is that copying is necessarily a sequential process in which the spatial relationship of the parts is more important than in simple discriminations. Whereas form perception is based primarily on the whole shape, copying requires fractionation of a stimulus into its parts and relating the parts to the whole. In support of her hypothesis, Maccoby reported an experiment in which the ability to copy forms improved following discrimination training on the components of the forms—angles and horizontal, vertical, and diagonal lines. Another group of children, trained on tracing outlines in grooved drawing boards, showed no improvement in copying ability. These findings lend partial support to her theory since the discrimination of components is a necessary first step. But the major hy-

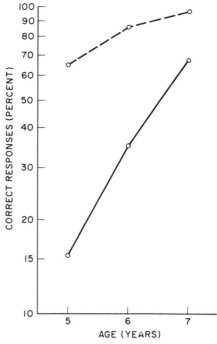

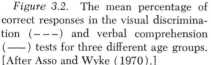

Figure 3.2. The mean percentage of correct responses in the visual discrimination (– – –) and verbal comprehension (——) tests for three different age groups. [After Asso and Wyke (1970).]

pothesis requires further testing and research—the importance of providing training in organizing and relating the components to each other.

I have reviewed only a few studies in this section but I hope they convey some idea of the importance of structure in perceptual development. Our goal, however, is to try to formulate a more detailed theory of what is meant by a structural description. The development of such theories has not been by psychologists, but by computer scientists who are interested in computer pattern recognition. The next section describes some approaches to this problem and the section beginning on page 44 attempts to relate these ideas to psychological theories of pattern recognition.

Structural Models in Artificial Intelligence

Our discussion of formal models of pattern recognition has thus far been based upon the assumption that patterns can be analyzed into features and represented by listing the values of these features. This type of a methodology was particularly evident in the "classical" model of pattern recognition in which statistical decision theory was applied to the feature values in order to assign patterns to categories (discussed in Chapter VIII). Beginning in the early 1960s, a small number of computer scientists became dissatisfied with such an approach. Influenced by the type of structural models that were being used in the field of linguistics, they argued that what is really important is not pattern categorization but pattern description and particularly a description that would include how the parts of patterns are structurally interrelated.

One investigator who argued for such a change in emphasis was Narasimhan (1962). According to Narasimhan, pattern recognition could best be achieved by a specially designed computer with parallel processing facilities based upon the phrase structure model of the linguists. Utterances in a language can be analyzed into a hierarchy of syntactic units such as phonemes, morphemes, phrases, and sentences. An explicit statement of the relationship between these units and between different linguistic levels constitutes a grammar of that language. By using the linguistic model as a general guide, Narasimhan outlined a recognition procedure for line patterns consisting of the following operations.

(1) List the basic sets. These constitute the lowest level units and consist of terminals, crossings, junctions, corners, and bends.

(2) Form a table of primary connections specifying for each pair of basic sets whether they are connected, and if so, how they are connected.

(3) Apply grammar rules to form phrases. Phrases consist of strings of primary connections formed by concatenation. Classes of strings can be identified as specific phrases—straight lines, open curves, circular arcs, etc.

(4) Apply grammar rules to form sentences by linking phrases to other phrases at their vertices.

A more concrete example of the general procedure is illustrated by a grammar developed to describe letters of the alphabet. Narasimhan and Reddy (1967) developed a phrase structure grammar consisting of a finite vocabulary of basic strokes and a finite system of rewriting rules. Figure 3.3 shows the vocabulary of basic units. The vocabulary items are used to construct phrases and the phrases are used along with the vocabulary items to construct letters. Elements of the vocabulary, as well as phrases, may have associated with them a distinct set of vertices. The vertices are the points where a vocabulary item or phrase can be linked to another vocabulary item or phrase. Each rewriting rule must therefore specify (1) which two phrases or vocabulary items are to be joined, (2) the vertices at which they are to be joined, and (3) the correspondence between the vertices of the resulting phrase and those of its components. As an example, a phrase named SGMMA is defined by the rewriting rule:

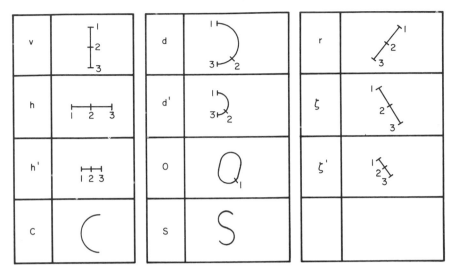

Figure 3.3. Terminal vocabulary of grammar in Table 1. [After Narasimhan and Reddy (1967).]

$$SGMMA(1, 2, 3) \rightarrow r \cdot h'(11; 2, 3; 3)$$

The rule expresses that the vocabulary unit r is joined to the vocabulary unit h' by linking vertex 1 of r and vertex 1 of h'. SGMMA has three vertices, the first corresponding to vertex 2 of r, the second to vertex 3 of r, and the third to vertex 3 of h' (see Figure 3.3). The rewriting rules specifying the generation of phrases and letters are given in Table 3.1. It should be noted that often more than one rewriting rule is listed (separated by vertical lines) and that alternative rewriting rules allow for either slight distortions of a letter or for alternative ways of grouping the parts of a letter into phrases.

Our purpose in presenting this example of a grammar is not to discuss its strengths and weaknesses, but rather to illustrate the general principles of a structural approach and to illustrate how such an approach differs from the feature model discussed in the previous two chapters. Although the theoretical development of structural grammars is still in its infancy, a number of important applications have already been made to the description of bubble chamber photographs, chromosomes, handwriting, fingerprints, cattle brands, and printed letters. It is these types of patterns, in which structural relations are so important, that are particularly difficult to characterize by a list of features.

The main unifying, theoretical impetus characterizing most of the early work on structural grammars for visual patterns has been the pre-

TABLE 3.1

LIST OF REWRITING RULES FOR A PARTIAL GRAMMAR FOR ENGLISH LETTERS[a]

LETTER	→	| A | B | C | D | E | F | H | I | L | N | O | P | Q | R | S | T | V | X | Z |
A	→	INVE·h (11,23;) | INVH·h (11,23;)
INVE (1·2)	→	r·ζ (11;2;2) | r·v (11;2;2) | v·ζ (11;2;2)
INVH (1,2)	→	SGMMA·ζ (31;1;2)
SGMMA (1,2,3)	→	r·h' (11;2,3;3)
B	→	PE·d' (11,23;)
PE (1,2,3)	→	v·d' (11,23;2,3;2) | r·d' (11,23;2,3;2)
C	→	c
D	→	v·d (11,33;) | r·d (11,33;)
E	→	BRKET·h (11;) | BRKET·h' (11;) | EFF·h (11;) | EFF·h' (11;)
BRKET (1)	→	GMMA·h (21;1) | GMMA·h' (21;1)
		SGMMA·h' (21;1) | ELL·h (11;2)
EFF (1)	→	GMMA·h (11;2) | GMMA·h' (11;2) | SGMMA·h' (11;2) | AITCH·h (11;2)
GMMA (1,2)	→	v·h (11;2,3;) | r·h (11;2,3;) | v·h' (11;2,3;) | r·h' (11;2,3;)
ELL (1,2)	→	v·h (31;1,2;) | r·h (31;1,2;) | v·h' (31;1,2;) | r·h' (31;1,2;)
F	→	EFF
H	→	AITCH·v (32;) | AITCH·r (32;)
AITCH (1,2,3)	→	v·h (21;1,3;3) | v·h' (21;1,3;3) | r·h (21;1,3;3) | r·h' (21;1,3;3)
I	→	TEE·h' (12;) | v | r
TEE (1)	→	v·h (12;3) | v·h' (12;3) | r·h (12;3) | r·h' (12;3)
L	→	ELL
N	→	ENN·v (13;)
ENN (1)	→	v·ζ (11; ;3) | r·ζ (11; ;3)
O	→	o
P	→	PE
Q	→	o·ζ' (12;) | o·ζ' (11;)
R	→	PE·ζ' (31;) | PE·ζ' (11;)
S	→	s
T	→	TEE
V	→	ζ·r (33;) | v·r (33;) | ζ·v (33;)
X	→	r·ζ (22;) | v·ζ (22;) | v·r (22;)
Z	→	SEVEN·h (11;) | SEVEN·h' (11;)
SEVEN (1)	→	h·r (31; ;3) | h'·r (31; ;3)

[a] From Narasimhan, R. and Reddy, V. S. N. A generative model for handprinted English letters and its computer implementation. *ICC Bulletin*, 1967, 6, Table 1.

vious work in the field of linguistics, particularly the work of Chomsky (1957). An important question is how far the analogy should be extended in developing grammars for visual patterns which may have little in common with linguistic sentences. Chomsky himself has cautioned against the overgeneralization of his theory (Chomsky, 1968):

> As I have now emphasized several times, there seems to be little useful analogy between the theory of grammar that a person has internalized and that provides a basis for his normal, creative use of language, and any other

cognitive system that has so far been isolated and described, similarly, there is little useful analogy between the schema of universal grammar that we must, I believe, assign to the mind as an innate character, and other known systems of mental organization. It is quite possible that the lack of analogy testifies to our ignorance of other aspects of mental function, rather than to the absolute uniqueness of linguistic structure, but the fact is that we have, for the moment, no objective reason for supposing this to be true [pp. 77–78].

More recently, Clowes (1969) has explored both the similarities and differences between grammars which describe sentences and grammars which describe pictures. According to Clowes, a syntax of a language may be thought of as a set of rules specifying how the primitive symbols of a language are grouped into functional units. A phrase-structure grammar consists of a set of rewrite rules expanding an initial symbol into a set of terminal symbols. The rewrite rule

$$X \rightarrow A \cdot B$$

expresses two relationships. First A and B are "parts of" X and second A is "followed by" B. The characteristic assumption underlying the use of phrase-structure grammars is that all the elements appearing in a structural description will be related in just these two ways. But pictures are characterized by many types of relationships. When we look at a square, we can see that a line meets two others, is perpendicular to two others, parallel to a third, and of equal length to all three. It is this multitude of relationships which are characteristic of pictures that has led Clowes to question the applicability of a phrase-structure grammar to pictures. Instead, he suggested formulating a pictorial language in terms of primitive relationships rather than primitive atoms as is prevalent in linguistic theory.

Not all the theoretical approaches in artificial intelligence have been motivated by linguistic grammars. One example, a program called SEE, attempts to isolate three-dimensional objects in a two-dimensional scene (Guzmán, 1969). Figure 3.4 shows a simple scene and the successful analysis by the program that regions 1, 2, and 6 form one body; regions 10, 11, and 12 form a second body, and regions 3, 4, 5, 7, 8, 9, and 13 form a third body. The successful analysis of very complex scenes demonstrates that it is possible to separate a scene into the objects forming it without knowing the definition of those objects. The program does not require a description of a pyramid or a cube to isolate them as objects even when they are partially occluded by other objects. Instead, SEE analyzes vertices, regions, and associated information to find clues that two regions form part of the same body. An important source of informa-

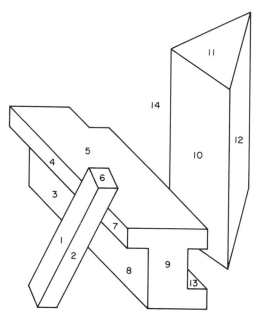

Figure 3.4. A simple scene analyzed by SEE. [After Guzmán (1969).]

tion are the different types of vertices (Figure 3.5) which are distinguished by the slope, disposition, and number of lines which form them.

The work in artificial intelligence suggests that a richer descriptive language is necessary to represent the types of patterns discussed in this section. In addition to listing the features of a pattern, we must define various relations and composition rules which specify how the features are related to each other. Our objective in the next section is to explore how these ideas might be useful to psychologists. The attempt to incorporate these richer description languages into psychological theories is only beginning so high expectations are not yet in order.

Structural Models in Psychology

The view that structural descriptions, as formalized by computer scientists, might be relevant to psychology was put forth by Sutherland in 1968. He argued that current theories of pattern recognition, including his own which emphasized feature analyzers, were insufficient to explain the complexities of the pattern recognition capabilities revealed in animals and man. Influenced by the work of Clowes (1967), Sutherland

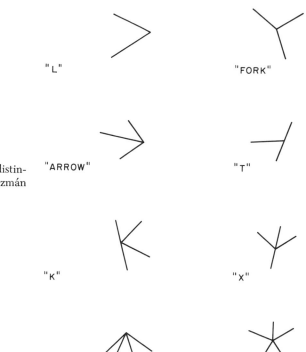

"L"   "FORK"

Figure 3.5. Vertices distin-   "ARROW"   "T"
guished by SEE. [After Guzmán
(1969).]

"K"   "X"

"PEAK"   "MULTI"

outlined a theory in which structural descriptions played a predominant
role. The theory has three parts:

(1) A processor that extracts local features from the input picture
preserving information about spatial relationships between the
features.

(2) A mechanism that produces an abstract description of the output
from the processor.

(3) A store in which such descriptions are held.

The visual input is first analyzed by a processor that extracts local features
simultaneously at all points on the picture. The nature of the feature
extractors should be consistent with physiological evidence, particularly
the findings of Hubel and Wiesel (1962). When a picture is memorized,
a rule is written into a store describing the output from the processor in
highly abstract language. Such a language would express how the features are interrelated and would allow for the possibility of segmenting
a picture in different ways. Recognition of a picture occurs when the out-

put from the processor matches a stored description. What we see is determined by the descriptive rule selected to describe the picture, so that a person is unable to respond to details of a picture not represented in the rule.

Sutherland argued that the advantage of such a theory is that it is sufficiently powerful to explain most of the experimental results obtained in investigating human and animal pattern recognition. He listed the following twelve conditions as results which should be accounted for by a satisfactory theory of visual pattern recognition.

(1) *Size invariance:* Animals trained to discriminate between a pair of shapes will transfer the discrimination when the size of the shapes is altered.

(2) *Retinal position:* If a man learns to identify a shape using one part of his retina, he is able to identify the same shape when presented to many other parts of his retina.

(3) *Brightness invariance:* There is some tendency to transfer when the brightness of a shape and its background is inverted, although such transfer does not always occur.

(4) *Equivalence of outline and filled-in shapes:* Many species transfer a learned discrimination between filled-in and outline shapes.

(5) *Nonequivalence of rotated shapes:* It is not true that any rotation of a shape will be treated as equivalent to the original shape.

(6) *Confusions between shapes:* An adequate theory of shape recognition should be able to explain confusions between shapes and why some shapes are more easily discriminated than others.

(7) *Jitter:* A shape can be recognized as the same shape when subjected to varying amounts of local distortion.

(8) *Segmentation:* Pictures can be segmented in different ways and ambiguous figures can be seen in more than one way.

(9) *Recognition of complex scenes:* A large, but not a small, inconsistency is noticed when complex scenes are briefly exposed.

(10) *Perceptual learning:* Man has the capacity to learn to identify specific objects and the ability to learn about classes of objects that will enable him to recognize new members of the class.

(11) *Redundancy:* Our recognition capabilities take advantage of the redundancy of the visual environment.

(12) *Physiological evidence:* An adequate theory must not only explain facts about pattern perception derived from behavioral experiments, but must also be consistent with what is known about the neuroanatomy and physiological functioning of the visual system.

In a later paper, Sutherland (1973) pointed out that a single object can be characterized in terms of many different discriptive domains. To illustrate his point, he used as an example the two objects shown in Figure 3.6. One way of characterizing the objects would be in terms of the brightness levels stored at each point in the retina. Storing such a description would be useless however, since the retina is never stimulated twice in exactly the same way. An alternative way of representing the objects would be as eight straight lines of specified lengths and orientations, joined at certain points. But since the lines can be grouped to form regions, one can also say that the object is composed of three regions—a square and two parallelograms joined in certain ways. Or finally, we could say that each object is a two-dimensional representation of a cuboid with two square surfaces and four rectangular surfaces. Each description belongs to a different domain in which the basis is either black and white picture points, lines, regions, or surfaces. According to Sutherland, the ability to go from one level of description to another depends upon the existence of a set of rules relating each domain. It is only under the last description, in this case, that the two patterns could be considered identical.

Reed (1971) attempted to formalize the idea of structural descriptions in terms of a grammar and use the grammar as a model of the operations used by people in encoding line patterns. Since predictions derived from such a model have not yet been tested, the grammar is presented here more as an illustration than as a final version of a model. Reed developed the grammar to represent only geometric line patterns of the type shown in Figure 3.7. It was hoped that such patterns would prove sufficiently simple that they could be described in terms of a simple grammar based on a few primitives and sufficiently complex that a variety of tests could be used to determine how people encode and change their descriptions of patterns.

Following Narasimhan's (1969) definition of the components of a grammar, let $G = G(P,A,R,C,T)$ be a *pictoral language,* where G is specified by a set of primitives, P; a set of attributes, A; a set of relations, R; a set of compositional rules, C; and a set of transformations, T. The set of *primitives* consists of four straight lines defined by orientation: (1) horizontal, (2) vertical, (3) negative oblique, and (4) positive oblique. Thus, $P = (-, |, \backslash, /)$. The set of *attributes* consists of the length of each line. Primitive lines are assumed to be of length X, with deviations

Figure 3.6. Alternative views of a cuboid. [After Sutherland (1973).]

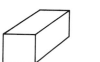

in size specified relative to X, i.e., .5X, 2X, etc. A set of *compositional rules* are specified in terms of a single operation and its inverse. The operation is that of joining or connecting two lines at their endpoints. The inverse operation consists of disconnecting two lines. The point at which two or more lines join is called a vertex. No *relations* are formally specified except for "join." Many relations (left, right, above, below) are implicit, however, but are not necessary to generate or describe the class of patterns being considered other than to label the endpoints of a line. One *transformation* is specified, that of changing one structural description of a pattern into an alternative structural description. The transformation is specified by changing the connections of the primitives.

It should be noted that a deliberate attempt is being made to develop a very elementary pictorial language. The language, in fact, consists primarily of four primitives and a single relation, that of joining primitives at their endpoints. As Clowes (1969) has pointed out, there are many pictorial relations, which are evident to the eye, that need not be expressed formally. For example, although a square consists of two pairs of parallel lines, the relation "parallel" is not necessary to describe a square.

My objective here is to specify the minimal components of a grammar that are both necessary and sufficient for generating a given class of patterns. The same is true of transformations. Only one transformation is defined and this can be specified in terms of the primitives and their connections. The order in which the connections are made is important, however, and is specified in terms of a hierarchical model. Four hierarchical levels of structural descriptions are distinguished: Level 1, primitives; Level 2, composite lines; Level 3, subpatterns; and Level 4, patterns. Primitives have been listed previously. A *composite line* is a straight line consisting of two or more lines of the same orientation joined at their endpoints. A *subpattern* consists of two or more joined lines and is a part of the total pattern. A *pattern* consists of two or more joined subpatterns.

The transformation of one structural description of a pattern into an alternative structural description will be used to illustrate how the grammar might be applied. Figure 3.7 shows four different ways of structuring or articulating a pattern. How are these different articulations related according to the proposed grammar? First, the alternative articulations are all based on the same number of primitives and involve the same number of connecting operations.

This is a nontrivial statement and, in fact, depends upon the choice of primitives. More specifically, it depends upon allowing primitives to be joined only at their endpoints and not at interior points as in one of the

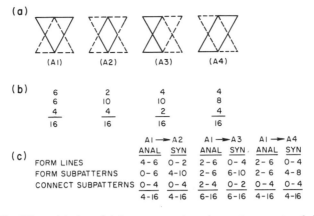

Figure 3.7.   Hierarchical model for representing alternative structural descriptions.
[From Reed (1971).]

grammars referred to previously (Narasimhan & Reddy, 1967). The advantage of the present approach lies in the transformational nature of the alternative articulations of a pattern. For example, if the first pattern in Figure 3.7 is analyzed into two three-sided triangles and the second pattern is analyzed into a four-sided diamond inside a six-sided hourglass, it is not obvious how the two patterns are related. Figure 3.7 illustrates the transformational nature of their relationship according to the present formulation. The transformation maps one structural description into an alternative structural description through an analysis and resynthesis of the first description.

The term *analysis* is used here to refer to the application of disconnecting operations; that is, analysis begins with the structural description and, by disconnecting lines, eventually produces the primitives. *Synthesis* refers to the application of connecting operations: beginning with the primitives and joining them in certain ways to form a structural description. Although different articulations of a pattern are based on the same number of primitives and connections, they differ on the number of connections made at each level in the hierarchy. For example, in forming an articulation of two triangles (A1), six connections are needed to form composite lines (the three sides of each triangle), six connections are needed to form subpatterns (joining the three sides of each triangle), and four connections are needed to join the two subpatterns (specifying how each triangle is joined to the other). The second column of numbers under synthesis (SYN) in Figure 3.7 shows the number of connecting operations required at each level in the hierarchy for the other three articulations. The example illustrates at what level in the hierarchy disconnections and connections have to be made to transform the triangle articulation into each of the other three articulations. For each transformation, the first column under analysis (ANAL) shows at what levels disconnections are made in the triangle articulation and the first column under synthesis shows at what levels the connections are remade in the new articulation. Whether or not such a model can be used to predict the amount of difficulty Ss have in restructuring a pattern is not yet known, but some current research is being directed toward this problem.

A related issue is how Ss form a description of a pattern. Each of the articulations shown in Figure 3.7 requires Ss to make decisions regarding how lines are to be joined. The decisions would have to be made in some organized fashion in order to avoid random connections resulting in an ill-structured pattern. This would require an active model in which the formation of connections would determine how other connections are to be made. Such a theory has been advocated by Hochberg (1970).

> What I shall argue is that (a) the mature observer has a vocabulary of sequential visumotor expectancies (e.g., "If I look along this edge to the left, I will see a corner concave to the right"), and that some of these expectancies (like phonemes in hearing) span a small period of time, and space whereas others, (like morphemes and phrases in hearing), span longer intervals in time and require multiple spatial fixations to encompass; (b) the perception of form over multiple fixations involves active looking, (like active listening in speech perception), and it is the plan of such active looking-and-testing that is stored over successive fixations, not the myriad details that are glimpsed with each independent fixation; (c) as the structure of linguistic expectancies provides the basis for selective perception of speech, the structure or organization of visumotor expectancies provides the basis for the selective perception of visual form. There is, thus, a vocabulary and a grammar of vision to be found, and both attentional and organizational phenomena arise as that visual language is applied to mapping and remembering the world to which we are exposed [p. 114].

Noton (1970) proposed a similar theory, emphasizing that patterns are stored in memory in the form of a feature network recording the attention shifts that are required to pass from one feature to another. Recognition involves matching a pattern to a feature network, the matching being carried out sequentially feature by feature. According to Noton, the order of scanning a picture should reveal the structure of the feature network since the theory predicts that Ss use a consistent scan path when becoming familiar with a pattern. The problem with a theory that emphasizes the importance of eye movements is that the stimuli have to be presented at artificially large visual angles in order to obtain eye movements. Noton used a 20° visual angle and a low level of illumination to limit peripheral vision. Kaufman and Richards (1969) reported that sequential processing correlated with eye movements only for very large figures having a visual angle of greater than 10°. They found that generally, and particularly for small forms of less than 5°, the eye focuses near the center of the figure and rarely wanders from that position. Such results question the importance of eye movements during perceptual learning of patterns. But the emphasis on the sequential organization of pattern structure is an important part of Hochberg's and Noton's proposals and their further development of this part of the theory would be very useful.

One remaining question is which factors determine the organization imposed upon a pattern. The old Gestalt idea that Ss will structure a pattern in a way that minimizes its complexity still provides a good answer. Complexity was an important factor in an experiment by Hochberg and Brooks (1960). The stimuli were ambiguous drawings which could be seen as either flat, two-dimensional forms or as three-dimensional forms. Subjects perceived some forms in two dimensions and other forms in three dimensions, depending on which organization was simpler. Leeuwenberg (1968) developed a theoretical measure of the information content of a pattern based on the assumption that the perceptual system operates on efficient principles which structure patterns in a manner that minimizes their complexity. Predicted complexity correlated very highly with S's ratings of complexity. Reed and Angaran (1972) found that the difficulty in finding an embedded figure is a function of the degree to which the combined complexity of the individual parts (figure and ground) exceeds the complexity of the whole. Although complexity was determined by Ss' ratings in this experiment, other investigators have developed theoretical measures of complexity which correlate very highly with Ss' judgments (Leeuwenberg, 1968; Vitz & Todd, 1971).

Vitz and Todd (1971) proposed that the perception of geometric figures involves sampling the elements of the figure at three hierarchical levels—lines, angles, and areas. The sampling process begins with lines, ends with areas, and requires that all elements at a given hierarchical level are sampled before sampling begins at a higher level in the hierarchy. The model assumes that elements are sampled independently with replacement and that the probability of sampling an element is proportional to the magnitude of that element. Long lines, wider angles, and large areas have a greater chance of being sampled than do shorter lines, narrower angles, and smaller areas. The complexity of a figure is determined by its symmetry and by the number of trials needed to sample its elements at each level in the hierarchy.

The purpose of this section was to illustrate the application of structural models in psychology. We may conclude that there are several proposed models, but a lack of basic research findings. Sutherland (1968) outlined a general theory, but presented no new experimental findings to test the theory or make it more specific. Reed's (1971) example illustrates how a formal language might be used as a basis for predicting the structural similarity of alternative articulations of a pattern. It is not known, however, if such an approach is useful. Two different proposals of how patterns are perceived are the sequential scanning interpretation (Hochberg, 1970; Noton, 1970) and the hierarchical sampling interpretation (Vitz & Todd, 1971). Neither proposal has been tested in detail. Noton reports sequential scanning for very large visual patterns, in which eye movements are necessary, but did not report evidence for smaller patterns. Vitz and Todd were successful in using their model to predict the complexity of patterns, but did not investigate the details of the sampling process over time.

Despite this lack of experimental evidence, the approaches described here are important for two reasons. First, they illustrate some of the challenging problems that arise when we use patterns that cannot be simply represented by a feature list. Second, they suggest possible approaches to these problems, and such approaches will hopefully encourage investigators to develop and test other structural models. Because this area of research is very recent and there have been few developments, most of the examples of formal models in subsequent chapters assume a feature-list representation.

Summary

Although representations based on a feature list are adequate to describe some patterns, they fail to capture all the relationships that exist among other patterns. Patterns consisting of interconnected lines are particularly difficult to represent by a feature list, since it is necessary to describe how lines are joined to one another. An important aspect of perceptual development is learning the structural interrelation of parts: how they are integrated into subpatterns, and how subpatterns can be reorganized to form new subpatterns. A task which requires such a reorganization is the embedded figures task, which is particularly difficult for younger children, since they often have to break up lines or form complex subpatterns. Matching one pattern to another pattern or to a verbal description and the drawing of a pattern are other skills that require the learning of structural relationships.

The development of detailed structural models is primarily the result of the work of computer scientists who were dissatisfied with the classical methods of pattern recognition based on lists of independent features. These investigators argued for procedures which would give a description of a pattern and particularly a description which would include how the parts of a pattern are structurally interrelated. The initial impetus came from the phrase structure models in linguistics, but later developments emphasized the need for capturing a multitude of relationships inherent in two- and three-dimensional representations of objects. A grammar for describing letters of the alphabet and a technique for analyzing a scene into its component objects are examples of this approach.

Sutherland argued that such ideas were relevant to psychology and outlined a theory in which structural descriptions played a predominant role. His model has three parts:

(1) A processor that extracts local features from the input picture, preserving information about spatial relationships between features.

(2) A mechanism that produces an abstract description of the output from the processor.

(3) A store in which such descriptions are held.

Sutherland listed the major experimental findings that should be accounted for by a pattern-recognition theory and argued that his proposed theory satisfied these requirements.

In order to formalize the notion of a structural description, a formal grammar was developed and applied to a limited class of patterns. Although people usually structure patterns so as to minimize their complexity, little is known about the temporal course of their decisions. The greater descriptive power of structural grammars suggests their usefulness despite the current lack of experimental findings.

Part 2 | **TEMPORAL EFFECTS**

IV | Serial or Parallel Matching

One of the important problems of pattern recognition concerns how people compare two patterns to determine whether they are identical. When patterns are composed of a number of well-defined dimensions, the values along each of the corresponding dimensions can be compared to determine whether the two patterns are the same. A comparison between two patterns will result in either a match or a mismatch depending upon whether the degree of congruency exceeds the S's criterion of identity. The speed with which people are able to compare two patterns depends upon whether the dimensions or attributes can be examined in parallel or must be examined serially, one at a time. The term *parallel* means that all dimensions of one pattern can be compared simultaneously to all dimensions of a second pattern. The term *serial* means that at any moment during the comparison, only one dimension of the patterns is being compared.

If all dimensions require an equal amount of time to make a comparison, predictions regarding the time needed to compare two patterns are very simple. Reaction time (RT) in a serial process increases linearly with the number of dimensions, whereas RT in a parallel process remains constant, independent of the number of dimensions. Predictions are more complicated when comparison times differ for the different dimensions. Reaction time in a parallel process, for example, is limited by the time required to compare values on the slowest dimension. Additional complications would of course occur if a combination of serial and parallel matching were used to compare two patterns. Townsend (1971b) has discussed various factors which determine whether we can distinguish between a serial system and a parallel system.

This chapter is organized into four sections. The first section is concerned with the case just considered: the comparison of two multidimensional patterns. The next two sections consider two important experimental paradigms developed by Sternberg and Neisser. The crucial area examined in these experiments is how the concept of serial and parallel matching relates to the comparison of whole patterns, as compared to the attributes of patterns. The final section examines how both identification and categorization influence decision time.

Multidimensional Matching

A variety of studies on pattern matching have used stimuli composed of well-defined dimensions. For example, Ss in an experiment by Nickerson (1967) judged whether two patterns were the same or different. The stimuli differed with respect to three attributes—color, size, and shape. The dependent variable was the time taken by Ss to make a "same" or "different" decision. In Experiment 1, the two stimuli were drawn side by side and presented simultaneously. In Experiment 2, the pairs were presented sequentially with a separation of 2 sec. Figure 4.1 shows the results. The two upper curves are for simultaneous presentation; the lower curve is for sequential presentation. In each case, the time taken to make a "different" decision was inversely related to the number of dimensions along which the stimuli differed. Results such as these are basically consistent with a serial, self-terminating model in which S compares one dimension at a time and responds "different" as soon as a difference is detected.

Although such a model adequately accounts for the "different" RT's, it fails to account for the "same" RTs. The reason for this is that the model predicts that RT should be a linear function of the average number of comparisons Ss have to make. The expected RT function for two "different" stimuli would be quite like that shown in Figure 4.1 since Ss make an average of 1, $\frac{4}{3}$ and 2 comparisons when stimuli differ along three, two, or one dimension. However, Ss must compare all three dimensions before deciding that two stimuli are the same and "same" responses should therefore result in the longest response times. The data clearly indicate otherwise, so what went wrong? A possible explanation is that Ss first attempt a template match and examine the features serially only if a template match fails. This model predicts that "same" responses should be the fastest, a prediction consistent with the response times found for sequential presentation of the two patterns. When two patterns are presented sequentially, Ss have time to encode the first pattern, resulting in faster RTs than when the two patterns are presented simultaneously (Figure 4.1). Apparently, the encoding takes a form which will allow for a rapid template match when the two patterns are identical.

The "same" response is not the fastest when the two patterns are presented simultaneously. The shape of the RT curve is shown by the two upper curves in Figure 4.1, and the results are very similar to results obtained by Egeth (1966) in an experiment using nearly the same procedure. Such findings are nearly impossible to interpret in terms of a simple model, but could be accounted for by a model proposed by

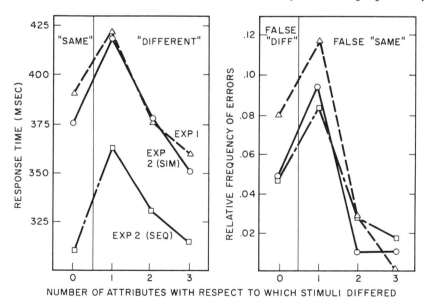

Figure 4.1. Mean response time and relative frequency of errors as functions of the number of attributes with respect to which two stimuli of a pair differed. [After Nickerson (1967).]

Bamber (1969). Bamber suggested that Ss simultaneously use two different procedures for comparing stimuli. One type of comparison is a serial,
self-terminating processor, which initiates a "different" response as soon
as a difference is detected on one of the dimensions. A second comparison
operation is made by an *identity reporter*, which is relatively fast and
initiates a "same" response whenever two stimuli are identical. One
problem with such a model is that it can predict any type of relationship
between same and different responses depending on the relative speed
of the identity operator. Such extreme flexibility makes it difficult to test
such a model rigorously, but may also be necessary to account for such
data as is shown in Figure 4.1.

Bamber did not elaborate on the exact nature of the identity reporter,
but it would possibly involve some type of template match. According to
Smith (1968), the notion of a template usually implies a point-to-point
isomorphism between the template and stimulus. He suggested that
while it can often be thought of as a spatial representation and visual
image, most proponents of template models have said very little about its
exact nature. One possibility is that a template match is nothing more
than a parallel comparison of dimensions. To the extent that this is correct, Bamber's explanation would suffer from having to postulate that Ss
were simultaneously comparing features serially and in parallel (for the
identity reporter). There would be no conflict if the identity reporter
finished its task before the serial testing began, but if both types of
processing occurred simultaneously, serial and parallel testing would have
to occur simultaneously.

As pointed out previously, the advantage of the Bamber model is that
it can account for any possible relationship between the relative speed of
"same" decisions and "different" decisions. This robustness led Nickerson
(1972, p. 312) to conclude that, of all the models proposed to date,
Bamber's appears best able to explain the existing data. An alternative to
the Bamber model would be to propose that Ss always first attempt an
identity match based on a parallel comparison of features. If they are
uncertain regarding their decision, they test each feature sequentially and
respond "different" as soon as a difference is detected or "same" if no
differences are detected. To account for the data, the model would have
to predict that sequential testing usually follows whenever the two patterns are different and usually does not follow whenever the two patterns
are identical. The exact formalization of the model would be very similar
to the model proposed by Juola, Fischler, Wood, and Atkinson (1971) to
account for performance in a different type of task (discussed on page
70). Like the predictions of the Bamber model, any type of relation between "same" and "different" reaction times would be possible depending

on the relative probability of sequential testing following same patterns, as opposed to different patterns. The advantage of the model suggested here is that the idea of parallel feature testing, followed by sequential feature testing, seems more intuitively plausible than the idea of simultaneous serial and parallel testing which seems to be implied by the Bamber model.

Evidence from the previous experiments suggests that, under certain conditions, observers are capable of matching all dimensions in parallel. The possibility of making such parallel comparisons is reduced when the two stimuli occur simultaneously in which case both patterns have to be encoded. A second factor which can reduce the possibility of template matching is the presence of irrelevant dimensions. In the second part of Egeth's (1966) experiment, "same" RT was measured as a function of the number of relevant dimensions. Trials were grouped into one-, two-, and three-dimensional blocks and Ss were told which dimensions were relevant before each condition. Reaction time increased between one and two relevant dimensions, as a serial model would predict, but decreased when all three dimensions were relevant. It is likely that some parallel processing of dimensions was occurring when all dimensions were relevant which was not possible when some dimensions had to be ignored. It would be more difficult to process dimensions in parallel when only some of them are relevant to the decision.

Another condition which may involve parallel processing is when a stimulus occurs very frequently. Lindsay and Lindsay (1966) presented Ss with random sequences of 32 distinct stimuli which assumed one of two levels for each of five dimensions. Two of the 32 stimuli occurred with probability .33 each and the remaining 30 stimuli occurred with probabilities summing to .33. Subjects responded by depressing a negative key to one of the frequently occurring stimuli, a positive key to the other, and a zero key to any of the remaining 30. The positive stimulus was the complement of the negative on each of the five dimensions. Mean RTs over all Ss and sessions for the negative, zero, and positive responses were 597, 684, and 617 msec, respectively. All Ss gave shorter mean RT for the negative response, next shortest for the positive, and longest for the zero response. The investigators proposed that frequently occurring stimuli are identified as total patterns, perhaps by some sort of template matching that compares all dimensions simultaneously. The template matches are made serially (since Ss responded faster to the negative template), however, and the infrequent stimuli are identified by a serial examination of stimulus dimensions.

An experiment conducted by Biederman and Checkosky (1970) is, in some respects, a simpler version of the Lindsay and Lindsay study. Each experimental condition consisted of simply two stimuli assigned to two responses. In the size condition, the two stimuli differed only in size, and brightness was held constant. In the brightness condition, the stimuli differed in brightness, while size was constant. In the redundant condition, they differed on both dimensions, either of which was sufficient for determining the correct response. The question asked by the experimenters was whether an excess of relevant information would facilitate or retard the speed of responding. Reaction times proved to be faster when stimuli differed on both dimensions. To account for these results, Biederman and Checkosky proposed a model in which both dimensions are processed in parallel and the S responds as soon as he knows the value of one of the dimensions. It is by capitalizing on the variability of the processing times for each dimension that a gain in redundancy can be achieved. This is possible only when the processing times for each dimension are statistically distributed, the two distributions overlap and are less than perfectly correlated. If these conditions are met, then Ss will sometimes finish processing the brightness dimension first and will at other times finish processing the size dimensions first. Since knowing the value of either dimension is sufficient for responding correctly, RTs should be faster when both dimensions are potential sources of information.

The patterns that we have considered so far have been geometric forms differing on such attributes as color, tilt, brightness, and size. Although the dimensions of such stimuli are well defined and easy to vary, they do not seem to be as realistic as other patterns, such as faces. It has recently been possible to construct very realistic looking faces from a set of Identa-Kit features (Bradshaw & Wallace, 1971). Figure 4.2 shows some examples. Are such familiar stimuli as faces perceived as perceptual Gestalts or are two faces compared feature by feature? In order to find out, Bradshaw and Wallace constructed lists of 45 pairs of faces. Five faces on each list were identical and 40 faces were different. The different faces on each list all differed on either two, four, or seven features. For each list, Ss were required to categorize each pair verbally by saying "same" or "different" while scanning down the list. The number of differing features proved to be a highly significant variable, since the greater the number of differing features, the faster Ss scanned. The investigators concluded that faces are perhaps compared by a sequential self-terminating scan in which Ss serially compare each feature and report a difference as soon as two values of a feature fail to match. Bradshaw and Wallace emphasized, however, that their conclusion might only be applicable to the particular demands of their experiment.

The results of previous research do, in fact, suggest that the task conditions favored a serial comparison of features. First, the comparison was

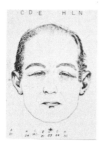
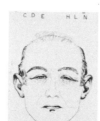
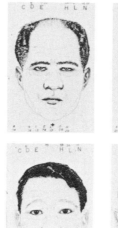

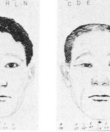

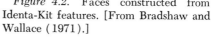

Figure 4.2. Faces constructed from Identa-Kit features. [From Bradshaw and Wallace (1971).]

between two simultaneously presented faces. Second, the Ss were responding primarily to differences and serial models have been more successful in predicting "different" than "same" responses. Would Ss be able to make a template match if two identical faces were successively presented? Results obtained by Smith and Nielsen (1970) suggest that they can, but only if the interval separating the two faces is not too long. In the Smith–Nielsen experiment, the Ss' task was to judge whether two schematic faces—separated by a retention interval of 1, 4, or 10 sec— were the same or different. When two identical faces were separated by only 1 sec, RT was independent of the number of relevant features that required testing. "Same" RTs increased with the number of relevant features only at the longer retention intervals, suggesting a loss of visual information which mediated a template match at the shorter retention intervals. Smith and Nielsen interpreted the findings as indicating parallel testing of features against a visual image at short intervals and serial testing of features against a verbal store at the longer intervals. "Different" RTs decreased with the number of features that differed between the two patterns at all intervals.

The results of these experiments suggest that when Ss have to decide whether two successively presented patterns are the same or different, they first attempt an identity match. The identity match involves a parallel comparison of features with a visual image of the first pattern. If the identity match succeeds, the subject responds "same." If the identity match fails, the subject tests the features sequentially and responds "different" as soon as a mismatch is obtained. Such an explanation accounts for the finding that same responses are usually faster than different responses and different responses take longer as the number of identical attributes is increased.

Although the experiments discussed here are representative of the research findings in this area, more complicated theories may be necessary to explain all the results. Grill (1971) has argued that the capability of the human organism to process information in many different ways makes it impossible to find a simple answer to the question of serial versus parallel processing. She found, using an experimental procedure similar to that used by Nickerson (1967), that processing was serial in the successive comparison task and the response times suggested that there were no differences between the decision processes for "same" and "different" decisions. When the stimuli were presented simultaneously, a shift from serial to parallel processing of dimensions occurred after 5 days of practice. Grill emphasized the importance of the role of specific experimental factors in determining the manner of processing.

An important factor in successive presentation as demonstrated by Smith and Nielsen (1970) is the temporal separation of the two stimuli.

The interstimulus interval in Grill's study was 4.4 sec which may have made it difficult to maintain a visual image for use in the identity match. An important factor in the simultaneous condition was the amount of practice. Another important factor, demonstrated by Egeth and Blecker (1971), is the familiarity of the stimuli. They found a significant inter-action between the familiarity of the stimuli and the type of response— same versus different. Two letters were presented simultaneously in either a familiar (normal) or unfamiliar (inverted) orientation. For "different" judgments there was no significant difference between the speed of response to familiar and unfamiliar pairs, but for "same" judg-ments the familiar orientation resulted in substantially faster responses than did the unfamiliar orientation. Apparently, the superiority of the identity match depended upon the use of familiar stimuli, whereas the detection of differences was independent of familiarity.

In the next two sections we examine whether whole patterns can be matched in parallel the same way that the attributes of a single pattern can be matched in parallel. For example, can the letter **A**, which is itself composed of a number of features, be simultaneously compared to several other letters? Inherent in such a question is the relationship between features and patterns. Marcel (1970) has suggested that letters and digits can be described as conjunctions of similar features. If this is so, then comparing a letter simultaneously against several alternatives should be equivalent to testing several conjunctions of attributes simultaneously. His experiment showed that while two conjunctions of features on differ-ent dimensions may be analyzed in parallel (green and square, *or* bar vertical and bar solid), two conjunctions of features on the "same chan-nel" may not (bar vertical and bar solid, *or* bar horizontal and bar broken). That is to say, Ss could test for a solid, vertical bar at the same time they were testing for a green square, but they could not test for a solid, vertical bar at the same time they were testing for a broken, hori-zontal bar. Marcel hypothesized that we may attend to events simul-taneously if they are on two functionally separate channels, but not if they are functionally on the same channel. If digits are perceived as conjunctions of variously oriented bars and curves on the same dimensions, then it may be that only one internal representation may be set up and tested against an exposed digit. This issue has been extensively studied using a paradigm developed by Sternberg.

Sternberg's Theory

Once the features of a letter or digit have been identified, we still are left with the problem of how this information is encoded in order to search for a match with a memory representation. Sternberg (1967a) proposed that there are at least two separate operations in the recognition or classification of a character. The first encodes the visual stimulus as an abstracted representation of its physical properties. The second compares the stimulus representation to a memory representation, producing either a match or a mismatch. Table 4.1 shows the alternative theories of character recognition considered by Sternberg.

The theories fall into three broad classes. In theories of Class A, encoding (Operation 1) is inconsequential, and matching (Operation 2) is carried out directly on a raw image of the stimulus. In theories of classes B and C the stimulus representation is a processed version of the stimulus. In B1 and B2 it is a refined image; encoding involves a normalizing process. In B3 the representation is a list of relevant features of the stimulus; encoding involves the extraction of features. In theories of classes A and B, encoding produces a representation based on physical properties of the stimulus that can be specified without identification of the stimulus. The memory representation then used in matching is either a template or feature-list. According to theories of class C, encoding identifies the stimulus, producing a representation based on its meaning or name, which is matched to names stored in memory.

Sternberg used a disjunctive reaction time experiment to test the various theories. Subjects first received a positive set of one, two, or four digits. Each S was then given blocks of 18 trials during which he indicated whether a test digit was or was not a member of the set. The test digit was either intact or degraded, and the dependent variable was the time taken to make a positive or negative response.

TABLE 4.1

Some Alternative Theories of Character Recognition[a]

Theory	Operation 1	Stimulus representation	Memory representation	Operation 2
A1	—	Raw image	Template	Template matching
A2	—	Raw image	Feature list	Feature testing
B1	Image refining	Refined image	Template	Template matching
B2	Image refining	Refined image	Feature list	Feature testing
B3	Feature extracting	Feature list	Feature list	Feature-list matching
C1	Identifying	Imageless concept	Imageless concept	Concept matching
C2	Identifying and naming	Image of spoken name	Image of spoken name	Acoustic or articulatory matching

[a] From Sternberg (1967a).

According to Sternberg's model, reaction time should be a linear function of the number of items in the memory set (s):

$$RT = a + bs$$

The zero intercept a is a measure of the mean time taken by events before and after the series of comparisons. This includes the formation of the stimulus representation, which is Operation 1 in Table 4.1. The slope b of the function is a measure of the mean time taken in the comparison of one stimulus representation with one memory representation. This comparison process corresponds to Operation 2 in Table 4.1.

If stimulus degradation is found to increase reaction time, the increase may be due either to Operation 1 or Operation 2. If it is due to the encoding of the stimulus, we would expect an increase in the intercept of the reaction time function, but not in its slope:

$$RT = (a + da) + bs$$

In this case, the stimulus representation would be sufficiently processed so that it incorporated none of the degradation. Such results would support a theory of type C.

A second possibility is that degradation might increase the mean duration of the comparison process. We would then expect the slope of the function to increase, but not its zero intercept:

$$RT = a + (b + db)s$$

For this case, Operation 1 is inconsequential and the stimulus representation is a replica of the stimulus, as in theories of class A.

The results of the experiment are shown in Figure 4.3. Degradation greatly affected the intercept in both sessions. The intercept increased 67 msec in Session 1 and 64 msec in Session 2. The effect of degradation on the slope was substantially smaller than its effect on the zero intercept, and was significant only in Session 1. The mean increase in slope was 7.6 msec per character in Session 1 and 2.7 msec per character in Session 2.

The major effect of test-stimulus degradation, then, was on Operation 1. The representation was apparently not a raw image of the stimulus, as theories of Class A would suggest. It was sufficiently abstracted so that, in Session 2, the degradation of the test stimulus did not lengthen the comparison operation. But degradation can influence the comparison operation as well, as was indicated by the slope differences in Session 1. It would seem, that contrary to theories of Class C, physical properties of the stimulus are represented rather than the identity or the name of the character. Sternberg concluded that the observed reaction time functions appeared to be consistent only with theories of class B. The image was

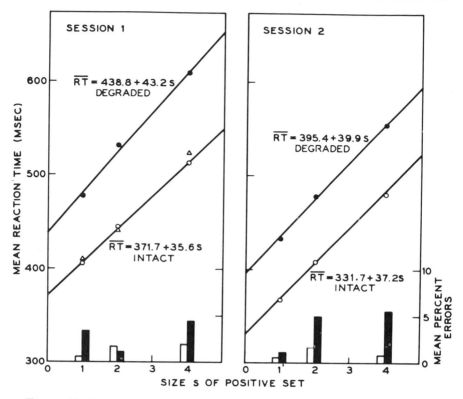

Figure 4.3. Mean reaction-time and error percentage as functions of size positive set for intact (□) and degraded (■) test stimuli. [From Sternberg (1967a).]

refined during Operation 1, but processing was not sufficient for complete identification.

In the previous paragraphs it was assumed that scanning was serial and that reaction time would increase linearly with the number of elements in the memory set. The findings, in fact, provided additional support for a serial scanning theory. Figure 4.3 shows that in both sessions and for both intact and degraded test stimuli, reaction time increased linearly with the size of the positive set. These results were consistent with Sternberg's previous findings. In an earlier experiment (Sternberg, 1966), Ss judged whether a test symbol was contained in a memorized sequence of from one to six digits. Mean reaction time was found to increase linearly with the length of the sequence. The linearity and slope of the function implied the existence of an internal serial comparison process, the average rate of which was between 25 and 30 symbols per second.

A second important issue concerning the scanning process is whether it continues throughout the entire memory set. According to Sternberg's analysis, a positive response should be initiated as soon as a match occurs if the scanning process is self-terminating. In general, a positive response requires an average of $(s + 1)/2$ comparisons in a list of s items. The reaction time for positive responses in a self-terminating search should therefore be:

$$RT = a + b(s + 1)/2$$

A negative response would require the examination of all s items and so reaction time should be expressed by:

$$RT = a + bs$$

For an exhaustive search, the second equation should hold for both positive and negative responses since all s items are always examined.

Two aspects of Sternberg's data suggested that Ss were making an exhaustive search of the memory set. First, the slope of the function relating RT to memory-set size was approximately the same for both positive and negative responses. An exhaustive search would predict such a result, but a self-terminating search would predict that the slope for positive responses should be only half as much, since Ss would, on the average, be testing only half the items in the memory set. Second, Sternberg found that RTs were independent of the serial position of the matching item. Such a finding would be expected from an exhaustive search, but not from a self-terminating search unless the search began from a randomly chosen serial position.

The trouble with an exhaustive search is that it would seem to be a very inefficient strategy to use. Why should testing continue once a match had been found? Before considering Sternberg's answer, let us quickly review a task in which searching of a memorized list was terminated by a match. Sternberg (1967b) presented Ss with a list of from three to seven digits, and found that mean RT increased linearly with list length when Ss were required to name the item that followed a test item. The linearity and slope of the function, and the effect of the test item's position suggested that the test item was located in the memorized list by an internal self-terminating scanning process. The average rate of scanning was about four items per second, much slower than the 25 to 30 items per second scanned by Ss who had to indicate only whether the digit appeared in the previous list.

Sternberg suggested that the results could be explained if we assumed that memory was scanned very rapidly, but checking for a match took considerably longer. When the required response depended only on presence or absence, sufficient information could be obtained by checking the register for a match just once, after performing comparisons throughout the entire list. Exhaustive scanning would then be a more optimal procedure than self-terminating scanning, since it would require only a single check for a match. But when the response depended upon locating an item in the list, the high-speed process could not be used. In order to determine location, the register would have to be checked after each comparison.

The experimental paradigm developed by Sternberg is popular and it has been extensively used by the other investigators since 1966. Readers who have not closely followed this literature should be warned that not all studies have yielded results supporting Sternberg's theory. Morin, Derosa, and Stultz (1967), for example, found that reaction times were markedly influenced by the serial position of items in the memory set. A large recency effect was particularly evident, since the recent items were recognized most rapidly. In some cases, conflicting results are most likely the result of procedural differences. In the experiment just cited, the test item was presented immediately following the memory list, which may have caused the recency effect. In other cases, conflicting findings may be more fundamental, requiring revision of the theory.

One of the more interesting extensions of Sternberg's model involves a combination of his sequential scan model with a modified signal-detection model (Juola, Fischler, Wood, & Atkinson, 1971). The model assumes that items in the memory set (target words) have a distribution of familiarity values that is greater than the distribution of familiarity values for items not in the memory set (distractor words). The memory set, in this case, was a list of either 10, 18, or 26 words which Ss had learned prior to the experiment. During the experiment, Ss responded "yes" or "no" as quickly as possible to indicate whether they thought an exposed word was a target word. Response time increased linearly with the number of items in the memory set, confirming Sternberg's results. Although this aspect of the results could be accounted for by Sternberg's model, several other findings could be more easily accounted for by an extension of his model. Response latency to "no" was greater if distractor words were visually or semantically similar to a target word or if the distractor word was tested earlier in the experiment. Response latency to "yes" was less if a target had been presented earlier, particularly if there were few intervening words tested between the two presentations of the same target word.

In order to account for these latter findings Joula *et al.* proposed that when an S sees a word, he first judges its familiarity. The familiarity values of target words are usually greater than the familiarity values of distractor words, but the two distributions overlap (see Figure 4.4).

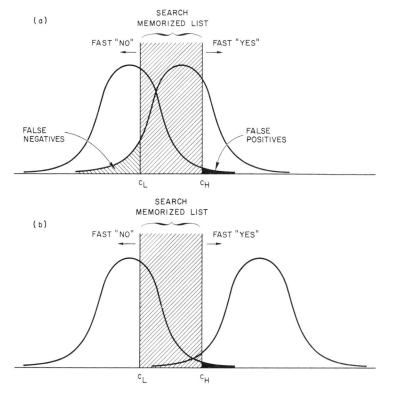

Figure 4.4. Distribution of subjective familiarity values for distractor words (left) and target words (right) with means μ_D and μ_T, respectively, on the familiarity continuum. Part (a) represents the relative locations of the distributions at the start of the session, whereas (b) shows the increase in μ_T immediately after the presentation of a specific target word. [From Juola, Fischler, Wood, and Atkinson (1971).]

Furthermore, the model assumes that the S has two criteria such that whenever the judged familiarity is greater than C_H, he responds "yes" immediately and whenever the judged familiarity is less than C_L, he responds "no" immediately. Words with familiarity values between the two criteria are compared by searching the memorized list. The search accounts for the effect of list length and for the slower responses to distractor words that have been presented previously or are similar to target words. These words are of intermediate familiarity and require a memory search. Previously exposed target words are very familiar and can be responded to immediately causing the fast RTs for these words.

In the next section, we consider a theory due to Neisser which differs from Sternberg's in that the emphasis is on feature-list matching and its implications for parallel processing. The theory proposed by Neisser has been applied to a somewhat different experimental paradigm and so does not necessarily conflict with Sternberg's theory if Ss use different types of processing in the different tasks. Nonetheless, it will be of interest to contrast the two theories, because they differ on the fundamental issue of this chapter: whether or not a pattern can be simultaneously compared to more than one internal representation.

Neisser's Theory

In 1963, Neisser reported the first of a series of studies on decision time in scanning. The Ss were given a list of 50 items and were asked to find one or more target patterns. The items were a string of either two or six consonants. The experimenter made several assumptions:

(1) A S's scanning rate should be limited only by the speed with which he can analyze the items except for physiological limitations such as eye movements.

(2) The process of recognition is hierarchically organized—the recognition of a Z involves prior decisions about subordinate features such as parallel lines and angles.

(3) Processing times should depend upon the depth of the required hierarchy, but if several operations are at the same level in the hierarchy, the S may be able to execute them simultaneously.

The model proposed by Neisser to account for how Ss process patterns when searching for a target should be thought of more as an outline of a theory, rather than as a detailed model. We still do not completely understand how Ss carry out such scanning tasks and Neisser's account does not specify all the details. His general theory has been greatly influenced by the Pandemonium model of pattern recognition (Selfridge & Neisser, 1960) which is shown in Figure 4.5. At the lowest level in the hierarchy are feature analyzers which report the features present in the input pattern. Features may be quite general and include such information as whether there are two parallel lines or whether there is a closed perimeter. A key aspect of the model is that feature tests are carried out in parallel. Features are tested simultaneously and the outcome of one test does not influence another test. Letters are specified by a weighted combination of the feature tests which give the amount of evidence for each of the possible patterns.

The model is very flexible in that it allows for both parallel and hierarchical processing. The problem for the psychologist is to specify both

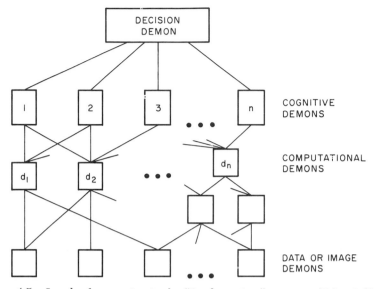

Figure 4.5. Levels of processing in the "Pandemonium" program. [After Selfridge (1959).]

those operations which can be carried out simultaneously and those which are sequential or hierarchical. Early experiments on the effect of context on search time supported the view that different tasks require different levels of processing (Neisser, 1963). These experiments revealed that the similarity of the target letter to the nontarget letters was an important determinant of scanning speed. On the second day of practice, Ss took only .08 sec per six-letter item to locate a **Q** embedded in angular letters, but .46 sec per item to locate a **Q** embedded in round letters. Similarly, Ss took .09 sec per item to find a **Z** embedded in round letters and .22 sec to find the same letter embedded in angular letters. Apparently a greater depth of analysis was required when the features of target letters were similar to the features of nontarget letters. The details, however, are unknown. One possibility is that all feature tests are carried out in parallel, but some tests are much faster than others. If the difference between curves and lines could be detected very rapidly, observers could quickly reject the nontargets without awaiting the outcome of the slower tests. A second possibility is that some tests might depend upon the outcome of other tests and therefore be sequential. This would be particularly likely for tests based upon the relationships of the more primitive features. Subjects would first have to detect two lines before determining whether they were parallel. Finding a **Z** in angular letters would require a closer inspection of relationships than finding a **Z** in round letters.

Neisser favors a model in which feature tests are carried out in parallel based on Ss' performance on a task requiring them to scan for a number of targets simultaneously (Neisser, Novick, & Lazar, 1963). In one task, Ss had to scan for any one of ten possible targets. Although initially quite slow, after 12 days of practice Ss could scan for any one of 10 targets as rapidly as they could scan for a single target (Figure 4.6). Furthermore, their error rate was actually slightly higher when scanning for the single target. Neisser (1967) accounts for such results by postulating a model in which operations at the feature level are carried out in parallel. Although more feature tests are needed in a multiple search task, scanning speed eventually becomes equivalent to searching for a single target because the additional feature tests operate in parallel. Practice is effective because it enables Ss to discover different and faster feature tests.

The hypothesis that improvement in visual search depends upon learning the optimal set of feature tests that will discriminate between relevant and irrelevant items was tested by Rabbitt (1967). Rabbitt argued that the extent to which improvement with practice depended upon learning a specific cue system could be measured by how much Ss were slowed down when the set of nontargets was changed to a different set. Subjects were asked to sort a deck of cards into two piles based upon the target

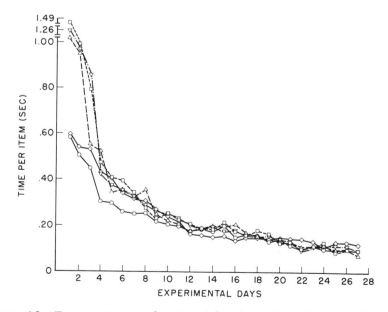

Figure 4.6. Time per item as a function of day of practice and number of targets. *Main experiment:* (□) ten; (▽) AFKU9; (△) HMPZ4; (○) K. *Control experiment:* (◇) K. [After Neisser, Novick, and Lazer (1963).]

letter appearing on the card. The target letter was always embedded in a string of nine letters. One group of Ss searched for two targets; placing all cards containing the letter **A** in one pile and all cards containing the letter **B** in another pile. A second group of Ss searched for eight targets; placing all cards containing the letter **A, B, C,** or **D** in one pile and all cards containing the letter **E, F, G,** or **H** in another pile. In addition to the relevant target letter, each card contained eight irrelevant, nontarget letters. After a variable number of practice trials, Ss were transferred to a trial in which the target letters remained the same, but were embedded in a new set of irrelevant letters. If Ss had learned a specific set of feature tests enabling them to discriminate between relevant and irrelevant letters, their scanning speed should slow down with the new set of irrelevant letters.

Figure 4.7 shows the results. Subjects searching for two targets did slow down and showed a slightly greater decrement the more practice they had with the original set of irrelevant letters. The effect of practice was much more dramatic for the Ss searching for eight targets. Subjects with only a single practice sort actually improved on transfer, but with increasing practice, showed greater amounts of negative transfer. Rabbitt concluded that Ss had to learn more cues to distinguish between eight relevant and eight irrelevant symbols than to discriminate between two relevant and eight irrelevant symbols. It would therefore take longer to learn a specific

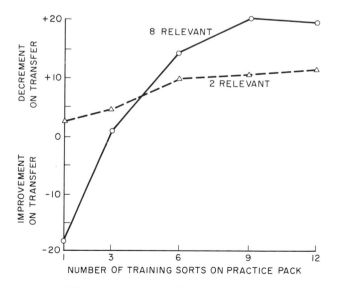

Figure 4.7. Mean difference score (sec) between transfer trial and last practice trial. [After Rabbitt (1967).]

cue system and once learned, a greater loss should occur on transfer. The results of a second experiment suggested that search time is less affected by the relative sizes of the relevant and irrelevant sets than by the particular physical characteristics of symbols in the sets. Subjects searching for two rounded targets (c and o) showed no decrement in search speed when transferred from an irrelevant set of angular letters to another set of angular letters. They did show a decrement, however, when transferred from irrelevant angular letters to irrelevant rounded letters. Rabbitt argued that Ss were able to use the same feature tests in the first case, but not in the second. The results of the Ss showing no decrement were more enlightening than the results of the Ss showing a decrement, since it was already known that increased similarity slows down scanning (Neisser, 1963). Thus, practice may or may not have been beneficial relative to a group who had no prior practice.

A modified, and more sensitive, version of Rabbitt's transfer paradigm was devised by Yonas (1969) to study the effects of learning specific feature tests to discriminate between targets and nontargets. Three groups of Ss participated in a transfer experiment in which differential training conditions were inserted between a pre- and posttest. The pre- and posttests were the same for all groups, consisting of the target letters (**Q, C, R**)+ and the nontarget letters (**N, F, V**)−. The presence of a curve distinguished the positive set from the negative set. Each group received 200 trials on one of three training conditions, differing on whether a discriminating feature distinguished between the positive and negative sets: (1) curvature useful, (**O, S, G**)+ and (**E, Z, A**)−; (2) curvature not useful, (**O, S, J**)+ and (**G, U, D**)−; and (3) diagonality useful, (**A, X, Z**)+ and (**T, H, L**)−. The task was similar to the Sternberg paradigm in that Ss responded positively whenever a target letter appeared on the screen and negatively whenever a nontarget letter appeared. The participants were told the target letters, but were not told what other letters might appear. The amount of improvement in RT between the pre- and posttest was 60 msec for the curvature useful group, 23 msec for the curvature not useful group, and 20 msec for the diagonality useful group. Yonas interpreted the findings as supporting the view that subjects in the curvature useful condition were able to learn to test for the optimal feature (curvature), whereas Ss in the other two groups learned some other strategy, which was not efficient on the transfer task.

Yonas's findings are informative, not only because they demonstrate feature learning, but because they were achieved on a task very similar to the one used by Sternberg. You will recall that in Sternberg's model, a pattern is compared sequentially to items in the memory set, whereas in Neisser's model, a pattern can be tested in parallel against the items in the memory set. What accounts for the opposing results? Neisser (1967) has suggested the following explanation:

> Extra targets to look for do not add to the decision time in search ex- periments, nor in certain highly compatible disjunctive reactions, but they definitely do increase latency in most character classification studies. Perhaps the principle involved is simply this: conditions which encourage the subject to *synthesize* each pattern *individually* generally produce "sequential" re- sults, while "parallel" data tends to appear where these conditions are ab- sent. Presenting one stimulus at a time, penalizing the subject for errors, and allowing him relatively little practice are all conditions which might lead to separate figural synthesis and thus to sequential processing [p. 99].

It is the ability of Ss to use feature testing very efficiently which enable them to make parallel comparisons at a feature level, rather than at a template level following synthesis. Even in the Sternberg paradigm, Ss can apparently use feature tests to achieve some economy of processing when a discriminating feature distinguishes between the positive and negative set.

Further evidence that tests can be carried out at a feature level prior to a complete synthesis was provided by Checkosky (1971). Checkosky combined the procedure used by Nickerson with the paradigm used by Sternberg in order to vary both the number of dimensions (D) that needed to be examined and the number of stimuli in the memory set (M). For example, if the memory set were a red circle and a blue square, possible negative instances would be (a) a red square—two attributes in common, (b) a blue triangle—one attribute in common, and (c) a green cross—no attributes in common. Both the number of items in the memory set and the number of shared attributes had a significant effect on reaction time, but the two variables did not interact as would be predicted by Sternberg's sequential matching hypothesis. If increasing the number of shared attributes slowed down each attempted match to an item in the memory set, increasing the number of shared attributes should increase the slope of the RT function, as discussed in the previous section. The lack of interaction between M and D suggested that the two variables affected independent stages of processing.

In order to account for the obtained independence, Checkosky pro- posed that the task involves the following stages. First, visual information from the incoming stimulus is passively registered. Second, a visual code is generated for each of the items in the memory set. This would account for the significant effect of memory set size (M). Third, the visual code is checked dimension by dimension, but the interrogation does not in- volve a serial search through the memory set items. Instead, Ss have direct access (presumably through a parallel comparison) to the required information for each dimension. This would account for the independence of M and D. Fourth, when sufficient information is obtained to allow the selection of a response, the memory interrogation terminates and the appropriate response is selected. The serial, self-terminating interrogation of dimensions would account for the significant effect of D.

Further evidence for the independence of M and D was obtained by Dumas (1972). Dumas repeated Checkosky's experiment but gave Ss 8 days of practice. During the early stages of practice, he found similar results—a significant effect of M and D but no significant interaction. However, continued practice had differential effects on the two variables. By the eighth day, the size of the memory set was no longer a significant variable, whereas the number of shared dimensions remained significant. The differential effects of practice supported the contention that the two variables influenced separate information-processing stages.

In summarizing the results presented in this section, we have examined evidence for matching at the feature level, particularly as a possible explanation for Neisser's finding that Ss can eventually learn to scan for many targets as quickly as they can scan for a single target. Since this ability is only achieved after much practice, our problem is to identify what is learned. Let us consider three possibilities. First, Ss may be able to test for all features in parallel, given sufficient practice. The number of targets should not matter, since increasing the number of feature tests would not matter if they could be executed in parallel. Second, Ss may eventually discover a small set of feature tests that would distinguish between targets and nontargets. This would correspond to the stage in Gibson's cognitive hierarchy (Figure 2.1, p. 12) of finding an economical set of feature tests. Third, Ss may become more efficient at maintaining the target items in memory so they can be easily accessed for matching.

These alternative forms of perceptual learning are more easily tested using stimuli with obvious dimensions and there is evidence for all three in the experiments presented in this chapter. Evidence for learning to test features in parallel was reported by Grill (1971). Grill found that Ss initially responded much faster to two identical simultaneous stimuli when only a single dimension was relevant than when three dimensions were relevant. After 5 days of practice, differences in response time became nonsignificant, indicating parallel processing of the three dimensions. Learning was not a function of improving access to a memory set (since the stimuli were simultaneous) nor finding a smaller set of features (since it was necessary to test all three dimensions).

Evidence for learning a more economical set of features was provided by Rabbitt's (1967) experiment in which transfer to a new set of nontargets slowed response time. Since the target set remained the same throughout the experiment, Ss' response times should have continued to improve over trials if they were learning the target set. The response times did improve for the eight-item target set during the initial stages of learning (see Figure 4.7, p. 75) indicating that Ss were still learning the target set for this condition of the experiment.

The third type of perceptual learning, gaining quicker access to the target set, is illustrated more directly by Dumas's (1972) experiment. Dumas found that with sufficient practice, the number of items in the target set (two or three) did not significantly affect response time. However, the number of features that had to be compared remained a significant variable, indicating that improvement was not at the feature level.

Any one of these three types of learning could account for Neisser's finding that Ss can learn to scan for ten targets as quickly as they can scan for a single target and I would hesitate to eliminate any explanation on the basis of available evidence. However, it is my contention that learning an optimal set of features is an inadequate explanation unless the set includes conjunctions of features. One reason is that there do not appear to be any reasonable candidates for an optimal feature set in Neisser's study. The positive set consisted of the 10 patterns **AFKU9HM PZ4** and the negative set consisted of the 20 patterns **BCGIJNOQRSTVW XY13567**. It seems that it would be more reasonable to assume that learning occurred at a higher level in the Pandemonium model, involving conjunctions of features. Since some features would be fed into a number of different conjunctions, this type of learning should be quite slow and could account for the extensive practice required by Ss to achieve high scanning rates for ten targets. Although testing for conjunctions would occur at a higher level in the hierarchy than testing for features, it would still occur at a lower level than complete synthesis. Such learning might require two stages: first learning what conjunctions to test for and second, learning to make these tests in parallel.

This is not to deny the importance of learning an optimal set of features when an optimal set is sufficient for distinguishing between positive and negative items. But even here we have more to learn. First, it is difficult to define a set of features for letters and attempts to find a useful set of dimensions from a confusion matrix have not been very successful (Townsend, 1971a). Second, it is not clear exactly how feature learning occurs. Do observers begin by applying a complete set of tests and gradually eliminate the inefficient ones or do they continually shift from one small set of tests to another until an optimal set is found? And finally, even when we have a fairly good idea of what an optimal feature set might be, it is not always obvious how it is used. For example, when Ss search for a **Z** in round letters, there are two basic strategies which they could use:

The first is a search for **Z** features and the second is a search for non-**Z** features. Whenever a subject detects a curve, he could stop processing that item because it contains a non-**Z** feature. Searching for curves would be a fairly good strategy for Neisser's Ss, who were mainly required to process nontargets. But this is not a part of the Pandemonium model, which bases its decision on the presence of **Z** features rather than the presence of features which are not part of a **Z**. This distinction should not make any difference to the extent that all feature tests occur in parallel and take an equal amount of time. However, the very fact that context has an effect suggests hierarchical processing in which some questions can be answered sooner than others. We saw in the first section how Ss' ability to utilize the degree of dissimilarity between two patterns depended upon their ability to terminate the comparison as soon as they located an inconsistent feature. A similar strategy would seem appropriate when scanning for targets that are quite dissimilar from nontargets.

In the next section we consider the relationship between three stages of information processing: stimulus examination, identification, and memory examination. The stages occur serially in the sense that a person knows something about the physical features of a letter before being able to identify it and he may have to identify it before deciding whether it is a consonant or a vowel. The latter decision involves a classification which follows identification, but some classifications may precede identification such as deciding that a round letter is a nontarget without knowing whether it is an "o" or a "c." The relationship between these various stages implies a hierarchical decision process, which is our next topic of investigation.

Identification and Classification

Neisser and Beller (1965) have suggested that the identification of a stimulus is not an isolated process in itself, but the termination of one kind of activity and the beginning of another. They distinguished between three stages of information processing: (1) stimulus examination, (2) identification, and (3) memory examination. *Stimulus examination* refers to those processes which precede identification. The activity in the receptors is analyzed for the possible presence of a variety of features and the information about these features is somehow combined to arrive at an identification. At some particular point, a cognitive subsystem is aroused which corresponds to the linguistic unit of what is seen. This tentative decision by the perceiver about what the object is, Neisser and Beller refer to as *identification*. Processes following identification operate upon very different information. Physical dimensions become irrelevant and there is a *memory examination* involving stored information such as associations, images, or properties of the stimulus. Memory examination can be used to classify a stimulus as a member of a set defined by some particular rule, such as "animals" or "vowels."

Neisser and Beller (1965) reported two experiments in which Ss searched through lists of words looking for either a known word, members of a small fixed set, or for words defined only in terms of their meaning, such as "any animal." In Condition 1, Ss searched for the word "Monday"; in Condition 2, for any member of a fixed set of 11 states; in Condition 3, for a word containing the letter "K"; in Condition 4, for any name of a person; in Condition 5, for any name of an animal; and in Condition 6, for the name of an animal or person. The results indicated that scanning is much slower when targets are defined in terms of their meaning than when the target is a known word, or a member of a small, fixed set. Neisser and Beller argued that printed words are processed in two stages, termed "stimulus examination" and "memory examination." The findings confirmed their hypothesis that scanning would be faster when the target could be distinguished by stimulus examination alone than when its identification required memory examination.

However, two other hypotheses were disconfirmed. The prediction that all searches for targets defined by stimulus examination alone ("Monday," "states," and "K") would be equally fast was not confirmed. The results also failed to confirm the hypothesis that all searches requiring memory examination would be equally fast. Although the difference between "name or animal" and the two single conditions ("name," "animal") became very small with practice, it did not vanish entirely.

Neisser's distinction between stimulus examination, identification, and memory examination is similar to the theoretical analysis by Posner and Mitchell (1967) of successive stages of information processing based on physical identity, name identity, and rule identity. These investigators were interested in bridging the gap between the very early stages of perception and the complex classification underlying learned concepts. The stimuli were always pairs of items—letters, digits, nonsense forms— to which the S had to respond "same" or "different" as quickly as possible. Subjects' decisions were based on one of three levels of instructions defining "sameness" in terms of physical identity (AA), name identity (Aa), or rule identity (both consonants or both vowels). Decisions concerning physical identity were made most rapidly and decisions concerning rule identity were made least rapidly.

Figure 4.8 shows the results obtained from Experiment 4. The Ss were instructed to respond "yes" if the stimulus pair were both vowels

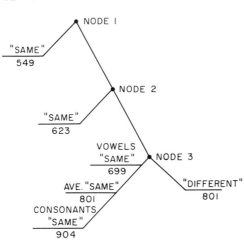

Figure 4.8. Reaction times for decisions based on physical identity, name identity, and rule identity. [After Posner and Mitchell (1967).]

or both consonants and "no" otherwise. Although Ss' decision always concerned rule identity, it could be made more rapidly if the two letters had the same name (Node 2) and most rapidly if the two letters were physically identical (Node 1) It is also evident from Figure 4.8 that it took longer to identify two consonants as being the same than two vowels. Posner and Mitchell suggested, based on this finding and Ss' introspective reports, that the outputs from the naming detectors are fed into a system which searches for vowels; a consonant pair then being identified by the absence of a vowel.

It is also of interest to look at the results from Experiment 2 and compare RTs across different levels of instructions. Under level-1 instructions, to respond "same" when the two stimuli were physically identical, the mean RT for the "same" response was 420 msec. This was substantially less than the 549 msec (Node 1, Figure 4.8) taken by Ss to indicate rule identity when the stimuli were physically identical. Under level-2 instructions to respond "same" when the two stimuli had the same name, the mean RT for the "same" response was 523 msec, or 100 msec less than the time Ss took to indicate rule identity when the two stimuli had identical names (Node 2, Figure 4.8).

Although the previous two studies both indicated that identification preceded classification, Brand (1971) has argued that classification of patterns can occur without identification in a visual search task. This suggestion is not novel, since Neisser's pattern-recognition theory depends upon classification of stimuli as nontargets before they are identified. In the same way, we can classify an approaching person as a man or a woman before we can identify the person. What is common to these two examples is that fewer physical attributes have to be known to make the classification than to make the identification. Brand's argument differs in that classification is supposed to occur immediately before Ss can identify any features of the stimulus. She found that Ss were capable of scanning for a digit more rapidly in a context of letters than in a context of digits, and were able to scan for a letter more rapidly in a context of digits than in a context of letters. But if there were features that distinguished letters from digits, classification could precede identification in the same way that detecting a curve would indicate a nontarget when one is searching for a **Z.**

Although the discrimination between letters and digits resulted in some economy of processing in the previous study, the time taken to name, as opposed to categorize a letter, suggests that naming precedes categorization in the following experiment (Dick, 1971). Only one item at a time was shown to Ss, whose task was to name the item or to categorize it by saying "number" or "letter." The number of items in the stimulus set varied from 2 to 16 and were evenly divided between numbers and letters. Naming time increased as the stimulus set size increased and categorization time could be predicted by the time required for naming plus a constant. Dick argued that both the faster times for naming and the parallel increase of naming and categorization times over set size (in which case the number of different name responses equaled the set size but the number of category responses remained constant—"letter" or "digit") indicated that naming must precede categorization.

In general, this research is consistent with the view that there are three stages of information processing: stimulus examination, identification, and memory examination. The stages are serially organized in that stimulus examination precedes identification which precedes memory examination. There is a subtle distinction between stimulus examination and memory examination as it applies to classification. For example, Brand's (1971) finding that it was easier to search for a letter in a number context than in a letter context could be explained as stimulus examination if there are features that distinguish letters from numbers. It could also be explained as memory examination if all items were classified and the letter context caused more associative interference than the number context. This would not be an optimal strategy, since, according to the results obtained by Neisser and Beller (1965) and Posner and Mitchell (1967), classification involving memory examination requires more time than identification.

Dick (1971) also found that classification required more time than identification, in contrast to the explanation offered by Brand (1971). These results are puzzling but again may be related to the question of whether classification is stimulus examination or memory examination.

Brand's experiment was based on Neisser's scanning paradigm, and, according to Neisser, scanning occurs at the level of stimulus examination
insofar as it is based on feature detection. Dick's experiment was more
similar to the Sternberg paradigm in that only a single item was exposed.
Both of these results could therefore be interpreted within the framework
of Neisser's theory (as presented in the previous section) by assuming
that looking for a target in a multi-item array enables Ss to make a classification on the basis of a feature analysis, whereas the identification of a
single item results in a full synthesis and a subsequent classification.

Although this explanation initially seemed to me to be the most attractive one, the results of two more recent studies (Ingling, 1972; Jonides
& Gleitman, 1972) question whether the scanning results are due to a
different set of distinctive features for digits and letters. Ingling (1972)
argued that if categorization applies to symbolic rather than physical
categories, it is necessary to show that the categories are not distinguished
on the basis of general physical features. She therefore chose letters and
numbers to equate closely the general physical features of each category
and found results similar to those found by Brand (1971). Subjects were
able to scan more rapidly for a digit when it was in a letter background
and for a letter when it was in a digit background.

Since it may be difficult to equate letters and digits perfectly for
physical similarity, the experiment by Jonides and Gleitman (1972) is
particularly interesting. Subjects had to indicate whether a target was
present or absent from a display of two, four, or six items. When the
target and background items were of the same category (both letters or
both digits), reaction time increased with display size. When the target
and background items were from different categories, reaction times were
independent of display size. The same results were obtained for the
ambiguous target **O** which was sometimes presented as the number "zero"
and sometimes as the letter **O**. Subjects could detect a "zero" more rapidly
in a display of letters and the "letter" **O** more rapidly in a display of digits,
even though the target was physically identical in both instances.

These results suggest that the categorization effect may be caused by
factors other than a different set of physical features for letters and digits.
It seems logically implausible to me, however, that a pattern can be
classified as a letter or digit without being identified unless fewer features
are needed to classify than to identify. An alternative interpretation is
that the patterns are fully identified and then classified. The classification
could then cause semantic interference whenever the targets and nontargets were from the same category. If Ss were conservative and re-
checked their identifications whenever they classified a pattern as
belonging to the same category as the target, their scanning speed would

be slower whenever targets and nontargets were from the same category. Although this interpretation is inconsistent with the view that decisions in scanning experiments are made at the feature level prior to identification, I think it should be considered a possible candidate because of the lack of explanations for the category effect. It should be noted, in addition, that the explanation is consistent with certain aspects of the Juola *et al.* (1971) model and my proposed revision of the Bamber (1969) model, both of which propose a rechecking procedure depending upon the outcome of an initial test.

Summary

A central issue of information processing models is the speed with which people can perform various operations. Two alternative formulations are that the features of a pattern, or entire patterns, may be compared either simultaneously (parallel) or one at a time (serial). When two multiattribute patterns are compared to determine whether they are identical, the time taken to reach a decision is greatly influenced by the number of differing attributes. Such findings imply that Ss compare each dimension, one at a time, and respond "different" as soon as a difference is detected. But the time required to respond "same" should be longer than the "different" response times according to a serial comparison model. Since the data indicate otherwise, it is likely that people use two comparison procedures: a parallel, template match to report identity and a serial, self-terminating match to report a difference. The efficiency of a template match is dependent upon the sequential presentation of the two patterns since this enables observers to construct a template of the first pattern before the second pattern is presented. It is also likely that the template match depends upon Ss' ability to retain a visual image of the first pattern. Therefore, shorter retention intervals should increase the possibility of parallel feature testing.

Other experimenters have studied whether entire patterns can be compared in parallel. Sternberg has found that the time required to decide whether an item is a member of a specified memory set increases as a linear function of the number of items in the memory set. His model postulates that the test item is first encoded and then compared serially to each item in the memory set. Sternberg's model has recently been extended to account for larger memory sets by assuming that Ss first judge the familiarity of the test item, responding immediately to items with extreme familiarity values and searching the memory set for items with intermediate values. The model accounts for the slower responses to distractor words which were presented earlier in the experiment or are similar to target words.

Neisser's theory differs from Sternberg's theory in that it postulates that decisions are made at a feature level before complete synthesis. The experimental paradigm used by Neisser also differs in that Ss scan a whole page of items looking for an item contained in the memory set. In contrast to Sternberg, Neisser has found that scanning time becomes independent of the number of items in the memory set with sufficient practice. In general, there is evidence for three levels at which perceptual learning can occur. First, Ss may learn to test for all features (or conjunctions of features) in parallel. Second, they may learn to test for an optimal subset of features. Although parallel testing would also be necessary for this condition, such testing might be easier for fewer features. And finally, perceptual learning might involve learning items in the memory set so that these items are more readily accessible for matching.

Neisser and Beller proposed that the identification of a stimulus is an intermediate stage of processing between stimulus examination and memory examination. Stimulus examination involves feature detection; feature detection leads to identification; and subsequent classifications (such as an "animal") require memory examination for stored associations or properties. Posner's finding that matching is quicker for physical identity (AA) than name identity (Aa), which in turn is quicker than rule identity (both vowels) is consistent with this type of hierarchical model. The question of whether an item can be classified before it is identified depends upon whether the classification is made at the level of stimulus examination or memory examination. When there are features that distinguish between the classes, classification can be made at the level of stimulus examination prior to identification.

V | Iconic Storage

In the previous chapter we discussed the question of serial versus parallel processing at two different levels. First, we asked whether the features of a pattern could be tested for in parallel and second, we asked whether patterns in the memory set could be tested for in parallel. A third question is whether more than one item in the perceptual array can be examined in parallel. For example, in Neisser's experiments Ss scanned a column of letters presumably using a number of fixations to get from the top to the bottom of the page. During each fixation a number of letters would be in the perceptual field, and the question is whether all these letters could be examined simultaneously in order to test for the target.

The advantage of Neisser's scanning experiments is that scanning is an important operation that we use daily in such tasks as reading. The disadvantage is that we have little experimental control over the perceptual array since successive fixations are determined by the subject. How many fixations he will make and how these fixations divide the material is under his own control. An experimental technique for controlling the perceptual array is to present a single brief exposure, small enough to be within the S's visual field and fast enough so that eye movements are eliminated. If a series of brief exposures is presented, one rapidly following another, the task becomes somewhat similar to the task used by Neisser except that the experimenter controls the content of each "fixation" and the speed of successive "fixations."

Sperling, Budiansky, Spivak, and Johnson (1971) used such a procedure to study whether the limiting factor in Neisser's search experiments might have been the rate of eye movements rather than the rate of information processing. Could Ss test for a single target faster than for ten targets if eye movements were not required? Subjects in Sperling's experiment searched a rapid sequence of a randomly determined number (from 6 to 12) of computer-generated letter arrays for the presence of a target. The highest scanning rates occurred when there were 9 or 16 letters in each of the arrays and new arrays were presented every 40 to 50 msec. Since these scanning rates are much faster than is possible by using eye movements, eye movements are a factor which significantly limit the rate of search.

The results of the experiment, however, supported Neisser's (1963) conclusion that Ss can test for ten targets as quickly as they can test for a single target—even at the very high scanning rates. In all conditions, Ss were instructed to search for a numeral in the letter arrays, but only in some conditions were they told to look for a specific numeral. There was little difference in the scanning rates between scanning for a particular numeral and scanning for any one of ten numerals. But there were large differences in the difficulty of detecting individual numerals suggesting that the similarity of numerals to letters was an important determinant of performance. As might be expected, numerals such as **0** or **1** were particularly difficult to detect.

In this chapter, we continue to examine the issue of serial versus parallel processing by reviewing the evidence on Ss' ability to perceive the content of a briefly exposed perceptual array. We shall emphasize the question of whether all items in the array can be tested in parallel or whether each item is scanned one at a time. A second, related issue concerns the effective duration of the display since the iconic storage (visual information store) which persists after the physical termination of the display enables the observer to continue to process its content. The first section of this chapter presents evidence for iconic storage; the second section discusses the earlier serial models which proposed that items in the array are scanned one at a time; the third section discusses more recent models which propose that items in the array are processed in parallel; and the fourth section reviews theories of masking and their relation to iconic storage.

One of the most explicit statements of the properties of iconic storage is Haber's (1971) discussion which distinguishes between feature extraction at the physiological and cognitive levels. When a visual stimulus is briefly exposed, feature detectors of the kind discussed by Hubel and Wiesel (1962) extract information about lines, angles, orientations, velocities, color, and retinal disparity. The features are extracted very rapidly and in parallel, since information comes from each receptive field at the same time. Haber assumes that feature extraction at a physiological level is an automatic process which is uninfluenced by memory, prior learning, or Ss' expectations. Thus, the perceptual stimulus is initially represented physiologically as an unorganized collection of primitive features of the visual array.

But it takes additional time for the subject to become aware of the features in the visual array and the iconic storage which persists briefly (about 250 msec according to Haber) after termination of the visual array. Iconic storage is particularly important for brief exposures, since it gives the observer additional time to extract information from the stimulus. Unlike the feature extraction that occurs at the physiological level, feature extraction at the cognitive level is assumed to be an active process that is greatly influenced by prior experience, expectancies, and the familiarity of the stimuli. Noticing what features are in the perceptual array and organizing these features into a pattern occurs after the physiological excitation of the receptive fields and is not identical with it. Haber's analysis is acceptable, except for the qualification that one way in which expectations can influence feature extraction at the physiological level is to tell the subject where to look, since Haber states that stimuli falling near the fovea probably have more precise features extracted than stimuli in the periphery of the retina. In Chapter X, we will have the opportunity to consider the effects of set in more detail. Our immediate objective is to examine the evidence for iconic storage.

Evidence for Iconic Storage

Evidence for iconic storage was reported by Sperling (1960) in a series of studies designed to measure the number of letters Ss could perceive during a brief tachistoscopic exposure. When an array of stimuli is briefly shown to an observer, he can report only a limited number of items in the display. One possible explanation of this limitation is that the observer can recognize only a few of the items because the exposure is so brief. A second explanation is that many items can be recognized but are not reported because of the limited number of items we can remember. To determine how much information is available to the observer at the time of exposure, Sperling (1960) developed a partial report technique in which Ss were cued to report only a part of the total information. The amount of information available was calculated by multiplying the probability of correctly reporting an item in the subset by the total number of items in the entire display. The partial report technique consisted of cueing Ss to report one of three rows of an array by presenting either a low-, middle-, or high-frequency tone. Each row of letters was small enough (three to four letters) to lie within the memory capacity so that errors or omissions would be the result of perceptual, rather than memory, limitations.

An important variable in Sperling's experiment was the delay interval between exposure of the stimulus array and presentation of the cue. To determine how the amount of available information decreases with time, the tone was delayed by various amounts up to 1 sec after termination of the display. The accuracy of the partial report was shown to be a sharply decreasing function of the delay in cue. For example, immediately following the exposure of an array of 12 symbols, Ss correctly reported 76% of the letters called for, indicating that 9 letters were available. After a 1-sec delay, the accuracy of the partial report was no better than the accuracy of a whole report which averaged slightly over four letters. Sperling interpreted these findings as providing evidence for a short-term information storage in the form of a persistence of sensation following a brief, intense stimulation. The high accuracy of partial report depends upon the ability of the observer to read a rapidly fading, visual image of the stimulus. Once the visual image has faded or its effectiveness reduced by a postexposure field, the tonal cue cannot be utilized and the accuracy of partial report becomes equivalent to the accuracy of whole report.

More recently, several other investigators have confirmed Sperling's suggestion that a decaying visual image persists following a brief exposure. Jackson and Dick (1969) investigated visual summation by varying the interval between two presentations of the same item. The experimenters first found the threshold at which their Ss could correctly identify the letters, **A, U, O,** and **Y,** 50% of the time. After the duration threshold was determined, 75% of the threshold value was used for each of two exposures. However, if a visual image persisted after the first exposure, it could summate with the second exposure to produce a suprathreshold duration. The results indicated that a persisting visual image from the first exposure produced visual summation if the second stimulus occurred within 60 msec after termination of the first exposure. Figure 5.1 shows that recognition accuracy declined over this interval as would be predicted from the concept of a decaying visual trace.

Eriksen and Collins (1968) also used the successive presentation of two stimuli to study the integration of a visual image with a second stimulus. Each stimulus by itself appeared to be a random collection of dots (Figure 5.2). However, when two corresponding stimuli were superimposed, a three-letter nonsense syllable was perceived. When a variable temporal interval separated the two stimuli, recognition of the nonsense syllable was found to be a decreasing function of the interstimulus interval over a range of 100 msec. Figure 5.3 shows the percentage correct as a function of the luminance of the two stimuli and the interstimulus interval. Eriksen and Collins argued that although these results provided evidence of a decaying sensory trace, this concept was unable to account for all of their findings. When two stimuli were exposed simultaneously at a luminance of 1 mL, Ss were correct on 80% of the presentations. Presumably a 5 mL exposure followed by a 1 mL exposure should, at

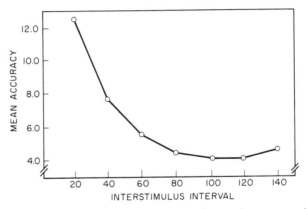

Figure 5.1. Mean accuracy (maximum = 20) for each interstimulus interval. [After Jackson and Dick (1969).]

Figure 5.2. The upper two dot patterns when superimposed result in the bottom stimulus pattern in which the nonsense syllable HOV can be read. [After Eriksen and Collins (1968).]

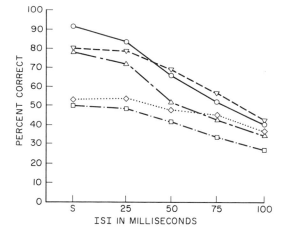

Figure 5.3. Percentage of correct nonsense syllable identifications as a function of the luminance of the corresponding stimulus halves and the interstimulus interval. ○: 5–5; ▽: 5–2; △: 2–5; ◇: 5–1; □: 1–5. [After Eriksen and Collins (1968).]

some interstimulus interval, also produce the same percentage of correct identifications. As is shown in Figure 5.3, recognition accuracy for this condition never exceeded 50%. It is for this reason that Eriksen and Collins suggested that additional concepts, such as a psychological moment or discontinuity detectors, may be necessary to account for the temporal organization of form. This suggestion requires further investigation, as does the possibility of some visual masking occurring with successive presentation of the two stimuli.

Serial Scan

Having reviewed some of the evidence supporting an iconic storage consisting of a rapidly decaying visual image, we now consider in more detail the processes involved when Ss observe a briefly exposed visual display consisting of many items. The first models proposed that Ss scanned the items in a sequential or serial manner. In 1963, Sperling proposed a model consisting of visual information storage, scanning, rehearsal, and auditory information storage. According to this model, contents of the visual information store usually decay very rapidly with decay times varying from a fraction of a second to several seconds. Decay rates depend upon such factors as the intensity, contrast, and duration of the stimulus in addition to the nature of pre- and postexposure fields. The contents of the visual information store can become available to subsequent components of the model as a sequence of items if they are first scanned. The rate of scanning high-contrast letters was found to be approximately 10 msec per letter for display sizes consisting of from one to four letters. These results suggested that Ss scanned one item at a time, requiring 10 msec to recognize a letter.

The next two components of the model consisted of rehearsal and auditory information storage. In order to remember the items until recall, Ss often reported rehearsing the items. Additional evidence was found when recall errors often appeared in the form of auditory confusions—producing a letter which sounded like the correct letter. This kind of behavior is represented in Sperling's model by rehearsal (saying the letters to oneself) and by auditory information storage (hearing the rehearsed letters). The advantage of the auditory information storage, as compared with the visual information storage, is that its contents decay much more slowly. Furthermore, items can be continuously recycled through the auditory information store by means of rehearsal.

We shall return in subsequent chapters to the process of rehearsal and the auditory information store. Our present concern is with the amount of available information in iconic memory and the manner in which the observer gains access to its contents. A remaining question concerns how many items an observer actually recognizes during a brief exposure of a multi-item array. Sperling calculated the "amount of available information," but how is this quantity related to the number of items recognized? This question is difficult to answer because equating the amount of available information with the number of items recognized depends upon the assumption that the proportion recognized in the cued row is identical to the proportion recognized over the entire display. A more sensitive technique for measuring the number of items actually perceived was developed by Estes and Taylor (1966). Their procedure is similar to a two-alternative forced-choice signal-detection experiment in that it requires reporting which of two critical letters appeared in the display. Estes and Taylor developed the technique as a means of obtaining estimates of the number of elements perceived when Ss did not have to process a cue or retain any information other than the name of the target letter.

The paradigm consisted of showing Ss a 50-msec exposure of an array of randomly selected consonant letters. Ss were instructed to report whether a B or an F appeared in the display and to guess if they did not perceive either of the two targets. The display size (D) was either 8, 12, or 16 letters. Theoretical interest focused on the number of letters actually perceived (P) by the subjects and how P varied as a function of display size. Equation (1) gives the probability of correctly reporting the target letters.

$$P_c = P/D + (1 - P/D)\tfrac{1}{2} \tag{1}$$

Since the targets were randomly located in the displays, P/D is the probability that S perceived the target and $(1 - P/D)\tfrac{1}{2}$ is the probability that S did not perceive the target but guessed correctly. Solving Eq. (1) for P, the estimate of the number of perceived letters is given by

$$P = (2\,P_c - 1)\,D \qquad\qquad (2)$$

By using this estimate of P, Estes and Taylor were able to investigate how the number of perceived elements varied as a function of display size. In particular, they were interested in discovering which of three models could best predict how P varied with increasing values of D. Figure 5.4 shows the theoretical predictions. The fixed-sample-size model states that Ss perceive a fixed number of elements and this number does not change as the display size increases beyond this limit. The fixed-area model states that Ss can perceive whatever occurs in a fixed area. The model predicts that the number of perceived elements increases linearly with display size, since the number of elements occurring in a given area is proportional to D in the Estes and Taylor displays. The third model, a serial scanning model, is somewhat more complicated. The model predicts that Ss scan the display items one at a time and that there is some fixed probability that each item scanned in the visual image will be the last item scanned as a result of the image decaying below threshold. The model predicts that the mean number of elements processed increases with display size, but the increase is not a linear function of D as predicted by the fixed-area model.

Experimental findings indicated that the mean number of perceived

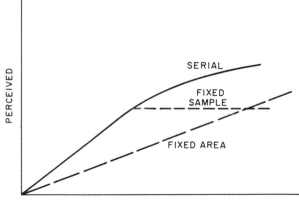

Figure 5.4. Predicted relation between the number of letters perceived and display size. Based on my interpretation of the models discussed by Estes and Taylor (1966).

elements increased with display size in a manner predicted by the serial processing model. This finding led Estes and Taylor tentatively to accept the serial processing model as giving the best account of the data. However, other aspects of their results could not be accounted for by a serial processing model. In one of their experiments they used displays of 16 elements in which there were either 1, 2, or 4 instances of the target. The proportion of correct detections as a function of the number of targets could best be predicted by the assumption that detections of multiple targets are independent events with a common probability of being detected for any given subject. Furthermore, the probability of a detection was relatively invariant with respect to the distance between two targets, in contrast to the prediction of a serial processing model that increasing the distance between the targets should increase the chances of detecting one of them. These results, along with additional findings to be discussed in the next section, led to the eventual rejection of a serial model.

Parallel Scan

In a 1967 paper, Sperling rejected the idea of a serial scan of the visual information store in favor of parallel processing of items. The result that led to his rejection of a serial scan was the observation that all items are reported with above chance accuracy before any one item can be identified with perfect accuracy. In contrast, in a purely serial process the nth location should not be reported better than chance until the $n - 1$st location is reported with perfect accuracy. Figure 5.5c illustrates that S was reporting locations occurring later in his preferred order (left to right or locations I to V) at above chance level before he achieved perfect recognition of items occurring earlier in his preferred order. An alternative interpretation of this finding is that Ss use a serial scan but vary the order of the scan from trial to trial. However, other aspects of the data suggested that this interpretation was unlikely. Sperling therefore concluded that items in the visual information store could be processed in parallel, but gave the illusion of being serial because items in different locations were processed at different rates.

The complete 1967 model is shown in Figure 5.6. Basically, it is quite similar to the 1963 version and contains a visual information store (VIS), a scanning device, a recognition buffer, a rehearsal component, and an auditory information store (AIS). One modification is that variation in scanning is now interpreted as changing the rate of acquisition at differ-

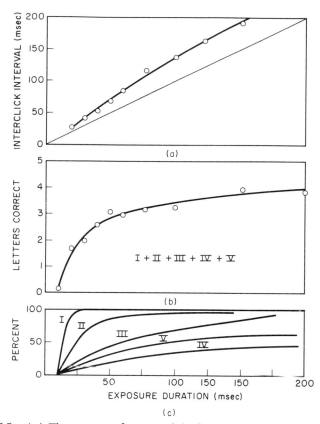

Figure 5.5. (a) The apparent duration of the letters in a letter-noise presentation. Abscissa is the exposure duration of the letters. Ordinate is the duration of an interval between clicks which was judged equal to the visual letters. Data for one typical subject. (b) The total number of letters reported correctly. Five letters were presented, one in each location, I to V. (c) The percentage of letters reported correctly, shown individually for each location, I to V. [After Sperling (1967).]

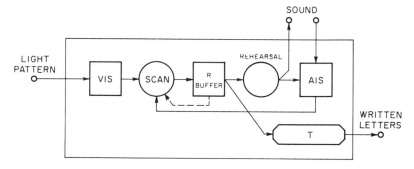

Figure 5.6. Model of processing stages in the Sperling paradigm. [After Sperling (1967).]

ent locations, with information processing beginning simultaneously at all locations. An addition to the 1963 model is the recognition buffer. Its purpose is to convert the visual image of a letter into a program of motor instructions for rehearsing the names of the letters. Sperling added the recognition buffer to the model because Ss would not actually have time to name the letters subvocally (rehearse) during the brief exposure of a stimulus array.

Further evidence for the parallel processing of items in a visual array was given in a paper by Wolford, Wessel, and Estes (1968). The experimental procedure was based on the Estes detection paradigm with the addition that response latencies were recorded. Subjects responded by pressing either a "B" or an "F" key following the brief exposure of a 4 × 4 array of Latin letters. The experimental variable was the number of target elements in the display. Assuming that the elements of the display are scanned serially until a target is detected, we must predict that response time should be a decreasing function of the number of duplicate targets present in the display. When the experimenters measured the latency of responses on true detection trials, they found that response latencies were independent of the number of target elements. In one experiment, mean reaction times (RTs) were 686 msec for one target and 694 msec for two targets. In a second experiment using different stimuli and different Ss, mean RTs were 705 msec for one target, 715 msec for two targets, and 698 msec for three targets. This finding, in addition to the finding that the probability of detecting a target is independent of the distance between two redundant targets, led Wolford *et al.* to conclude that the elements of an array are sampled independently, in parallel, with sampling probabilities varying over the display. They suggested, however, that once the sampling has occurred, a serial processing mechanism may take over when the results of the initial stimulus sampling are coded, or transferred to short-term memory.

A very impressive theoretical account of a wide range of data obtained from partial report, whole report, detection, and backward masking experiments was recently given by Rumelhart (1970). Figure 5.7 shows his more general theoretical assumptions. At the onset of the stimulus display a representation of the physical stimulus is registered in the visual information store (VIS). At the offset of the display, the clarity of the information in the VIS declines as the image decays. The rate at which information is extracted from the display also declines with decreasing clarity. As soon as enough information has been obtained from the display to recognize any of its elements, the name of that element is transferred to a short-term memory store (STM). The more detailed assumptions are as follows:

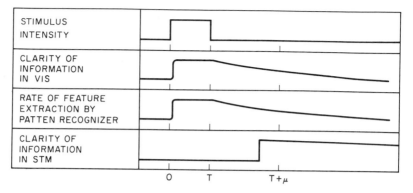

Figure 5.7. Time diagram showing the hypothesized relationships between the stimulus, the VIS, the pattern recognizer, and the STM. [After Rumelhart (1970).]

(1) When a display of N elements is presented for T msec the elements of the display are registered in some visual information store.

(2) Following the offset of the display, information in VIS fades away with decay constant μ.

(3) Each item is composed of a small set of features which are recognized sequentially.

(4) Recognition of c features is sufficient for recognition of any given item.

(5) If recognition occurs, the name of the item is transferred into STM store.

In order to consider the model in more detail, we first have to be able to represent the clarity of information in the VIS as a function of time. Let $v(t)$ be the clarity of the information at time t. Then

$$v(t) = \begin{cases} 0, & t < 0, \\ v, & 0 \leqslant t \leqslant T, \\ v \exp - [(t - T)/\mu], & T < t. \end{cases} \tag{3}$$

Equation (3) says that the clarity of the information remains at a constant value v during the T msec of the exposure and then begins to decay exponentially with time constant μ. Both v and μ are parameters to be estimated from the data, but their value should depend upon such factors as the duration and intensity of the exposure. Since recognition of an item depends upon whether the observer has extracted enough features from that item, it is necessary to know the probability of extracting c or more features from the ith item by time t. The probability of recognizing the ith item by time t is given by:

$$P[R_i(t)] = \sum_{K=c}^{\infty} \exp[-m_i(t)] \frac{\{m_i(t)\}}{K!} \qquad (4)$$

since the recognition of features is given by a Poisson process with parameter

$$m_i(t) = \theta_i \int_0^t v(t')\,dt' = \theta_i v[T + \mu] \qquad (5)$$

if the trace has completely decayed. Thus the probability that the ith element of a display will be correctly perceived is given by the probability that a Poisson variable with parameter $\theta_i v[T + \mu]$ exceeds or equals some value c. The parameter of the Poisson distribution represents the total clarity of the ith item which depends upon the amount of attention allocated to the ith item (θ_i), the clarity of the initial exposure (v), and the decay constant (μ).

When applying the model to the whole report technique used by Sperling, Rumelhart assumed that Sperling's results were primarily due to limitations of the perceptual system so that all items recognized would be remembered and reported. The expected number of reported items should therefore be given by the probability of recognizing an item multiplied by N, the number of items in the display. This would result in a linear increase in reported items with display size if it were not for the additional assumption that the amount of attention given to any item is inversely related to the number of items in the display. By using the value $\theta_i = 1/N$ in Eq. (5), Rumelhart was able to predict the number of reported letters as a function of display size. Figure 5.8 shows the data

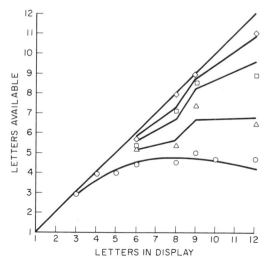

Figure 5.8. Predicted and observed values of "letters available" for whole report and partial report procedures as a function of display size and delay of the instruction tone. ROR: ○: whole report; △: 550-msec delay of cue; □: 200-msec delay of cue; ◇: 50-msec delay of cue. [After Rumelhart (1970).]

and predictions for one of Sperling's Ss. According to the model, the reason the subject never reported more than four items is that although he was extracting information from all the items in the display, increasing display size was compensated for by the slower rate of extracting features from each item.

Basically the same idea is used to make predictions for the partial report procedure. Rumelhart assumed that Ss began processing all items in the display, thus $\theta_i = 1/N$. When a cue was given at time τ to report only a particular row, Ss shifted their attention to process only the r items in that row. Thus $\theta_i = 1/r$ after time τ and the rate of extracting features from the items in the critical row increased relative to the whole report technique. Equation (4) was again used to calculate the probability of recognizing an item in the cued row, but the parameter $M_i(t)$ is now found from the sum of two integrals. The first integral is over the interval 0 to τ in which case $\theta_i = 1/N$ and the second integral is over interval τ to ∞ in which case $\theta_i = 1/r$. Figure 5.8 shows the number of available letters and the theoretical predictions for three delays of the cue. Three parameter values c, v, and μ were calculated to fit all the data in Figure 5.8 as well as additional data presented in Rumelhart (1970).

The third area of application of the model was to the detection paradigm developed by Estes. Rumelhart applied the model to data obtained by Estes and Taylor (1964) using the detection and the whole report procedure. Equation (4) was again used to calculate the probability of recognizing an item. Rumelhart speculated that the difference between the two experimental procedures is primarily the amount of time needed to process the items in the display. Each item of the display should require somewhat more processing if it had to be recalled than if the S merely had to determine whether a letter was a "B" or an "F" or neither. In a comparison of the detection and report procedures, all the parameters should therefore be the same except for the criterion. The criterion for detection c_d should be less than the criterion for report c_r. Figure 5.9 shows the fit of the model to data obtained from the two experimental procedures.

The parameters estimated from the data were $c_d = 1.15$ and $c_r = 1.92$ supporting the prediction that a greater amount of processing per item is necessary in the report procedure.

It should be noted that by using a model in which items are processed in parallel, Rumelhart was able to predict the relationship between the number of elements processed (P) and the display size (D). This prediction is important because it was the relationship between P and D that Estes and Taylor could not originally account for except by a serial model. In addition to predicting the relationship between P and D, Rum-

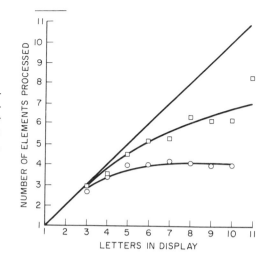

Figure 5.9. Predicted and observed numbers of "elements processed" as a function of display size for both whole report (○) and detection (□) procedures. [After Rumelhart (1970).]

elhart's model predicts the other findings of Estes and his co-workers that suggested the need for a parallel processing model. A second point of interest is the difference between the two criterion parameters: $c_d = 1.15$ and $c_r = 1.92$. If the estimates imply that only about one feature is necessary for detection and two features for recall, the results would support Neisser's (1967) interpretation that when searching for a target, it is not necessary that S recognize the nontargets. It is only necessary that he process the item long enough to classify it as a nontarget. A possible alternative interpretation is that a greater amount of processing time is necessary for reporting items, not because more features have to be detected, but because Ss would have to prepare to rehearse the items. This is the recognition buffer of Sperling's (1967) model. It is not clear, however, if the recognition buffer should be identified with recognition in which case it would use processing time in the report procedure, or whether it occurs after recognition in which case it would not necessarily require processing time until after the visual image had decayed.

One experimental variable which should clearly lead to differences in the number of features that have to be detected is the degree of similarity between targets and nontargets. It has been shown by McIntyre, Fox, and Neale (1970) that the number of letters processed depends upon both the similarity and the redundancy of the nontarget letters. Redundancy referred to whether the nontargets consisted of letters drawn randomly from the alphabet or the repetition of a single letter. The similarity dimension was defined in terms of the number of physical features shared by the target and a redundant (repeated) nontarget. To manipulate similarity, four nontarget letters (O, U, I, E) were selected that

varied in their similarity to the target letters, **T** and **F**. Table 5.1 shows
the number of elements processed in the different experimental conditions. The results indicate that, with one exception, more elements were
processed with a redundant background. This finding supports a parallel
model in that Ss would have to be processing the entire display in order
to use the redundancy. The second variable also had an important effect,
since increasing the dissimilarity between target and nontargets resulted
in more elements being processed. This finding is in agreement with
Neisser's and lends some support to his interpretation that a feature
analysis of nontargets can lead to their rejection before they are completely recognized. Both the effects of redundancy and similarity are also
consistent with Rumelhart's model which proposes parallel processing of
items in the array but sequential recognition of features for each item.

Although Rumelhart's model accounts for an impressive number of
experimental findings, it is unlikely that all his assumptions would go un-
challenged. The main point of controversy is whether increasing the
number of items in the display reduces the rate of processing individual
items (Eriksen & Spencer, 1969; Shiffrin & Gardner, 1972). Eriksen and
Spencer presented 10 letters sequentially and varied the rate between
letters from 5 msec to approximately 3 sec. They found that the rate of
presentation had no effect on performance (reporting whether the letter
A appeared in the sequence) despite the phenomenal experience that all
letters appeared simultaneously at the 5-msec rate of presentation. The
5-msec rate of presentation should have resulted in poorer performance
according to a limited-capacity assumption since Ss would have to
divide their limited attention among all 10 letters. The failure to find
such an effect suggested that there was no overloading of the encoding
mechanism. The only significant effect was the number of letters in the
sequence which primarily increased the number of false alarms—incorrectly reporting that the target was in the sequence. Eriksen and Spencer

TABLE 5.1

NUMBER OF ELEMENTS PROCESSED AS A FUNCTION OF MATRIX SIZE
AND NOISE CONDITION[a]

Noise condition		Matrix size	
		8	14
Random		2.848	3.444
Redundant	O	5.200	9.240
	U	5.008	6.804
	I	4.368	5.320
	E	2.320	4.564

[a] From McIntyre, Fox, and Neale (1970).

interpreted the significant effect of the number of letters as affecting the judgmental rather than the perceptual aspects of the task. The more letters that are in the display, the greater is the probability that one of the letters would be confused with the target letter.

Shiffrin and Gardner (1972) extended the Eriksen and Spencer experiment and introduced additional methodological improvements. Subjects reported which of two targets was present in briefly exposed four-letter displays. The methodological improvements included presenting the letters simultaneously as well as sequentially, informing Ss of the order of presentation for the various locations, and using a masking field to control the duration at each location. The data indicated that processing four letters simultaneously was as efficient as processing four letters presented sequentially, implying that there was no perceptual limitation, at least up to four letters. Shiffrin and Gardner agree with Eriksen and Spencer in interpreting the effect of increasing the number of letters in the display. The more letters there are in the display, the more that will be confused with target letters thus making the judgment more difficult.

There are currently two interpretations based on parallel-processing models that can account for the effect of display size in Figure 5.9. One model (Rumelhart's) postulates a perceptual limitation and the other (Eriksen and Spencer, Shiffrin and Gardner) postulates a judgmental limitation. It should be noted, however, that the judgmental process would be more difficult if there were also a perceptual limitation. The perceptual limitation results in a slower rate of feature extraction according to Rumelhart's model so that fewer features are extracted from each pattern as the number of patterns increases. Since less information is available, there would be a greater chance of confusions making the judgmental task more difficult than if there were no perceptual limitations. More recently, Rumelhart (1971) has extended the multicomponent model to predict how partial information (an insufficient number of features for complete recognition) is used to select a response. We will return to this issue when examining response selection in Chapter XI (pp. 213–216).

Visual Masking

Our interest up to this point has focused upon the properties of iconic memory which enable the observer to continue processing information beyond the termination of the physical stimulus. In this section, we will be looking at ways of reducing the effectiveness of iconic memory. The short-term sensory storage of a stimulus can be interfered with by pre-

senting a second pattern or a bright exposure field immediately following the termination of the first stimulus. Both types of interference are
referred to as visual masking, but the first example involves masking by
noise and the second example, masking by light. A second distinction is
between forward masking and backward masking. In forward masking,
the masking field occurs before the stimulus field and in backward masking, the masking field follows the stimulus. A recent review paper by
Kahneman (1968) describes various masking paradigms, results obtained
from studies using these paradigms, and theories constructed to explain
the results. Three theories discussed in Kahneman's paper are Eriksen's
luminance summation theory, Sperling's interruption theory, and Kinsbourne and Warrington's degradation theory.

Eriksen's luminance summation theory has been used primarily to
account for backward and forward masking by light (Eriksen, 1966). The
theory is based upon two assumptions about the visual system. The first
assumption is that recognition accuracy at brief exposures increases
with increased luminance contrast of the form with the ground. The
second is that the visual system summates the luminance from successive
stimulations within a brief time interval of about 100 msec. The degree
of summation, of course, declines with increasing time between successive stimuli. We have already seen how visual summation can improve
recognition when the same stimulus is repeated twice (Jackson & Dick,
1969). However, when the second exposure is a brightly lit field, visual
summation results in a lower contrast between figure and ground and
hence poorer recognition. Eriksen tested the first assumption by simultaneously presenting a brightly lit second field with a field containing
a black form on a white ground. The forms consisted of the capital letters, **A**, **T**, and **U**, presented singly and requiring a forced-choice recognition response from the observer after each presentation. The results supported Eriksen's prediction that recognition accuracy would increase
with the ratio of the luminance of the figure to the luminance of the
ground.

A second experiment was designed to study the successive presentation
of the stimulus and masking fields. The results confirmed the expectation
that when the adapting field and the interstimulus interval were dark,
recognition accuracy would increase with increasing separation of the
stimulus and masking fields. Forward masking was more effective in
preventing recognition, one reason being that a form preceded by a masking flash has its contrast impaired right from its onset. In a second condition, the stimulus and masking fields were always superimposed upon
a bright adapting field. Eriksen predicted that the mask would have little
effect in this condition because the added luminance would only very
slightly change the already low contrast ratio of the figure. This predic-

tion was confirmed for both forward and backward masking in that form identification remained relatively constant as the interstimulus interval was varied.

The addition of visual noise to the masking field complicates theoretical predictions. Although luminance summation may still be involved, the presence of contours in the masking field may further degrade or interrupt the processing of the test stimulus. Sperling (1963) was able to reduce the effectiveness of the icon by presenting a visual noise field composed of letter parts immediately following the exposure of a letter array. Sperling argued that the noise field interrupted further processing of the letter array. Such a view implies that a very clear and legible image is initially available to the observer, but he has too little time to recognize much of its content. An alternative view is that the stimulus and masking fields appear to be simultaneous causing the degrading of the test stimulus by the visual noise (Kinsbourne & Warrington, 1962). According to this view, the test stimulus is never very legible, but appears degraded from its initial onset.

In order to test these alternative views of masking, Liss (1968) studied the identification of letters under three different procedures: (1) backward masking by visual noise, (2) concurrent masking by visual noise, and (3) no masking. Liss argued that backward masking and concurrent masking, in which the visual noise and stimulus are presented simultaneously, should produce similar results if the effect of backward masking is to degrade the stimulus input. The results supported the view that backward masking interrupts stimulus processing rather than degrades the stimulus input. Subjects reported that the letters which were followed by the noise field appeared to be of high contrast but there was not enough time to identify them before the mask appeared. Their reports were supported by direct judgments of the brightness, contrast, sharpness, and duration of the letters. Paired-comparison judgments supported the view that backward masking stops stimulus processing. As an example, letters presented for 40 msec with backward masking appeared much brighter than letters presented for 9 msec with no masking. Liss concluded that the appearance of a mask stops preimage processing by disrupting the processing which occurs after retinal stimulation but prior to the appearance of a complete image of the pattern.

There is also evidence which supports a degradation theory of masking and the opposing arguments are discussed by Kahneman (1968). One such argument in favor of the degradation theory is the similarity of results for forward and backward masking (Kinsbourne & Warrington, 1962). The interruption theory has only been developed as a theory of backward masking. It is, of course, possible that both theories are correct, depending upon experimental conditions such as exposure duration, luminance and contrast of the test stimulus, luminance and contrast of the masking stimulus, and degree of similarity between the test and masking fields. Liss reported that tests with a variety of masks indicated that backward masking disrupts stimulus identification to a greater degree the more the mask resembles the form qualities of the stimulus. As a mask, Liss chose rows of 0s superimposed on rows of Ns because it was the most effective in stopping the perception of letters presented prior to it. It is likely that other masks could be devised which would degrade the stimulus without totally preventing its further perception.

A quantitative model of backward masking has been developed by Rumelhart (1970) as a part of his multicomponent theory. A quantification of Eriksen's luminance summation theory is used to predict the results of using a homogeneous flash to mask the perception of a single letter. The effect of the mask is to reduce the clarity of the stimulus and the rate of feature extraction. Rumelhart successfully applied the model to data collected by Thompson (1966) in which he varied both the luminance and delay of the mask. The multicomponent model was also applied to data obtained by using a small ring to encircle the target stimulus. Such data is usually best fit by nonmonotonic masking functions, with the greatest amount of masking occurring at about a 20-msec delay of the mask. A successful fit of the U-shaped masking function was made possible by applying the multicomponent theory to a hypothesis suggested by Werner (1935). Rumelhart assumed that if no features of the target have been recognized by the time the second stimulus is presented, the observer sees both patterns; the target encircled by the ring. If some features of the target have been extracted from the target, the second pattern has the effect of destroying this information and only the second pattern is perceived. If, however, enough features have been extracted so that the first pattern is recognized before the masking stimulus is presented, the two figures are perceived sequentially. According to this interpretation, masking has its greatest effect at an intermediate delay between the simultaneous and sequential perception of the two patterns. The successful fit of the masking data provides additional confirmation of Rumelhart's model and extends its range of application to an important aspect of the temporal processing of visual information.

Summary

The visual information store consists of a decaying sensory image, existing beyond the physical termination of the stimulus. If the interstimulus interval between two stimuli is short enough, the second stimulus can summate with the image of the first stimulus. If the two stimuli are the same, the summation of two subthreshold exposures can result in recognition. If the two stimuli are different, the second stimulus may mask and prevent recognition of the first. Additional evidence for iconic storage was provided by a partial report technique in which observers were cued to report a certain part of the array. Partial report improves Ss' performance only if the cue is given before the complete decay of the sensory image.

A model of how observers report information from an array has been proposed by Sperling. The model consists of a visual information store, a scanner, a recognition buffer, a rehearsal mechanism, and an auditory information store. Early models assumed that items in the array are scanned serially, but more recent models emphasize that items are processed in parallel. A particularly sensitive technique of studying the perceptual processing of multielement arrays is Estes' detection paradigm requiring Ss to report which target element appeared in the array. Rumelhart has constructed a detailed, quantitative theory of the perception of briefly exposed visual displays. The theory assumes that items are processed in parallel but the features of each item are recognized sequentially. The model has been successfully applied to data from whole report, partial report, detection, and backward masking experiments. A controversial part of the model is whether increasing the number of items in the display slows the perceptual processing of each item or only makes the final decision more difficult.

There are several theories of masking which are partially dependent upon the nature of the masking field. It is likely that luminance summation causes a poor contrast between figure and ground when a bright, homogeneous field is used as a mask. The presence of contours in the mask can cause additional degradation of the stimulus or even completely interrupt the processing of the stimulus. Task variables, such as the similarity between the stimulus and masking fields, most likely determine whether the mask degrades the stimulus or completely interrupts further processing of the stimulus.

Part 3 | MEMORY CODES

VI | Visual and Verbal Codes

In the previous chapter we saw that patterns could exist for a very short time as a decaying visual image. In this chapter we examine whether patterns can have a more permanent existence in some form of visual representation or whether they must be encoded verbally. The visual images discussed in this chapter differ from iconic storage in a number of important ways. The main function of iconic storage is to lengthen the effective duration of a brief exposure. A 10-msec exposure, if followed by a dark postexposure field, will appear equivalent to a much longer exposure that is followed by a masking field. The preservation of stimulus information during iconic storage gives the observer additional time to recognize the content of the display. Iconic storage preserves the stimulus information in its original sensory modality and does not require recognition of the patterns (see page 89). In contrast, the visual memory codes discussed in this chapter assume that the patterns have been recognized. Although both types of visual images become less clear over time, the rate of decay is much slower and less susceptible to masking following recognition.

As an alternative to a visual image, a verbal code can also exist at a number of different levels. At one level the pattern may have a name so that the *S*'s task is simply reduced to remembering the name. At another level, the pattern may not be familiar so that Ss have to remember a verbal description of the pattern. In trying to determine whether patterns are encoded as a visual image or as a verbal code, we will have to review a number of experimental procedures. The first section contains a discussion of the various matching paradigms developed by Posner, Sternberg, Neisser, and Estes. Interest focuses on whether names or images are being matched. Visual representations in long-term memory are studied in the second section with an emphasis on the capacity of visual memory. The third section is concerned with the role of verbal descriptions in recognition and recall, and the final section discusses the decline in the accuracy of the visual code over time.

Before beginning, we shall first consider some general properties of a visual memory and, in particular, those properties which differ from a verbal short-term memory. The experiment that will serve as the vehicle for this discussion (Sanders, 1968) was designed to study memory for spatial positions so care must be taken in generalizing to visual patterns. Nonetheless, Sanders provides an excellent comparison of visual and auditory STM and raises a number of fundamental issues which will be important later. Sanders repeated a number of traditional experiments on STM with visual spatial positions as stimulus material. Subjects were seated in front of a display which contained two long rows of lights. A sequence of three to seven lights was successively presented and the *S*'s recall task was to point to the lights in the correct order of presentation. The results deviated in many respects from those obtained with verbal items (Table 6.1).

TABLE 6.1

SHORT-TERM MEMORY FOR SPATIAL POSITIONS OR VERBAL MATERIAL:
MAIN CONCLUSIONS[a]

	Spatial positions	Verbal material
Memory span	3–4	6–7
Serial position	Primacy effect	Primacy + recency effect
Set of alternatives	Effect	No effect
Presentation rate	No effect	Effect
Confusion errors	Visual	Auditory
Repeated lists (Hebb effect)	No effect	Effect
Retention after learning	Very instable	Moderately stable
Rote learning	Gradual improvement	Gradual improvement
Rehearsal	Not effective	Effective

[a] From Sanders (1968).

The memory span was between three and four positions, compared to six to seven items for verbal memory. Subjects made visual confusion errors—they frequently chose positions adjacent to the correct position. Performance declined as a function of the set of alternatives (2 to 12 lights in a one- or two-dimensional array), but variation of presentation rate (.8–2.4 items per second) had no effect. Retention appeared deficient and Ss did not recognize repeated sequences (the Hebb effect) when they were repeated five times and separated by four trials. Sanders concluded that these results are difficult to explain in terms of a unitary STM, but rather suggest a conception of short-term activation of a modality specific memory.

The conception of separate visual and auditory short-term memories received additional verification in a study by Sanders and Schroots (1969). The experimenters investigated the effects of similarity on short-term recall by presenting lists of six consonants followed by short lists of additional remote cognitive categories: digits, tones, or spatial positions. Improved immediate recall resulted when the additional items came from more remote categories. The effect was small and questionable when consonants were followed by digits, more clear with consonants and tones, and approached additivity of the memory spans when consonants were followed by spatial positions. An average span of about 10 items was found for the last condition, which was only slightly below the sum of the two memory spans, due possibly to a slight decay factor. The investigators attributed the large effect to different coding, acoustical with consonants and visual with spatial positions, resulting in very little interference.

The lack of interference between the two memory stores is useful for several reasons. First, it provides an experimental procedure for determining the modality of the memory code by testing whether a visual or a verbal intervening task is most effective in disrupting memory. This technique is used in several studies that are described later. Second, the advantage of two memory stores is that they can increase the capacity of STM if the information can be divided between the two stores, as illustrated by the previous experiment.

Another advantage is that if information about each item is stored in both modalities (in contrast to the previous experiment), Ss should have a greater chance of recalling the item. The formation of a visual image from a word and the naming of a visual pattern represent alternative ways of changing the modality of the memory code. Paivio and Csapo (1969) demonstrated that forming a code in the opposite modality can result in improved performance on a memory task. The task involved the presentation of a nine-item list of familiar pictures, their concrete noun labels, or abstract words at a fast rate (5.3 items per second) or a slow rate (2 items per second). The two rates were chosen so that Ss would have time to name the pictures at the slow rate but not at the fast rate. The fast rate of presentation caused the greatest performance decrement for pictures and the least performance decrement for abstract words. Paivio and Csapo argued that Ss had insufficient time to generate an additional memory code for the pictures (a verbal label) and the concrete words (a visual image) at the fast rate of presentation. Abstract words were least affected by rate of presentation because imagery is seldom used even at the slower rates. The following sections describe other experiments on memory codes for visual stimuli. Paivio's (1971) recent book discusses the research on memory codes for verbal stimuli.

Matching Names and Images

One of the major advances in our understanding of how patterns are coded has been the development of a number of experimental procedures for studying how patterns in the perceptual world are matched to patterns stored in memory. Table 6.2 shows four experimental paradigms associated with the work of Posner, Sternberg, Neisser, and Estes. The experimental techniques have all been presented previously but the emphasis here is on the modality of the memory code. The procedures have in common the requirement that a subject search an array of one or more patterns in order to discover whether any items in the array match the items he has stored in memory. The procedures differ primarily in the number of items in the memory set and the number of items in the perceptual array. The items are invariably alphanumeric patterns.

There are a number of alternative operations which can be used to match an item in the preceptual array to an item stored in memory. Sternberg described different matching procedures (Table 4.1, page 66), which are illustrated by Nickerson (1973) in a more detailed flow chart. Figure 6.1 shows four possible comparison procedures for the Sternberg

TABLE 6.2
MODALITY OF COMPARISONS FOR DIFFERENT
RECOGNITION PARADIGMS

Paradigm	Modality	Memory	Perception
Estes	Visual	2	1–16
Neisser	Visual	1–10	Many
Sternberg	Visual?	1–6	1
Posner	Both	1	1

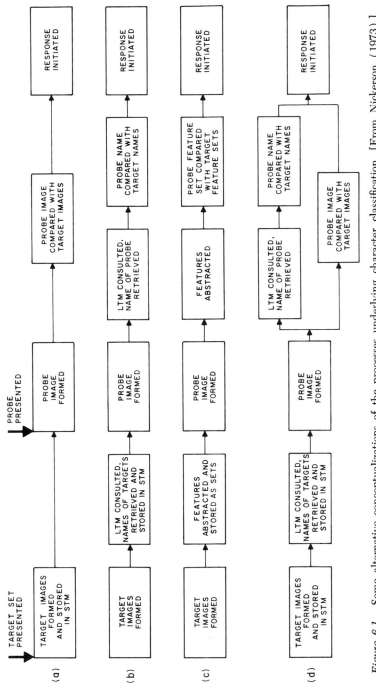

Figure 6.1. Some alternative conceptualizations of the processes underlying character classification. [From Nickerson (1973).]

task, although we can apply them to all the experimental paradigms listed in Table 6.2 if a "probe" refers to any item in the perceptual array. Procedure (a) is a visual comparison based on two visual images. It assumes that the probe is compared as a whole and serially against the target images stored in memory. Procedure (b) is a name match based on the names of the patterns. Procedure (c) is a visual comparison but is made at a feature level rather than at the level of a complete visual image. The distinction between procedures (a) and (c) is essentially the distinction between the theories proposed by Sternberg and Neisser, discussed in Chapter IV. Procedure (d) involves a parallel comparison using both the visual and verbal codes.

The simplest experimental paradigm is the one used by Posner in which a single letter is presented, followed by a second letter after a delay lasting from 0 to 2 sec. Posner and Mitchell (1967) demonstrated that a stored letter can be matched more rapidly with a physically identical letter (AA) than it can with a letter having only the same name (Aa). This discovery provided Posner with a technique for exploring the memory code used in making the match. If only the name of a letter is present in memory, it should not make any difference whether or not the second letter has the same physical form. However, if the subject has stored a visual representation of the first letter, his reaction time should be faster whenever the second letter is physically identical to the first letter. In order to test the relative efficiency of physical matches, Posner, Boies, Eichelman, and Taylor (1969) studied the difference between physical and name identity matches as a function of the interval between the two letters. Figure 6.2 shows their results. Immediately after the presentation of a letter, a physical match is about 90 msec faster than a name match, but this difference is lost after 2 sec. As the retention interval increases, physical matches begin to take more time and name matches begin to be made in less time.

In a second experiment, Posner et al. (1969) sudied the effect of an interpolated task on physical and name matches. Three conditions of an interpolated interval were used. Either the interval was filled by a blank field, by a black and white random noise field, or by a pair of digits whose sum had to be reported after responding to the second letter. The addition task abolished the difference between physical and name match RTs, but the visual noise had no effect on this difference. The results of both experiments suggested that it is difficult to maintain visual information, particularly if the Ss' attention has to be used elsewhere such as in the addition of two numbers. The importance of attention in maintaining a visual representation was demonstrated in a third experiment designed to give Ss a greater incentive in using physical matches. In this experi-

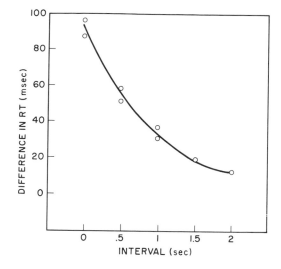

Figure 6.2. Difference between physical and name identity matches as a function of
the interval between the two
letters. [After Posner, Boies,
Eichelman, and Taylor (1969).]

ment, "same" matches were always physically identical since only upper-
case letters were used. When the physical aspect of a letter was made a
completely reliable cue, the efficiency of a visual match was maintained
over a 1-sec interval. According to Posner, visual and name codes of
letters are separately stored, have their own time courses, and can be
searched independently and in parallel.

A model for recognition with visual and acoustic comparisons operating in parallel was recently proposed by Cohen (1969). The Ss were
presented letter trigrams (lowercase) which were the "same" or "different." The stimuli were separated by a retention interval of 5 sec, making
it likely that physical matches would take the same time as name
matches. The experiment was designed to test the following hypotheses,
derived from the parallel matching model shown in Figure 6.3 [similar
to procedure (d) Figure 6.1]:

(1) The main effect of confusability occurs at the comparison or matching stage, rather than during identification;
(2) If matching is either visual or acoustic, confusability of the relevant kind should either slow RTs or increase errors;
(3) If both matching procedures were used in parallel a single type
confusability would produce little or no effect;
(4) But RTs would be increased if visual and acoustic confusability
were both present.

In order to test these hypotheses, the different stimuli were divided into
four groups: not confusable (NC), acoustically confusable (AC), visu-

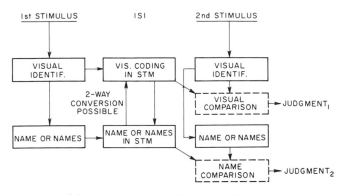

Figure 6.3. A model for recognition with visual and acoustic comparisons operating in parallel. [After Cohen (1969).]

ally confusable (VC), and both visually and acoustically confusable (VC & AC). As predicted by the parallel comparison model, only double confusability resulted in a significant increase in RTs and errors. Mean RTs for the four kinds of different judgments were 436 msec, NC; 437 msec, AC; 452 msec, VC; and 529 msec, VC & AC. The error distribution followed the same trend as the RTs. Perhaps one reason that visual confusability slightly increased RTs, is because acoustic matching cannot be entirely independent of visual information, since visual identification must precede naming (Figure 6.3).

In a second experiment, Cohen designed a task such that under one condition, Ss would have to make visual matches by judging only physically identical trigrams the same (hsb and hsb), while under a second condition, Ss would have to make acoustic matches by judging mixed-case trigrams having the same name (hsb and HSB). According to her model, acoustically confusable stimuli should produce slow RTs in the acoustic matching task and visually confusable stimuli should produce slow RTs in the visual matching task. Only the second prediction was confirmed. The results therefore give partial support to a parallel comparison of visual and name codes, but the visual comparison may be the more fundamental of the two matching routines.

The model proposed by Cohen is in agreement with Posner's argument that visual and verbal codes can be examined in parallel, but further requires that visual information be still available after a 5-sec delay. Posner proposed that incentive is an important factor in maintaining the visual code and the possibility of acoustic confusions may have provided the incentive in Cohen's study. Other evidence (Parks, Kroll, Salzberg, & Parkinson, 1972) indicates that Ss can maintain a visual image over an interval as long as 8 sec if there is verbal interference. The incentive in this study was an intervening task that was designed to interfere with the maintenance of the name code and thus encourage the retention of the visual code. During the 8-sec retention interval between a pair of letters, Ss shadowed and repeated aloud a series of spoken letters. After the 8-sec interval, correct affirmative decisions that the two letters had the same name were significantly faster when the two letters were of the same case suggesting that a physical match was used for this condition.

The incentive to maintain a visual image should be particularly great when the patterns cannot be named and are difficult to describe verbally. Phillips and Baddeley (1971) used as stimuli a 5 × 5 matrix of randomly filled squares and asked Ss to report whether two successively presented patterns were the same or different. Reaction times steadily increased and the percentage correct steadily declined over a 9-sec retention interval, although Ss were still responding slightly above chance after a 9-sec delay. The investigators concluded that the rate of decay of information in visual STM is slower than that suggested by Posner, although the lack of a name code may have resulted in greater attention to the visual code.

An experiment in which parallel matching of visual and name codes was not found was a study by Tversky (1969) using unfamiliar stimuli with unfamiliar names. The stimuli and their names are shown in Figure 6.4. The Ss had previously learned to associate the names to each of the eight schematic faces. A name or a face was presented for 1 sec, followed by a second stimulus (name or face) after a 1-sec delay. Names were presented visually so a stimulus was either a schematic face or a printed word. Subjects responded "same" if the two stimuli had the same name (i.e., were either two identical faces, two identical names, or a face and its correct name) and "different" otherwise. There were four sessions of the experiment in which the first stimulus was either always a name or always a face and the second stimulus was either a face on 79% of the trials or a name on 79% of the trials. Significantly faster reaction times were obtained for the more frequent stimulus "modality," regardless of the "modality" of the first stimulus. The average RT for the more frequent modality was 705 msec compared to 873 msec for the more infrequent modity. The evidence suggests that not only could Ss generate a visual image of a face from the name (and vice versa), but that whether either verbal or pictorial material is verball or pictorially encoded depends upon Ss' expectations as to which encoding will produce the fastest match. That both codes could not be examined simultaneously was most likely due to the unfamiliarity of the material or to the fact that faces and names were both presented visually so that Ss had to prepare for a specific type of pattern.

Figure 6.4. Faces and associated names used as stimuli. [After Tversky (1969).]

The second matching paradigm which we will consider is the paradigm developed by Sternberg. The paradigm differs from the one used by Posner in that Ss may have as many as six items stored in memory. Sternberg (1969) has argued that Ss compare the presented pattern to the patterns stored in memory by using an exhaustive serial scan based on matching visual images. His argument is based partially on the finding that degrading the test stimulus increased the slope of the RT function such that the comparisons themselves took longer (Session 1, Figure 3.3). This could only occur if the output of the encoding stage was still degraded and not if the subject had completely identified or named the test stimulus. The slope was not affected in the second session, although this may have been the result of Ss forming a more refined visual image with practice.

A more direct test of whether Ss were using visual or acoustic matches was undertaken by Chase and Calfee (1969). Unfortunately, the results do not give strong support to either alternative. Chase and Calfee used the Sternberg memory procedure to study the effects of auditory and visual presentation of memory and test stimuli. In addition, three types of material were used: visually confusable letters, acoustically confusable letters, and neutral letters. The major finding was that search rate was substantially slower when different presentation and test modes were used (visual–auditory or auditory–visual) than when the same mode was used. The search rate was slowest for acoustically confusable lists but this finding was statistically reliable in only one of their two experiments. There was no difference between visually confusable and neutral letters in either experiment. It would have been of interest if letters which were both visually and acoustically confusable had been used, since this was the only condition producing a significant effect in Cohen's (1969) experiment.

One possible difficulty for a visual matching hypothesis is Posner's

(1969) finding that it requires an active use of attention to maintain a visual image. As the size of the memory set is increased from one to six items, it may become increasingly difficult to maintain a visual image for each item. Another important variable is whether a fixed memory set is used in which the items in memory remain the same throughout the experiment or whether a variable memory set is used in which the items change from trial-to-trial. Presumably, a fixed set procedure would favor visual matching in that verbal rehearsal would not be as necessary and Ss would have practice in maintaining the visual representation. An example of visual matching in a fixed set procedure was reported by Sternberg (1969). Item-recognition was studied using nonsense forms and photographs of faces as stimuli. Reaction time data were qualitatively the same as for digit sets except that the scanning rates were slightly slower. All in all, experimental evidence to date gives some support of the hypothesis that visual matching is used in the Sternberg memory task, but the issue is certainly not resolved and may depend on specific experimental variables.

Visual matching does seem to be established in the scanning tasks used by Neisser and Estes. We have already seen the importance of visual confusability in determining scanning rates in Neisser's task (page 73) and the number of letters processed during a brief tachistoscopic exposure (page 101). What distinguishes both of these tasks from the paradigm used by Sternberg and Posner is that Ss are searching an array of items, processing many items in parallel. Subjects are apparently capable of examining items for physical features, rejecting many items as nontargets before they are completely recognized. A direct test of the role of visual and acoustic confusability in a visual search task was undertaken by Kaplan, Yonas, and Shurcliff (1966). Rate of scanning was found to be significantly slower when the target and background were visually confusable, but acoustic confusability had no effect.

To summarize the results of this section, we considered four matching paradigms shown in Table 6.2. I have indicated in Table 6.2 what I think is the modality of the memory code, based on the experimental results presented here and the two previous chapters. When there is only a single item stored in memory and that item can be named, the evidence suggests that matching can occur at both visual and name levels. It is likely that both codes can be tested in parallel for familiar items, supporting procedure (d) of Figure 6.1 (page 115). I have listed the visual modality as the basis for making comparisons in experiments using the Sternberg paradigm, mainly because of Sternberg's own arguments in favor of the visual code. Sternberg supports procedure (a) in which the completely synthesized visual image is compared serially against visual images stored in memory. The question mark indicates that I am not completely convinced, particularly for large, variable memory sets of letters or digits. The alternative possibility in this case is procedure (b) in which matching is based on the names of the patterns. The basis for matching is more clear in the Neisser and Estes paradigms in which an array of letters rather than a single pattern is presented. Scanning would be very slow if every item in this array were named; instead, the evidence indicates a visual match based on a feature comparison [procedure (c) of Figure 1]. Since we have now exhausted all four experimental paradigms listed in Table 6.2 as well as the four matching procedures in Figure 6.1, we can consider a new topic—the capabilities of recognition memory for visual material.

Visual Representations in Long-Term Memory

The results indicating that visual images decay in STM do not imply that we totally lack more permanent visual representations, but that these visual representations may lack much of the detail of our original perceptions. If you are asked to describe the living room of a friend's home, it is likely that your visual image of the room will assist you in your description. It is also likely that your visual image is not clear enough to provide a completely accurate description. I have entitled this section "Visual Representations in Long-Term Memory" because retention is measured over much longer intervals than the 30-sec period often associated with the temporal limits of STM. Atkinson and Shiffrin (1968, 1971) make a distinction between STM and LTM and emphasize the importance of rehearsal for maintaining information in STM and transferring information to LTM (see Figure 1.1, page 3). Their 1971 paper provides additional experimental support for this distinction.

An interesting question concerns the relevance of their model to visual codes, since experimental support is typically based on material that can be verbally coded. We saw in the first section of this chapter that attention is important in maintaining a visual image and there seems to be an analogy between attending to a visual image and using rehearsal to maintain verbal information in STM. But is there an analogy between attending to a visual image and using rehearsal to transfer verbal information into LTM?

Shaffer and Shiffrin (1972) reasoned that if visual material could be rehearsed, memory for visual material should be improved when more time is allowed for rehearsal. They presented 120 pictures to Ss and varied the exposure duration of each picture (from .2 to 4.0 sec) and the time between pictures (from 1 to 4 sec). Subjects were instructed to think about a slide and try to remember it during the interval between slides. After viewing the pictures, Ss saw a random series of 30 new slides and 30 old slides and judged how confident they were that they had previously seen each slide. The longer exposure duration significantly increased confidence ratings for the previously presented pictures, but the interval between pictures had no effect, suggesting that rehearsal could not be used to improve visual memory. Shaffer and Shiffrin proposed that complex pictures appear to be processed almost entirely during the period in which they are physically exposed and there is no direct analogue of visual rehearsal in the processing of complex visual information. They suggested, however, that visual rehearsal does seem to be used in experiments where the visual input is of low information content, so their results do not necessarily contradict Posner's statement that attention is a form of visual rehearsal.

An alternative, perhaps more attractive, explanation emphasizes the distinction between the separate functions of rehearsal in maintaining information in STM and transferring information into LTM. Posner's results are concerned with using rehearsal to maintain visual information in STM, whereas Shaffer and Shiffrin's results test whether rehearsal tranfers visual information into LTM producing a slower decay rate after rehearsal is terminated. The combined results indicate that visual rehearsal is effective in maintaining information in STM but is not effective in producing slower decay rates by transferring additional information into LTM. Memory for a visual image is established only during the exposure of the pattern and a visual image therefore has its maximum clarity (memory strength) immediately following the termination of the stimulus. In contrast, the memory strength of verbal information can be increased by rehearsal following the termination of the stimulus (Atkinson & Shiffrin; 1968, 1971).

The classical experiments on memory capacity for visual material have been primarily concerned with the number of items that can be stored, the degree of similarity among the items, and recognition accuracy over various retention intervals. In one of the early experiments, Nickerson (1965) showed Ss 600 photographs representing a wide range of subject matter. The first 200 photographs contained no duplicates but half of the subsequent 400 photographs were duplicates of the first 200. The Ss' task was to decide whether each of these photographs had been previously presented. The number of items that intervened between the first and second occurrence of a photograph ranged from 40 to 200. The number of intervening items had a significant effect on performance but 87% of the old items were correctly identified even at the maximum delay. Nickerson concluded that recognition memory is quite good, but it remains to be determined exactly what information was stored for each picture. He proposed that whatever is stored must be sufficient for differentiating that item from others and for determining the correspondence between the stored representation and its recurrence as a visual experience.

Shepard (1967) also found that recognition accuracy for visual material was very high in an experiment which was first reported in 1959 at a meeting of the Eastern Psychological Association. Subjects viewed 612 pictures at a self-paced rate. A two-alternative, forced-choice task immediately followed the inspection series. Some Ss returned after either 2 hours, 3 days, 1 week, or 4 months and were tested on pairs which differed from the stimuli in the immediate test. They were quite accurate in choosing which picture in each pair had been shown previously. Percentages correct were 96.7% for the immediate test, 99.7% after 2 hours, 92.0% after 3 days, 87.0% after 7 days, and 57.7% after 120 days. Although the retention interval had a marked effect on performance, memory for pictorial material after a week delay was still nearly equivalent to memory for words when tested immediately.

The most impressive demonstration of our memory capacity for pictorial material was provided by Standing, Conezio, and Haber (1970). Three Ss were shown 2560 slides over four successive days. The test consisted of 280 two-alternative, forced-choice trials, given 1 hour after the final session. The percentages correct for three Ss were 95, 93, and 85%. The results are impressive not only because of the number of stimuli but because of their similarity. Unlike the pictures in Shepard's experiment which were selected for high saliency and low confusability, many of the pictures were from common classes. The slides included 300 pictures of single male adults and 200 pictures of single female adults.

Although visual recognition memory appears to be quite good, there are limitations on its accuracy, particularly for complex, unfamiliar patterns. Goldstein and Chance (1971) questioned whether the use of heterogeneous material may have caused some investigators to overestimate the capacity of visual memory. Each S in their experiment viewed only a single class of stimuli—either faces, ink blots, or snow. Ink blots and snow crystals were selected because, in contrast to faces, they are relatively unfamiliar. Subjects saw a series of 14 stimuli and were told that they would have to recognize the stimuli later. A recognition test consisting of the 14 old stimuli and 70 new stimuli was given either immediately or 48 hours later. The results cannot be directly compared to the previous studies because the probability of a correct guess is much lower, but the various experimental conditions can be contrasted. The percentages of correct recognition responses for the immediate and delayed test were 72% at both delays for faces, 51 and 43% for ink blots, and 37 and 30% for snow crystals. Goldstein and Chance concluded that recognition of pictorial stimuli is not clearly superior to recognition of nonpictorial stimuli when homogeneous arrays of stimuli are used and that familiarity improves recognition (although other factors such as interstimulus similarity are also important).

Fagan (1972) has shown that recognition memory for faces develops quite early. The experimental paradigm utilizes an infant's preference for novelty to test his recognition memory (see Fagan, 1970, for details). A previously shown pattern will appear novel if it is not remembered and so the infant should divide his attention equally between the old pattern and a novel pattern. If the pattern is remembered, the infant should show his preference for novelty by attending more to the novel pattern. Infants were first exposed to a face for 1 min and were then immediately exposed to the previous face and a novel face during two 5-sec tests. Evidence that the infant remembered the first pattern and could discriminate between the two test patterns was provided whenever the infant spent significantly more time looking at the novel face. The stimuli were always faces but were either line drawings, photographs, or three dimensional masks (Figure 6.5).

Four-month-old infants could discriminate between a rotated and an upright face but they could not discriminate between two upright faces. Females, 5–6 months old, could discriminate between photographs of two upright faces but they could not discriminate between line drawings or between photographs of inverted faces. Male infants of the same age lagged developmentally since they could not discriminate between upright photographs but they could discriminate between upright masks. Although memory was tested immediately in these experiments, more recent findings indicate that infants' recognition memory for faces exists over at least a 48-hour interval (Fagan, personal communication). The experimental paradigm is important not only because of its developmental implications, but because it enables us to study visual recognition memory in its pure form, free from verbal coding. Presumably, the visual code is predominate when pictorial material is remembered but verbal coding may also be used once language becomes available. In the next section, we examine the relative importance of visual and verbal codes as related to recognition and recall.

Verbal Descriptions in Recognition and Recall

Whether stimuli come from the same or different perceptual classes has important implications for verbal, as well as visual, codes. If all the

Figure 6.5. Alternative representations of faces: Line drawings, photographs, and three dimensional masks. [From Fagan (1972).]

stimuli are snowflakes, Ss utilizing a verbal code would have to remember verbal descriptions of the stimuli rather than names of the stimuli. A verbal description of a pattern might also be used if the pattern were unfamiliar and did not have a name. According to the verbal loop hypothesis proposed by Glanzer and Clark (1964), Ss in a perceptual task translate input-information into words, store the words, and use them in responding. One consequence of the hypothesis is that the complexity of a stimulus pattern should be determined by the number of words needed to describe it. By using overt descriptions to estimate the length of verbalizations it was possible to account for two measures of complexity of line drawings, which included the eight drawings shown in Figure 6.6. The first measure was a performance measure. The accuracy of reproducing a pattern following a brief exposure resulted in a correlation of .81 between difficulty and length of verbalization. A correlation of .87 was obtained between length of verbalization and judged complexity. Glanzer and Clark interpreted the results as supporting their theory as an alternative to Gestalt and information theory approaches to perceptual organization.

A series of experiments by Cohen and Granstrom (1968a,b) were designed to test more directly the role of verbalization in memorizing figures. Retention of visual figures in STM was studied by varying the type of material interpolated during the retention interval. Figure 6.7 shows the experimental patterns and Figure 6.8 shows the recognition and recall tests given to Ss after a 10-sec retention interval. The recognition task (Figure 6.8a) required that Ss select the pattern which matched the original, whereas the recall (reproduction) task required that Ss modify a basic pattern to match the original (Figure 6.8b). Reproduction was as good as recognition when the retention interval was empty, but was inferior when the retention interval was filled by a learning task. The interpolated task involved the paired-associates learning of either visual figures, auditory words, or both. Only the visual plus verbal condition

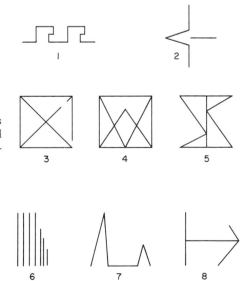

Figure 6.6. Eight stimulus figures differing in complexity of their verbal descriptions. [After Cohen and Granstrom (1968a).]

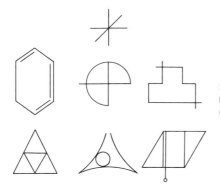

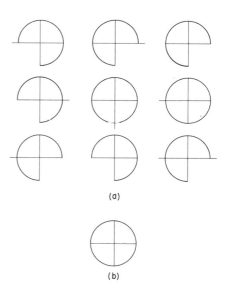

Figure 6.7. Figures used to measure the role of visual and verbal coding in recognition and reproduction. [After Cohen and Granstrom (1968b).]

caused a significant decrement in recognition performance, although the visual task produced a slight decrement. Cohen and Granstrom concluded that recognition STM has a major nonverbal component and a minor verbal component, and that interference is only apparent when the interpolated task contains both types of material. In the reproduction task, all three interference conditions caused a large retention loss. The loss was interpreted as being caused by the prevention of rehearsal, and they proposed that reproduction memory is primarily verbal since rehearsal is only possible with verbal material. In view of Posner's finding that the maintenance of a visual image is also an active process requiring attention, the possibility of a visual image also playing an important role in reproductive memory cannot be eliminated. What is dramatically illus-

Figure 6.8. (a) Recognition series for one of the experimental figures given in Figure 6.7. (b) A basic figure, to be corrected in reproducing the same experimental figure. [After Cohen and Granstrom (1968b).]

(a)

(b)

trated by the Cohen and Granstrom study is how much more reproduction is subject to interference, even when the reproduction and recognition tests appear to differ little in difficulty (Figure 6.8).

A more convincing demonstration of the importance of rehearsal in a
reproduction task was shown in a second study (Cohen & Granstrom,
1970). In the first experiment, the results confirmed that a S's ability to
reproduce visual figures correlated with his ability to describe them. A
significant correlation was not obtained between recognition and descriptive ability. A second experiment used two interpolated tasks that seemed
more purely verbal and purely visual than the previous tasks. Recognition
of three faces or the recall of three names served as the visual and verbal
interpolated tasks. Each of the patterns used in the previous study was
shown for 1 sec and had to be recalled by recognition or reproduction
after a 7-sec retention interval. A significant interaction between mode of
recall and type of interpolated material revealed that the visual interpolated task caused greater interference in recognition but less interference in reproduction relative to a verbal interpolated task. Figure 6.9
shows the interaction, which was particularly strong in Experiment 3.

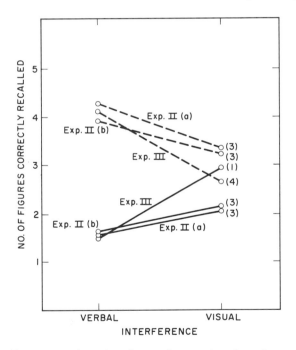

Figure 6.9. Recognition (– – –) and reproduction (——) performance for verbal
and visual interpolated material. The number of interpolated items is indicated beside
the appropriate plot. [After Cohen and Granstrom (1968b).]

That experiment was designed to equate the reproduction and recognition tasks for difficulty by using more interpolated items in the recognition task. The results support the view that reproduction has a verbal component which is lacking in recognition.

Somewhat the same conclusion was reached by Smith and Nielsen (1970) using a quite different technique. Smith and Nielsen studied visual and verbal processes in recognition and recall by successively presenting two schematic faces separated by a retention interval of either 1, 4, or 10 sec. In a recognition reaction time experiment, Ss decided whether the second face was the same as or different from the original. We saw in Chapter IV that "same" RT increased with the number of relevant features only at the longer intervals, suggesting a loss of visual information which mediated a template match at the shorter retention intervals. In a recall task, Ss indicated the size of a probed-for feature (ears, eyes, eyebrows, nose, or mouth). Recall RT increased with the number of relevant features at all intervals, suggesting retrieval from a verbal representation. These findings support the hypothesis of Cohen and Granstrom, but also suggest that a verbal description was used in recognition when the visual image was no longer available.

A dissertation by Frost (1971) argued that Ss' expectations regarding the type of test that they expect to receive influences their coding of the stimulus. The stimuli were 16 objects representing four different semantic categories: animals, clothing, vehicles, and furniture. Each object was drawn to fit one of four different shapes so that Ss could organize their recall either by categories (semantic dimension) or shapes (visual dimension). Frost considered three different retrieval models in which (1) one type of organization would be used exclusively—semantic or visual, (2) the memory codes would be searched successively, or (3) the visual and semantic searches would be combined. If the visual and semantic codes are combined, there should be a large number of double repetitions in which successively recalled stimuli have the same shape and are from the same semantic category. Subjects who expected a recognition task were tested on recall after a 15-min filled retention interval. There was a large proportion of double repetitions which supported the model postulating the combined use of visual and semantic codes (Model 3).

The use of visual information to aid recall is perhaps somewhat surprising in view of the previous studies which emphasized verbal coding in recall tasks. The second experiment in Frost's study suggests that Ss had utilized the visual code because they were expecting a recognition task. When expectations were varied as an experimental variable, the clustering scores indicated that recognition-set Ss clustered on both visual and semantic dimensions, whereas recall-set Ss clustered only by semantic categories. In addition, recognition-set Ss were superior in identifying the shape of each stimulus (2.75 errors compared to 4.67 errors) although the performance of both groups was well above chance (12 errors).

A third experiment confirmed the importance of the visual code when Ss expected a recognition task. Subjects were given either a recognition or a recall set and were then shown a series of drawings. They were later instructed to respond "yes" to objects they had previously seen regardless of whether the object had the same shape. Some of the objects were identical to the original stimulus, whereas other objects were redrawn to fit a different shape. Recognition-set Ss responded faster to same-shape objects than to different-shape objects suggesting that their decisions were influenced by visual coding. In contrast, recall-set Ss were equally fast in responding to the same- and different-shape objects. In order to account for her findings in all three experiments, Frost proposed that a recall-set and a recognition-set result in different aspects of the stimulus (name code versus visual code) being emphasized during the initial encoding. Although both codes may be retained, the emphasized modality provides the principal means of access to the stored information.

The results of the experiments reviewed in this section are remarkably consistent in suggesting that visual codes are primarily utilized in recognition and verbal codes are primarily utilized in recall. This conclusion has been established in experiments based on a variety of research paradigms—the correlations among the adequacy of a verbal description and task performance, the effectiveness of visual versus verbal interference, the effect of the number of relevant features on reaction time, the effect of task expectations on the differential use of semantic and visual codes in organizing recall, and the effect of task expectations on recognizing same- and different-shape objects.

Perhaps one reason that visual images are more useful in recognition than in recall is that they may be accurate enough for recognition but not accurate enough for recall. We may feel that our visual image of a face is insufficiently clear to allow us to describe that person, but that we would not have any trouble recognizing the person. If the recall task required recalling the name of an object rather than a description of an object, a visual image might be more useful because details would not be required. A visual image lacking in details might be of little use in Cohen and Granstrom's reproduction task but might be useful in recalling object names in Frost's study. There is some evidence to support such a view and we will consider this evidence in the next section on the accuracy of visual images.

Accuracy of Visual Images

It is clear that visual images decay over time and our visual memory becomes less accurate. It is not clear exactly how the images change or what factors contribute to their rate of decay. Some of the experiments reviewed in this chapter studied visual decay over a period of seconds, whereas other experiments studied decay over a period of weeks. There are several alternative hypotheses as to how images change over time. One possibility is that matching based upon a specific visual image is replaced by matching based upon a more abstract image as the prior stimulus is absorbed into the schemata of previous experiences (Posner, 1969). This suggestion is supported by Franks and Bransford's study (page 28) in which Ss had little memory for specific patterns but only for the central tendency of the patterns. It is more difficult to say whether images of common objects show a similar transformation. Images may simply become less legible or various parts may be lost while other parts remain quite clear. This issue will be one of the topics of the next chapter.

We do know that our internal representations of patterns do not always correspond exactly to the original patterns. An ingenious technique for learning something about our internal representations was developed by Shepard and Chipman (1970). The crux of their argument is that although it is difficult to learn anything about an individual representation of an object, we can explore the relations among different external objects and relations among their corresponding internal representations. They used two conditions to obtain similarity judgments regarding the shapes of states. In the first condition Ss were shown pairs of words naming two states of the United States. The Ss rated the visual similarity of the two states based upon their memory for how the two states were shaped. In a second condition, Ss were shown pairs of states consisting of the actual physical shapes. Each set of similarity ratings was analyzed separately in a multidimensional scaling program (discussed in Chapter IX) and the two solutions were superimposed. The superimposed two-dimensional solution is shown in Figure 6.10 illustrating how Ss' visual representations of the states corresponded to the actual physical shapes. A fairly close correspondence was found between the actual shapes and the imagined shapes with similarity judgments in both cases being determined by vertical versus horizontal elongation, general irregularity of form, and the straightness of the borders. The correspondence was not exact; however, the changes which occurred in the visual images do not appear to be systematic.

A more detailed exploration of how a visual image changes over time to become less like the original was carried out by Bahrick, Clark, and

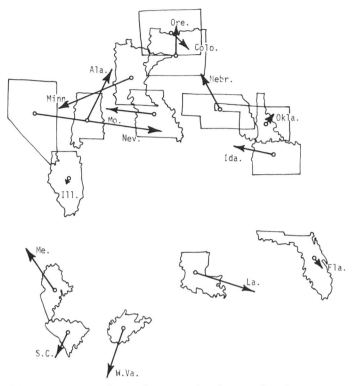

Figure 6.10. Superimposed two-dimensional solutions for the name condition (heads of arrows) and the picture condition (tails of arrows) based upon the two sets of similarity ratings averaged over all seven Ss. [From Shepard and Chipman (1970).]

Bahrick (1967). Subjects were required to select previously exposed pictures of common objects from among a series of alternative pictures which differed in similarity to the original. Figure 6.11 shows an original picture (second from the right) and the degree of dissimilarity of the alternatives. Generalization gradients were obtained following four stages of training (1, 3, 9, or 18 exposures) and four retention intervals (immediate, 2 hours, 2 days, or 2 weeks). The generalization gradients for the

5   3   1   4   2   5   1   3   4   0   2

Figure 6.11. Recognition test in which alternatives differ in their similarity to the original pattern (second from right). [After Bahrick, Clark, and Bahrick (1967).]

four retention intervals are shown in Figure 6.12. The generalization gradients become gradually flatter over time indicating a gradual loss of information about the original objects.

As a visual image becomes more impoverished over time, it becomes increasingly difficult to distinguish the image from similar objects of the same class. However, if someone has retained an impoverished image, he may still utilize the image to recall that a cup was presented even though he cannot remember enough details of the cup to distinguish it from other cups. This possibility was explored by Bahrick and Boucher (1968) in a study designed to test both the recall and the recognition of previously presented objects. In order to assess the role of verbal coding in memory, one group of Ss was instructed to call out the name of each object as it was presented. Overt naming of the stimuli led to improved recall of the objects but only when retention was tested immediately. The most significant finding was that the probability of a subject recalling the name of an object was uncorrelated with his recognition accuracy of that object, where recognition accuracy was defined as the amount of error on the generalization test. The experimenters considered two alternative

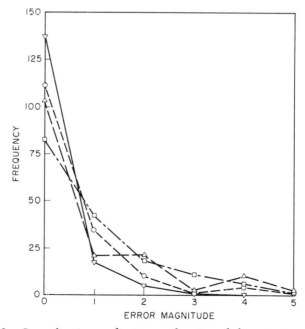

Figure 6.12. Generalization gradients as a function of the retention interval. △: Immediate; ○: two hours; ▽: two days; □: two weeks. [After Bahrick, Clark, and Bahrick (1967).]

explanations of the obtained independence between verbal recall probability and the accuracy of the visual image. Either recall of the objects depended entirely on retrieving the object names from a separate verbal memory, or recall was dependent on visual images but was unaffected by the completeness of the image. Bahrick and Boucher argued for the latter interpretation because overt verbalization of the names did not lead to improved recall after a 2-week retention interval; Ss reported using imagery to aid recall; and completely accurate images are not necessary to remember what objects had been presented.

The final technique that we will consider involves both visual and verbal presentations of the stimuli. In an experiment by Dallett and Wilcox (1968), Ss were shown a group of pictures intermixed with verbal descriptions of other pictures. Either immediately, 2 days, or 1 week later, they were asked to write down a brief phrase or label identifying each item they could remember. The free recall test showed that recall was better for pictures (P) than descriptions (D) but both were forgotten at equal rates (Figure 6.13). It is not clear why there is a better memory for pictures than descriptions, but one obvious possibility was eliminated by a second test. It could be hypothesized that Ss could more easily recode pictures into descriptions than descriptions into images. This would give Ss visual and verbal information for the pictures. In order to assess the effects of recoding, Dallett and Wilcox gave Ss a recognition test in which they had to indicate whether each item had been seen, described, or not encountered in the experiment. The recognition test showed some tendency for Ss to identify descriptions as pictures more often than they

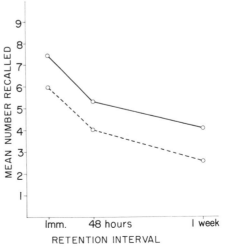

Figure 6.13. Mean number of items recalled for picture (—) and verbal description (– – –) conditions. [From Dallet and Wilcox (1968).]

wrongly identified pictures as descriptions. If they had primarily recoded pictures into descriptions, it is more likely that the opposite results would have been found—pictures misidentified as descriptions.

The Dallett and Wilcox experiment is similar to the Bahrick and Boucher experiment in that both tasks depended upon the recall of a label rather than the recall of a detailed description. In general, the results of the last two sections suggest that visual codes are dominant in recognition and verbal codes are dominant in recall. Visual codes seem to be useful in recall if the task involves recall of general concepts rather than of specific details. Presumably this is due to the possibility that visual images are not completely accurate and are therefore more useful sources of general, rather than specific, information.

Summary

We began by considering the general properties of a visual memory as it applies to spatial positions and found that it differed in a number of respects from a verbal memory. The memory span was shorter, retention was less stable, and there was little interference with auditory material. All these aspects have important implications for discovering how perceived items are matched to items stored in memory. Two stages are involved in this matching process: the encoding of the perceived item followed by its comparison to the memory items. When the perceived item is presented visually, a visual encoding of the item precedes retrieving the name of the item. Once encoded, however, matching can occur in parallel for both the visual and name codes. The result is that physical matches occur more quickly than name matches unless it is difficult to compare the two visual representations. This occurs if the encoded item and the items in the memory set are visually confusable or if the visual representations of items in the memory set have decayed, since the maintenance of visual representations requires an active process of attention. Thus the size of the memory set and whether it is fixed or variable may determine whether it is possible to use visual matching. Visual confusability is an important factor when Ss search an array of items for a target, implying visual matching based on a partial identification of features.

Although visual rehearsal (attending to the visual image) is useful in maintaining an image in STM, it does not appear to be effective in transferring information into LTM. Once rehearsal terminates, the rate of decay in the clarity of the image depends more upon the familiarity and complexity of the material than upon the amount of prior rehearsal.

Recognition memory for pictorial material is very good, even when Ss view as many as 2560 different pictures. The familiarity and similarity of the items is an important factor, however, since performance is much worse for recognizing snowflake crystals than for recognizing faces. The study of infants' recognition memory has important developmental implications and provides a pure test of visual memory, since the possibility of verbal coding is eliminated.

Once language develops, it can be used for both naming patterns and for verbally describing patterns which do not have names. The verbal loop hypothesis states that patterns are remembered by storing a verbal description and that the complexity of a pattern is determined by the number of words needed to describe it. Current evidence suggests that recall or reproduction of a pattern depends upon a verbal description, but recognition depends more upon a visual image. Ability to describe a pattern verbally correlates with success in reproduction but not with success in recognition. A verbal intervening task interfers more with reproduction but a visual intervening task interfers more with recognition. The time needed to recall the value of a feature depends upon the number of relevant features in the pattern suggesting retrieval from a verbal store. The time needed to recognize that two successively presented patterns are the same does not depend upon the number of features suggesting that the second pattern is matched to a visual image. Task expectations can influence what is stored during the initial encoding of patterns. Subjects expecting a recognition task emphasize the visual code whereas subjects expecting a recall task emphasize the verbal code.

Visual images exist in long term memory but are less detailed and less specific than the original patterns. They can be studied by obtaining similarity judgments for a set of physical patterns and for the same set of patterns as they are remembered by the Ss. A multidimensional scaling of the two sets of judgments revealed a close, but not an exact, correspondence. Generalization gradients for images become less and less steep over time suggesting a gradual loss of information, but there is no correlation between recalling what objects had been presented and the accuracy of the images. It is likely, however, that a visual image aids the recall of names since this type of recall does not depend upon the detailed accuracy of an image. One interpretation of these findings is that visual images are often accurate enough for recognition and the recall of general concepts but are not accurate enough for the recall of specific details.

VII | Memory Models: Components and Networks

The previous chapter was concerned with very general aspects of how patterns are represented in memory, namely, whether the representation is primarily visual or verbal. In this chapter we are interested in the structure, rather than the modality, of the memory code. The discussion parallels the presentation in Chapters II and III, since we begin with memory models which assume a feature-list representation and end with a presentation of experimental results that relate more to the structural aspects of patterns. The major issue is how the two representations can be used to test various aspects of the memory code. For example, if a pattern is stored as a list of features, do all the features have the same decay rates or are some parts of a pattern more likely to be remembered than others? When asked to indicate what part of a pattern has changed, does the S use the same criteria when considering each feature? Is it easier to learn a list of patterns if each pattern is unique or if some of the patterns are transformations of other patterns? These are a few of the questions that are discussed in the next three sections.

The first section considers the development of multicomponent models of memory which assume a feature-list representation. The first detailed presentation of a multicomponent model, together with its implications, was given by Bower in 1967. Bower's model has since stimulated the development of similar models; the most extensive being the proposal by Norman and Rumelhart (1970). Both proposals are very general and can be applied to all patterns that can be represented by a feature-list. We considered the application of Rumelhart's (1970) multicomponent theory to the perception of tachistoscopic displays in Chapter V, but the emphasis was on perception and the features were not specified. The second section shows how multicomponent models have been applied to specific patterns composed of well-defined features.

The final section differs from the previous two sections in that the emphasis is on structural models. There has been a recent development of network models of verbal LTM to interrelate semantic information in a network of nodes connected by relationships (see the papers in Tulving and Donaldson, 1972). Two general kinds of relationships are important in storing visual information: the relationships that join the parts of a pattern and the relationships that exist among different patterns. The network models enable us to describe highly structured patterns that are too complex for feature models. But feature models have the advantage that their greater simplicity makes it possible to formulate detailed predictions, as is illustrated by the multicomponent models. It remains to be determined whether similar predictions can be derived from the more complex structural models.

Multicomponent Models

Bower's (1967) paper was concerned with representing the formal structure of the memory trace and developing its implications for a variety of memory experiments. He hypothesized that following feature analysis, the stimulus is represented in memory as an ordered list of attributes with their corresponding values. Forgetting consists of an erasure or change in value of some of the components. It is assumed that the loss of any one component is an all-or-none event but the loss of information in the memory trace appears gradual because it consists of many components. As a result, the range of confusion errors in recognition or recall will increase directly with the number of forgotten components. As an example, we can think back to the cups shown in Figure

6.9. If I forgot the design on the side of the cup, I might pick a cup differing by one unit from the original. If I forgot the design, the shape, and the handle, I might pick a cup much less like the original.

One simplifying assumption of Bower's model is that the components of a pattern are forgotten independently and at the same rate. When this assumption is combined with the assumption of all-or-none forgetting, it becomes possible to use the binomial distribution to calculate the probability that a certain number of components are retained. Let $r(t)$ be the probability of a component being remembered at time t and let N be the number of components initially stored to represent the pattern. Then the probability that i components are retained at time t is given by the binomial distribution:

$$P(R = i) = \left(\frac{N}{i} \right) r(t)^i [1 - r(t)]^{N-i}. \tag{1}$$

By using this equation as a basis for further derivations, Bower was able to make detailed predictions for a variety of memory experiments including multiple choice and single stimulus tests of recognition memory, response latencies, amount of information transmitted, and confidence ratings in recall; effects of repetition and redundancy; and perceptual recognition of degraded stimuli.

In order to consider one example of the predictions derived by Bower, we will consider the single stimulus test of recognition memory. Subjects are asked to judge the familiarity of a test stimulus by comparing it to a memory trace of a previously presented stimulus. The theory assumes that S compares the feature values of the two stimuli and bases his familiarity judgment on the number of matches, the number of mismatches, and possibly the number of unknown values. Bower shows that the predictions based on a multicomponent model with all-or-none forgetting are very similar to the predictions derived from assuming that an item gradually declines in memory strength. In other words, an item with enough all-or-none components will give the same results as an item which varies on a continuous scale of memory strength. This makes it more difficult to distinguish between all-or-none forgetting of components and the gradual forgetting of components postulated in the next model.

Influenced by the work of Bower, Norman and Rumelhart (1970) developed a general model in which feature vectors played a predominate role. Figure 7.1 shows the general system with its two parts, perception and memory. The perceptual system was described in Chapter V as part of the discussion on the visual information store. Basically, it involves extracting features from each item and storing the features in perceptual

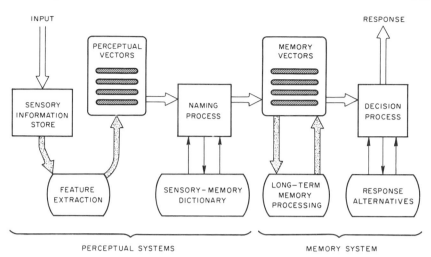

Figure 7.1. Outline of a multicomponent model of perception and memory. [After Norman and Rumelhart (1970).]

vectors. The perceptual vectors are then transformed by a naming process into a form meaningful to the memory system. The task is accomplished by matching the perceptual features extracted by the pattern recognizer against the features belonging to patterns in the set of possible stimuli it has been told to expect. The set of possible stimuli is referred to as a memory dictionary. If the features present in the perceptual vector match perfectly with only one dictionary vector, it is easy to identify and name the item. However, some features may be missing from the perceptual vector so that several dictionary vectors match the incomplete perceptual vector. In this case, Ss may elect either to discontinue processing that item (conservative naming strategy) by failing to name it or select a name by choosing randomly among the matching dictionary vectors (liberal naming strategy).

Items which are named are represented in the memory system in the form of memory vectors. Norman and Rumelhart, in presenting a general formulation of the model, deliberately avoided specifying the attributes of an item, but it is clear that the features composing the memory vector may differ from the features composing the initial perceptual vector. For example, the perceptual vectors representing letters in a tachistoscopic display would most likely be visual segments. Once named, however, letters could be represented in memory by auditory components such as phonemes. When an item is named, it is stored in STM where the clarity of its features or attributes decay exponentially. The probability that an attribute can be recognized at any given time is assumed to be proportional to the clarity of that attribute. Some attributes may transfer into LTM where they are represented more permanently. The rate at which attributes of an item are transferred to LTM is assumed to be proportional to the clarity of the information held in STM about that item and the amount of attention allocated to that item.

Both recognition and recall of items require Ss to make judgments about the context in which the attributes were originally stored. Since meaningful items are likely to be already stored in Ss' memory before the experiment begins, it is the fact that a particular item was presented within the context of the experiment that must be retained. When a subject is asked to recall material, he tries to retrieve the individual attributes by linking them to the context in which the attributes were originally stored. The probability of a correct recall depends upon how many of the attributes are still available in either STM or LTM and how successful a subject is in matching the attributes with the vectors of all possible responses. In a recognition experiment, the S's task is to decide whether he previously perceived a test item within the context of the experiment. The theory assumes that a subject checks the context associated with each attribute of the test item and responds positively if c or more attributes of the test item match one of his memory vectors. Mathematical derivations are used in making predictions from the model and the parameters estimated for various memory experiments include the number of attributes composing the memory vectors (N_m), the probability of an attribute being shared by any two stimulus items (δ), the decay component for STM (γ), the rate of transfer into LTM (λ), and the response criterion (c).

Applications of Component Models

In order to make the discussion less abstract, we shall consider several applications of multicomponent models. A computer simulation program developed by Laughery (1969) is an example of how a multicomponent model can be used to give a detailed specification of the structures and processes used in a complex memory task. The program was designed to simulate the standard memory span procedure in which a subject is presented with a sequence of digits or letters and asked to reproduce as many items as he can remember. Although the model is basically a simulation of STM, both LTM and STM are represented. Long-term memory contains the visual and auditory definitions of the stimuli and represents S's permanent knowledge about the items. Although all the items are specified in terms of both visual and auditory components, only the auditory components are assumed to be stored in memory since previous research has indicated that visual components are not important in determining performance. Auditory components consist of the 43 phonemes, and from 1 to 6 phonemes are need to define each of the stimuli. The STM consists of a series of memory structures containing information about the names of the auditory components, the times at which the components were stored, and their decay rates. Laughery's model consists of a number of separate programs which simulate the different aspects of Ss' performance in a memory task. Table 7.1 lists the programs and their descriptive titles.

When an item is presented, it is entered into STM by specifying for each auditory component, the name of the component, the time it was stored and a function describing its decay. Components decay independently according to exponential functions giving the probability of retrieving a component as a function of length of time in STM. Unlike the mathematical models discussed in the previous section, components can decay at different rates. Decay rates are assigned on the basis of some results obtained by Wickelgren (1965) indicating that the pronun-

TABLE 7.1

DESCRIPTIVE TITLE OF MODEL ROUTINES FOR LAUGHERY's COMPUTER SIMULATION MODEL[a]

Program name	Descriptive title
E1	Model executive
S1	Subject executive
S2	Input stimulus
S3	Is a new item in window?
S4	Net sorting
S5	Store and update in short-term memory
S6	Respond
S10	Interitem activity
S11	Find location (M) of next short-term memory structure
S20	Store basic component
S22	Store link substructure
S40	Select item
S41	Generate list of consistent items
S42	Generate list of items consistent with most components
S50	Retrieve auditory components of item from dictionary
S52	Update
S100	Rehearsal
S101	Retrieve remembered components of an item
S105	Is rehearsal continued?
S110	Recoding

[a] From Laughery (1969).

ciation time of a phoneme is related to the kinds of acoustic confusions made by *Ss*. Laughery therefore divided the phonemes into five categories according to their pronunciation time and assigned a different decay rate to the phonemes in each category. The decay rates are modified by rehearsal which occurs during the interitem interval. Each time an item is rehearsed, the storage time of each component in the item is reset and the decay function for each component is changed to a slower rate. The change to a slower decay rate is used to represent learning. In addition to rehearsal, *Ss* can improve their performance by recoding items into chunks consisting of more than one item. Chunks are formed if they are meaningful (such as the sequence of digits 1492) or if they are pronounceable (such as the letters DUP). Chunking improves the efficiency of *Ss'* performance, since it takes less time to rehearse the chunks and it is easier to remember the temporal order of the individual items composing the chunk.

Errors can occur by missing an item if the input rate is very fast, retrieving an incorrect item that will tend to have common auditory components, or mistaking the order of items. Forgetting results from the failure to retrieve components. When there are not enough components recalled to specify a unique item, the model chooses randomly from among the alternatives containing the phonemes which are recalled. For example, if only the first phoneme is recalled from the letter **F**, there would be six items consistent with the recalled information—**F L M N S X**. The result is that the model tends to make auditory confusion errors like those found in the performance of actual *Ss*.

A phonemic model of memory has also been developed by Sperling and Speelman (1970), although their model is limited to consonants specified by two phonemes. The model assumes that: (1) when letters are presented auditorily or rehearsed all phonemes of a letter are stored in memory; (2) once in memory, constituent phonemes of letters are retained or lost independently; (3) at recall, if only one of the two phonemes is available, a guess is made from among those letters of the alphabet that contain the retained phoneme in the same position. The assumptions of the two models are quite similar, although Sperling and Speelman primarily focus on capacity and how many phonemes can be stored in STM.

One difference between the various multicomponent models is that in the mathematical models proposed by Bower (1967) and Norman and Rumelhart (1970), the rate of decay is the same for all components, but as already stated, in the computer simulation model proposed by Laughery, components may decay at different rates. A factor that may influence the retention of features is their saliency. It has been found in concept identification experiments that some dimensions are more salient or noticeable than others and these dimensions are likely to be chosen first for testing (Trabasso & Bower 1968). Would saliency also determine which components of a pattern are better remembered? In order to explore this hypothesis, Friedman, Reed, and Carterette (1971) tested memory for schematic faces. The faces differed on four well-defined features: the height of the forehead, the distance between the eyes, the length of the nose, and the height of the mouth. Each feature could take on one of two values as is illustrated by the left and right faces shown in Figure 7.2. A recognition memory procedure was used in which Ss were shown two schematic faces separated by a delay of 6, 12, or 18 sec. Their task was to judge whether the second face was the same as or different from the first face. If they judged the two faces different, they indicated the feature or features of the two faces which differed. After the experiment, each S rank ordered the four features according to saliency.

Figure 7.3 shows the probability of a miss (failing to state that a feature changed) and the probability of a false alarm (incorrectly stating that a feature changed) for each of the four features. The features are

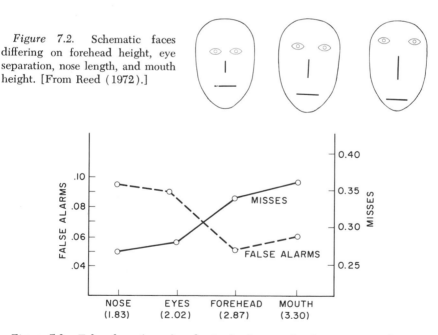

Figure 7.2. Schematic faces differing on forehead height, eye separation, nose length, and mouth height. [From Reed (1972).]

Figure 7.3. False alarm (– – –) and miss (——) errors for the component features. The features are ordered in terms of decreasing saliency. Mean rank saliency scores are given in parentheses for each feature. [After Friedman, Reed, and Carterette (1971).]

arranged from the most salient feature, nose, to the least salient, mouth. The results indicate that Ss made fewer misses but more false alarms on the more salient features. This finding suggests that saliency may influence response bias more than the retention of the components. A calculation of bias and retention parameters revealed this to be true. Assuming all-or-none retention of components as proposed by Bower, retention probabilities were found to be .63, .66, .63, and .53 for the four features in declining order of saliency. Although Ss' memory was not as good for the least salient component, there was little difference among the other three components. A more systematic decline was found for the bias parameters. The probability of Ss guessing that a particular feature changed declined from .33, .26, .22, and .17 in decreasing order of saliency. Although these results suggest that saliency had a greater influence on the decision aspects of memory, studies using different patterns may find retention differences as well (see Odom, 1972).

An issue related to feature saliency is whether some features are better than others in enabling an observer to identify a pattern. For example, are certain parts of a face particularly helpful in recognition? This problem was investigated by Goldstein and Mackenberg (1966). Children in kindergarten, first grade, and fifth grade were shown pictures of their classmates which they had previously been able to identify. In order to determine what features or parts of the face contributed to recognition, the experimenters used a variety of masks to partially occlude the photographs (Figure 7.4). The results indicated that some parts of the faces were more important than others for aiding recognition (Figure 7.5). The upper part of the face was more informative than the lower and the eyes (Condition M) aided the older Ss more than the nose (Condition J) or mouth (Condition K). The older children generally did better than the younger children, but the reasons for their superiority are not clear. One question raised by these results is whether the more informative features are better remembered or whether they are only more discriminative. More information is also needed to determine the relative importance of the individual features as opposed to the relations among features. Spatial relations is our next topic.

Network Models

Like the feature models of Chapter II, the multicomponent models have no direct representation of the structure of patterns. It is of interest that the principal developers of multicomponent models have more recently emphasized the importance of relations and organization as determinants

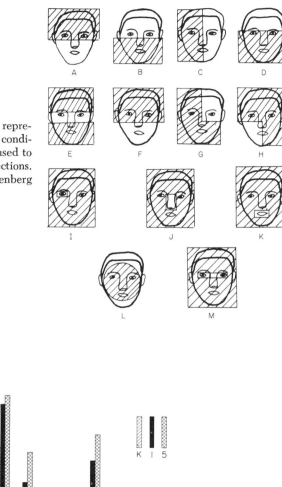

Figure 7.4. Schematic representation of experimental conditions. An opaque mask was used to occlude cross-hatched sections. [From Goldstein and Mackenberg (1966).]

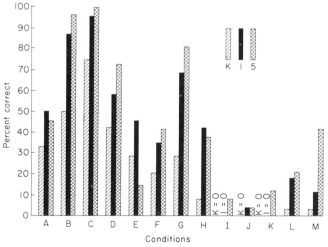

Figure 7.5. Percentage of correct identifications by kindergarten (K), first (1), and fifth (5) grade subjects on condition A to M of Figure 7.4. [From Goldstein and Mackenberg (1966).]

of memory storage and retrieval. Bower (1972) began a recent paper by reviewing the contributions of Gestalt psychology and pointed out its relevance to current experimental findings on organizational factors in memory. Rumelhart, Lindsay, and Norman (1972) proposed that information is stored as a set of nodes interconnected by various relations. For example, the relationship *isa* defines set membership as in the statement *a dog isa animal. Has* defines property relations: *a dog has feet.* In this case *dog* is a node and *isa* and *has* are relations attached to that node. The addition of more nodes and more relations can result in a large network of interrelated information.

Although these models have been primarily developed for verbal material, they are somewhat similar to the structural models discussed in Chapter III, particularly the network model proposed by Noton (1970). The emphasis on the many different kinds of relationships characterizing semantic memory is also similar to Clowes's (1969) emphasis on the many different types of relationships that characterize visual patterns. First, there are the relations that exist among the features and parts of a pattern and second there are the relations that connect different patterns with each other.

It was primarily the first type of relationship that was our concern when discussing structural models in Chapter III. But do people really store patterns as structural descriptions? Reed (1971) attempted to answer this question by testing Ss' ability to recognize the various parts of a previously exposed pattern. Twenty-four Ss served in an experiment requiring them to judge whether the second of two successively presented patterns was a part of the first pattern. The first pattern was presented for 3 sec, followed by a 3-sec delay, followed by the second pattern. Subjects responded by pushing either a positive switch or a negative switch, and reaction times were recorded. The instructions indicated that a repetition of the first pattern should be considered a part of the first pattern. Thus, patterns 1A–1E are parts of pattern 1 and patterns 2A–2E are parts of pattern 2 (Figure 7.6).

Since Ss are quite accurate at recognizing repetitions, we know that their memory for the first pattern is quite good, but we do not know whether their memory is in the form of a structural description or an unanalyzed template. It was hypothesized that if Ss were basing their decisions on a template stored as a visual image, they should recognize one part about as well as any other part of the pattern. They would simply have to examine their visual image for the presence of the part, as in the standard embedded figures task. However, if Ss had encoded the patterns in terms of a structural description, they should be more accurate on those parts which were specified in their description. The re-

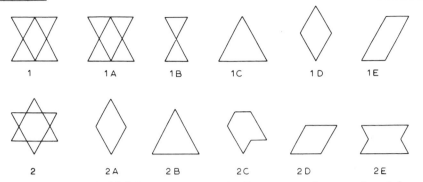

Figure 7.6. Embedded figures. Figures 1A–1E are parts of pattern 1 and figures 2A–2E are parts of pattern 2. [From Reed (1971).]

sults supported the latter prediction. Whereas approximately $\frac{2}{3}$ of the Ss recognized patterns 1B–1D, only 4 Ss responded correctly on pattern 1E. Only 2 Ss were correct on pattern 2D, compared to 17 correct responses for pattern 2B.

In general, these results support Sutherland's (1968) proposal that people store patterns in terms of an abstract description and that they can only respond to aspects of the pattern that are a part of that description. It is less clear what the modality of the memory code is, but I think the results argue against a very sharp visual image. If the Ss retained a clear image of the first pattern, recognizing any part of that pattern should be relatively easy (for adults) in the same way that the task would be easy if the pattern and part were simultaneously exposed. Some form of a structured image may be used, however, to maintain the relationship of the subpatterns. It would be easier to visualize how two triangles overlap than to describe verbally exactly how they are joined.

Shepard and Metzler (1971) proposed that a visual image can be used to compare two highly structured objects. Their task required that Ss compare two perspective line drawings to determine whether they were the same shape. Figure 7.7 shows three pairs. Half of the pairs could be rotated to match each other and half of the pairs were mirror images which did not match. The pairs differed in orientation from 0° to 180° in 20° steps. The time taken to decide whether the two objects were the same increased linearly with an increase in orientation suggesting that Ss were rotating a visual image of one of the forms until it had the same orientation as the other form. Introspective reports confirmed this explanation since Ss reported that they imagined one object rotating into congruence with the other and that they could only rotate an image at a certain rate without losing its essential structure. Since the reaction time

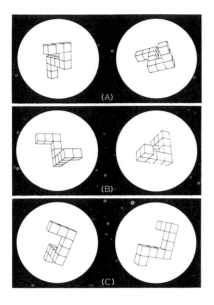

Figure 7.7. Examples of pairs of perspective line drawings. The two patterns of pairs A and B are different orientations of the same pattern. The two patterns of pair C are different patterns. [From Shepard and Metzler (1971).]

ranged from 1 sec at 0° to 5 sec at 180°, a visual image was maintained over this interval but it is likely that Ss continued to look at the exposed pattern to help them maintain the image.

The previous experiment illustrates the second relation referred to earlier—the relationship between different patterns rather than the relationship between the parts of a pattern. Different orientations of the same object, different photographs or views of the same person, the similarities and differences among dogs, and the similarity of a pattern to a prototype are all examples of this second relationship. The issue here is whether pattern descriptions are stored separately or whether the descriptions are related to other descriptions, perhaps, by some sort of network. Schema theory, considered in Chapter II, is one example of how patterns can be related to each other, in this case by reference to a central prototype.

If patterns are related to each other, can they be learned more easily? Royer (1971) sought an answer to this question by constructing three sets of patterns that differed in the number of patterns in the set which were identical except for orientation (Figure 7.8). Set A consisted of eight unique patterns; Set B consisted of four unique patterns and one orientational transformation of each pattern; and Set C consisted of three unique patterns, one transformation of two of the patterns, and three transformations of the third pattern.

Royer hypothesized that if figural information is more difficult to learn,

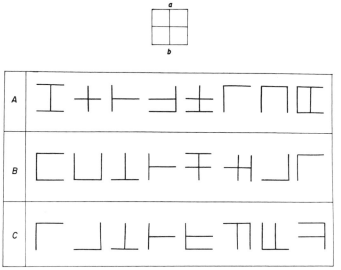

Figure 7.8. Three sets of patterns differing on the number of patterns in each set which are orientational transformations of other patterns in the set. [From Royer (1971).]

Set C should be the easiest but if orientational information is more difficult to learn, Set A should be the easiest. Subjects were assigned to one of the three sets and were told that they would have 3 sec to observe each stimulus and that they would have to reproduce each stimulus at the end of the series. There were 10 trials in a learning experiment. Performance differed significantly across the three lists, with list A being the easiest to learn and list C the most difficult. Royer proposed that orientation information is fairly well maintained in memory unless a pattern appears in several different orientations, in which case the indexing of the different orientations becomes more difficult. This view is supported by his finding that the increase in the number of errors in going from list A to list B to list C was entirely the result of orientational errors, rather than omissions or other types of errors.

These results are of interest because little is known about what type of interpattern relationships facilitate learning. The outcome might have been predicted from a knowledge of the difficulty children have in discriminating letters that differ only by rotations or reflections. But the patterns in Figure 7.8 are easily discriminated by adults. Schema theory would more likely predict that it should be easier to remember transformations rather than completely different patterns (although none of the patterns represented a central tendency as discussed in Chapter II).

The verbal loop hypothesis would also predict that it should be easier to remember transformations if less words were required to describe the transformations than were required to describe unique patterns. And finally, the results raise the question of whether they are interpattern relationships that facilitate learning rather than retard it. The investigation of this question might not only lead to network models that parallel those of verbal learning, but suggest a model for predicting the difficulty of learning various structures.

Summary

Multicomponent memory models assume that an item can be represented in memory by a vector of feature values. A formalized model, together with its implications for a large variety of memory experiments, was first presented by Bower in 1967. The model assumed that the loss of any one component occurs as an all-or-none event but the loss of information in the memory trace appears gradual because it consists of many components. With the additional assumption that components are forgotten independently and at the same rate, it is possible to specify the number of retained components by the binomial distribution. The multicomponent model was developed further by Norman and Rumelhart who extended the model to include perception as well as memory. The theory assumes that physical inputs are first stored in a sensory information store where critical features are extracted from each item and placed in perceptual vectors. The vectors of perceptual features are transformed into vectors of memory attributes by a naming system. Following the entrance of an item into STM, the probability of recognizing an attribute decays exponentially with a time constant which is identical for all attributes. Responding occurs through a decision process which considers the attributes remaining in each memory vector and the set of possible response alternatives.

A third multicomponent model was developed by Laughery in the form of a computer simulation program. The program was designed specifically to model the memory span procedure in which Ss are required to recall a sequence of numbers or letters. Items are represented in memory in terms of phonemes, which are lost independently and with possibly different decay rates. Both rehearsal and recoding can be used to maintain items in memory. A response process selects randomly from among those items consistent with the retained components resulting in acoustic confusion errors when a memory item is incompletely specified. One advantage of the simulation model is that it is not required to make the simplifying assumption that components are treated equally since feature saliency may influence decay rates or Ss' decisions in responding. The results of a recent experiment using schematic faces as stimuli indicated that feature saliency influenced Ss' decisions, causing a bias in favor of the more salient features. Some features were found to be more informative than others when children were asked to identify their classmates, although either differences in memory or discriminability could account for the results.

Recent theories of LTM have represented semantic information within a network of nodes connected by various relationships. Two different kinds of relationships which characterize visual patterns are the relationships that exist among the parts of a pattern and the relationships that exist among different patterns. The ability of Ss to identify correctly the parts of a previously exposed pattern illustrates the first relationship. Their poor performance in identifying certain parts suggests that they store a pattern as a structural description and have difficulty in responding to parts not represented in their description. The ability of Ss to make use of interpattern relationships in learning a list of patterns illustrates the second relationship. Experimental results indicated that Ss could learn a list of unique patterns faster than a list in which some patterns were orientational transformations of other patterns. The results raise the question of how patterns are related and what relationships would facilitate, rather than interfere with, learning.

Part 4 | PERCEPTUAL CLASSIFICATION

VIII | Probability Models

In this and the following chapter we discuss alternative theoretical approaches to the problem of perceptual classification. The experiments described in the previous chapters have generally used a single exemplar of a pattern and have not dealt with pattern variability. We now return to a fundamental issue: How people can recognize many different types of exemplars of a pattern, including novel exemplars not encountered before. We discussed this problem briefly in Chapter II when we considered schema theory and the formation of prototypes as one possible classification strategy. But the emphasis in that chapter was primarily on discrimination learning, particularly the discrimination theory of perceptual learning proposed by the Gibsons. What was not made explicit until recently is how categorization relates to this theory. This point is briefly discussed in E. Gibson's (1969) book:

> It would seem superficially, that practice in categorizing should lead only to more generalized, less specific perceptions and thus, result in the opposite of perceptual learning. But it is also possible that members assigned to a category actually share, potentially, some feature—either a minimal distinctive or some higher order one—that distinguishes the category from other

157

categories. If this is picked up with practice and processed without verbal
intervention, perceptual learning has taken place [p. 190].

It is usually not the case, however, that all patterns within a category
share a common feature. It is true in many concept-learning experiments
in which S's task is to find the single dimension which will enable him to
classify the stimuli correctly. Once he has discovered this dimension,
classification is trivial as he can respond on the basis of this one cue. It
is more usual in pattern-recognition problems that stimuli are composed
of a number of *partially valid* cues rather than a single, perfectly valid
cue. A decision rule is therefore required which will integrate the available information. This problem was attacked by Jerome Bruner, whose
approach to perception is quite different from the Gibsons'. In a 1957
paper, Bruner began by making the assumpton that all perceptual experience is necessarily the end-product of a categorization process; that
whatever is perceived achieves its meaning from a class of percepts with
which it is grouped. By a category, Bruner meant a rule for classifying
objects as equivalent. The rule must specify

(1) the critical properties of the stimuli,
(2) the manner in which the properties are combined,
(3) the weights assigned various properties, and
(4) the acceptance limits for each category.

Furthermore, Bruner believed that there was no reason to assume that
laws governing inferences of this kind were discontinuous as one moved
from perceptual to more conceptual activities.

Bruner's statement that "all perception is necessarily the end-product
of a categorization process" has not gone unquestioned. Neisser (1967, p.
49), for example, has argued that some kinds of perceptual experience,
such as visual tracking, may be more analogue than categorical. Nonetheless, other forms of perceptual experience such as pattern recognition
are, for the most part, categorical. One of the most popular approaches
to the problem in both artificial intelligence and psychology has been
the use of probability models in assigning patterns to categories. This
approach assumes that Ss learn the conditional probabilities or cue validities of the various features. A decision rule is also required and the first
problem we consider is whether the rule should be probabilistic or deterministic.

Probabilistic or Deterministic Decision Rules

One type of probability model was developed by Estes as part of his
work on stimulus sampling theory. Estes was concerned with the problem

of how Ss learn stimuli with overlapping cues and how this learning transfers to novel patterns composed of the previously learned cues (Estes & Hopkins, 1961). An important aspect of Estes's theory is the distinction between transfer mediated by individual cues or components and transfer mediated by patterns of cues. According to the component hypothesis, the probability of a response to any given component should be given by the probability of that reponse being reinforced over training trials on which the component occurs, either alone or in combination with other components. As an example, let us take three components represented by the letters a, b, c, and one pattern consisting of two components ab. S's task is to choose either response "one" or response "two" when shown a component or a pattern consisting of several components. Let us assume that as the result of previous reinforcement, the probability of response "one" being correct is 1.0 for a, .50 for b, .33 for c, and 1.0 for ab. According to the theory, the probability of a response to a stimulus compound is a weighted average of the probabilities of the constituent elements. If each component is responded to as a separate element, the predicted probability of response "one" to a novel test pattern abc would be $(1.0 + .50 + .33)/3 = .61$. If the pattern ab were treated as an element rather than a and b as separate elements, the predicted probability of response "one" would be $(1.0 + .33)/2 = .67$. In either case, the model is probabilistic in that it does not give a deterministic response rule but predicts Ss will give a certain response some percentage of the time.

One formulation of the theory, called the mixed model, assumes that learning occurs in terms of patterns but transfer to novel situations is mediated by responding to component cues. Friedman, Trabasso, and Mosberg (1967) tested the mixed model by having Ss learn to assign one of three responses to each of nine items. Each item was composed of two cues (Greek letters) and some items shared common cues. The experimenters assumed that learning occurs in terms of patterns (the compound item) and that all items in the list are learned independently with the same parameter values. However, transfer to unlearned or novel patterns is determined by the component cues. Since learning is assumed to occur at the same rate for all patterns, it is the response rules to unlearned patterns which form the basis of the theory and determine total errors and trial of the last error for the individual items. The model assumes that Ss select a component of a novel unlearned pattern and respond on the basis of the responses associated with that component. Probability parameters are used to specify the response rules and a parameter of particular importance is the probability of S selecting a *relevant* cue, one which is associated with only a single response.

An alternative, more normative model which does give a deterministic response rule is statistical decision theory. Lee (1963) has pointed out the essential difference between these two types of choice models. If Ss use categories, as postulated by the statistical decision theory model, they should divide the stimulus space into choice regions, and always respond to stimuli on one side of the boundary in one way, and to stimuli on the other side in another way. The theory specifies the regions in terms of a likelihood ratio. If f_A is the height of probability distribution A at some location, and f_B is the height of distribution B at some location, the likelihood ratio of A to B is $\lambda = f_A/f_B$. For equal costs and a priori probabilities, any stimulus resulting in $\lambda > 1$ should receive response A and any stimulus resulting in $\lambda < 1$ should receive response B. Lee has labeled the alternative theory "probability micromatching." It is similar to the component model of stimulus sampling theory in that it states that S chooses As and Bs for a given location probabilistically, and in the proportion equal to $f_A/(f_A + f_B)$.

As an example, let us assume that a stimulus can be represented by specifying its values on two dimensions and that each stimulus comes from one of two categories. Figure 8.1 illustrates that the stimuli in each category are normally distributed on both dimensions, x_1 and x_2. The two bivariate normal distributions overlap, as is indicated by the two circles and the projection of the distributions on each axis. The straight line between the two circles is the decision boundary separating the two distributions. The height of distribution A (f_A) is greater than the height of distribution B (f_B) above the decision boundary implying that it is more probable that a stimulus in this region of the stimulus space comes

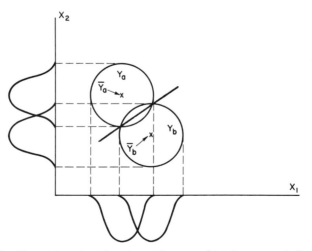

Figure 8.1. Two categories of patterns shown as bivariate normal distributions.

from distribution A. The opposite is true below the decision boundary so Ss should always choose category A for any stimulus above the boundary and category B for any stimulus below the boundary if they are basing their responses on decision theory. If they are basing their judgments on micromatching, they should always choose each category probabilistically, in proportion to the height of the two distributions at that point.

The predictions of the two different theories are illustrated in Figure 8.2 (Lee, 1963). The solid line represents the sharp boundary of decision theory whereas the dashed line represents the gradual transition in responses predicted by probability matching. The two categories were formed from the location of a dot on a white card, where the location (the coordinates) was determined by sampling from one of two bivariate normal distributions. The task was to judge whether each card belonged to Category A or Category B. As indicated in Figure 8.2, the responses of

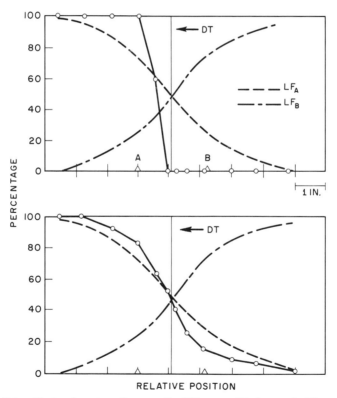

Figure 8.2. Choice functions for two Ss (S1, top; S2, bottom). The solid line, *DT*, gives the theoretical choice function for decision theory. The dashed line, *LF*$_A$, for micromatching. [After Lee (1963).]

S1 are more characteristic of decision theory and the responses of S2 are more characteristic of micromatching. One way of summarizing the results shown in Figure 8.2 is to calculate the percentage of crossover choices, that is the number of A and B responses on the wrong side of the decision axis. Decision theory predicts that there should be no crossover responses (line DT in Figure 8.3), since Ss should always choose the most probable category. Micromatching predicts that there should be a certain percentage of crossover responses (line M_μ in Figure 8.3) since Ss should not always choose the most probable category. In a second study, Lee and Janke (1964) investigated how Ss would categorize samples from three continua—dot position, grayness, and two-digit numbers. The results for the dot position continuum were closer to the predictions of decision theory, whereas the results for the other continua fell in between the predictions of the two theories. These findings are shown in Figure 8.3 as the percentage of crossover choices over trials.

One factor which should be considered in evaluating the predictions of decision theory is that Ss may attempt to use a deterministic decision rule and still make crossover responses due to failures in discrimination or failures in integrating information. Lee and Janke argued against failures occurring in discrimination, since a sharp boundary could be formed on the number dimension without perceptual error, yet the number of crossover responses was greatest for this condition. A second factor which may limit the successful application of a deterministic decision rule is the ability to integrate information when complex stimuli differ along a

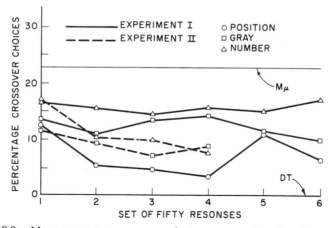

Figure 8.3.   Mean percentage crossover choices versus trials. Graphs would follow the abscissa for a perfectly sharp crossover. The result in the case of probability micromatching—M_μ—is indicated. [After Lee and Jahnke (1964).]

number of dimensions. A study by Kubovy, Rapoport, and Tversky (1971) indicates that deterministic strategies are used when conditions encourage the use of such strategies. Kubovy *et al.* used numbers as stimuli so that the stimuli would be discriminable, ensured adequate knowledge of the distribution by providing Ss with several thousand learning trials, and motivated Ss to behave optimally by using monetary payoffs which depended upon their performance. The results showed that the difference between the observed and expected frequencies of choosing each category was nonsignificant for the deterministic decision theory model, but was highly significant for the micromatching model.

In general, these studies support the deterministic decision rule although failures in discrimination, lack of knowledge about the alternative distributions, and the inability to integrate information from several dimensions are all factors which may limit the performance of Ss using a deterministic response strategy. The very fact that people are quite good at recognizing patterns suggests the use of an optimal response rule. People make mistakes, however, when learning new patterns and the probabilistic response rules have been successful in predicting the types of errors people make (Friedman, Trabasso, & Mosberg, 1967). Indeed, the mixed model uses both a probabilistic response rule, to account for errors on unlearned patterns, and a deterministic response rule, to account for the eventual learning of patterns. Kubovy *et al.* (1971) also emphasized the important role of learning in forming a deterministic response criterion. This is not to say that the issue is entirely resolved. Luce concluded a 1964 article by asserting that psychologists are still not able to decide even for the simplest situations whether a S's asymptotic decision process is primarily probabilistic as a result of adaptive learning or whether it is based on a more analytic evaluation of the situation. The problem is still an important one, but we will assume here that deterministic models are more appropriate in accounting for our ability to recognize. At the least, they are a good first approximation.

Discriminant Analysis

In our search for classification models, we shall first review the merits of discriminant functions. Rodwan and Hake (1964) proposed that the linear discriminant function can serve as a model for perceptual classifications in that it enables us to find the linear function of the features which allows for maximal discrimination between two categories. The linear discriminant function assumes that a pattern can be represented as a vector of feature values and that a weighted linear combination of these values determines how a pattern should be classified. If $X = (x_1, x_2, \ldots,$ $x_d)$ is a pattern with feature values x_m a linear discriminant function has the form:

$$g(X) = w_1 x_1 + w_2 x_2 + \cdots + w_d x_d + w_{d+1} \qquad (1)$$

The weights w_m determine how the pattern should be classified. The geometric interpretation of a linear discriminant function is that the decision boundary separating two categories is a straight line for two-dimensional patterns ($d = 2$) and a plane for three-dimensional patterns ($d = 3$). The decision boundary shown in Figure 8.1 can be represented by a linear discriminant function in which the orientation of the boundary depends upon the feature weights, w_1 and w_2, and the location of the boundary between the two categories is determined by w_3.

Rodwan and Hake (1964) applied the discriminant function to a classification task in which Ss were asked to classify schematic faces into one of two categories labeled "intelligent" and "nonintelligent." Each face varied along four dimensions: length of the nose, length of the chin, distance between the eyes, and the length of the forehead. After Ss had made their classifications, the experimenters calculated the linear discriminant function which would best separate each S's classifications. The discriminant model enabled the investigators to make a number of useful conclusions. First, a linear discriminant function could predict each S's classifications with relatively few errors, indicating that the judgments could be reproduced from a linear combination of the feature values. Second, the weights calculated for each feature indicated what features primarily influenced Ss' decisions. The relative importance of the features was quite similar for the three Ss and the dominant variable in each case was the length of the forehead. Finally, the results indicated that the judgments were stable and changed little over time.

The discriminant function calculated by Rodwan and Hake was the linear combination of feature values which best discriminated between the two categories formed by each subject. When there is an objective criterion for distinguishing between the two categories, the discriminant function calculated for each S's classifications can be compared to the discriminant function calculated to separate the objectively defined categories. If a S's classifications differ from the objectively defined categories, the two functions can be compared. This approach was used by Aiken and Brown (1971) to study what features Ss emphasize and whether their classifications could be predicted by a linear weighting of features when their classifications differed from the objectively defined criterion. The criterion was two schematic clusters formed by generating patterns (similar to those shown in Figure 2.9, page 27) about two prototypes. Subjects viewed a series of 150 patterns and classified each pattern into one of two categories. The results indicated that even when a S's classifications differed from the objectively defined categories, a linear discriminant function was fairly successful in predicting his classifications. The feature weights differed from the feature weights of the objective function, suggesting that Ss were using a linear combination rule but were emphasizing the "wrong" features.

Although the linear discriminant function can provide us with useful information, it is limited as a model for perception because it does not tell us what kind of decision processes Ss actually use in making their classifications. A process model should not only be able to make successful predictions, but should describe a reasonable set of psychological assumptions regarding how Ss actually carry out the task (Gregg & Simon, 1967). The linear discriminant function is too general to serve as a process model because a variety of decision strategies would result in classifications that could be predicted by the discriminant model.

One example of a process model assumes that Ss make their classifications on the basis of a likelihood ratio. Such an assumption would be consistent with statistical decision theory and with multivariate versions of signal detection theory. The different values of each feature would be distributed along a dimension and the number of dimensions would equal the number of features. Each category of patterns would have a probability distribution showing how the different values of each feature were distributed for that category. Let us assume that there are two categories and that patterns within a category are distributed according to a multivariate normal distribution. The distribution for each category is specified in terms of the mean vector, showing the mean value along each dimension, and the covariance matrix showing the variance along each dimension.

The two probability distributions could be used to form a likelihood ratio for each test pattern and the test pattern could be classified on the basis of the likelihood ratio. We saw in the previous section that a likelihood ratio of Category A to Category B is of the form $\lambda = f_A/f_B$, where f_A is the probability of pattern X for Category A and f_B is the probability of pattern X for Category B at each point in the stimulus space. If $\mu = (\bar{x}_1\ \bar{x}_2, \ldots, \bar{x}_d)$ is the mean and Σ is the covariance matrix of the multivariate normal distribution representing Category A, the probability of any pattern X for Category A, can be calculated from Eq. (2).

$$P(X|\text{Cat.A}) = [(2\pi)^{(1/2)p}|\Sigma|^{1/2}]^{-1} \exp[-\tfrac{1}{2}(X - \mu)'\Sigma^{-1}(X - \mu)] \quad (2)$$

If Category B has the same covariance matrix as Category A, $P(X)|$ Cat.B) can be calculated by an equation identical to Eq.(2) except for the difference in the mean vector. In this case, it is possible to greatly simplify the likelihood ratio $\lambda = f_A/f_B$ and rewrite it in the form of a linear discriminant function (Anderson, 1958, pp. 133–134). If Ss based their classifications on a likelihood ratio involving the preceding assumptions and were perfectly accurate in calculating the likelihood ratio for each test pattern, it would be possible to derive a linear discriminant function which would predict their classifications.

But the success of a linear discriminant function in predicting Ss' classifications would not enable us to conclude that their decisions were based on probability distributions and likelihood ratios. There are other types of decision criteria which could also be formulated as a linear discriminant function (Nilsson, 1965). One example discussed by Nilsson is a minimum distance classifier which is particularly relevant whenever the category patterns can be adequately represented by a prototype pattern (see the discussion of schema theory in Chapter II). The decision rule is simply to classify each test pattern into the category which has the closest prototype. Such a decision rule is a particular example of a distance model and will be discussed in greater detail in the next chapter. The important point to be stressed here is that two models involving very different process assumptions can both be expressed as linear discriminant functions.

This does not imply that the discriminant function calculated from the likelihood ratio assumption is the same as the discriminant function calculated from the closest protoype assumption. Both the category means and covariance matrices determine the discriminant weights in the case of the likelihood ratio, whereas only the category means (prototypes) determine the discriminant weights in the case of the minimum distance classifier. Figure 8.4 shows the discriminant functions for both cases. The decision boundary for the minimum distance classifier is the

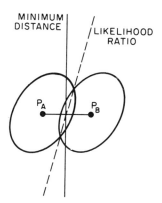

Figure 8.4. Decision boundaries for classifications based on the likelihood ratio and the distance to the two prototypes.

perpendicular bisector of the line segment joining the two prototypes (Nilsson, 1965, p. 20). Points right of the line are closer to prototype B and points left of the line are closer to prototype A. Decisions based upon the likelihood ratio depend upon the covariance matrix which is represented by the two ellipses in Figure 8.4. Points left of the likelihood ratio decision boundary are more likely to be from Category A and points right of the decision boundary represent patterns which are more likely to be from Category B. The relations that exist among different classes of discriminant functions are discussed in more detail by Minsky and Papert (1969, Chap. 12).

Our final example of how a discriminant function might be used in psychology is the trainable pattern classifier suggested by Dodwell (1970, pp. 213–216). Basically, the trainable classifier uses feedback to adjust the discriminant weights and position of the decision boundary. When a pattern is wrongly classified, the decision boundary is moved so as to try to classify it correctly. The adjustments are made step-by-step in such a way as to reduce errors gradually. The mathematical details presented by Dodwell are based on Nilsson's description, but the process assumptions are unclear as to how the decision boundary is represented by the organism. It is unlikely that anyone would propose that the organism calculates a value from the discriminant function equation by multiplying the value of each feature by a weight and summing the total. The geometric interpretation of the discriminant function might, in certain cases, be a reasonable process assumption if Ss knew what patterns were on the decision boundary. This strategy may have been used in Lee's (1963) experiment in which the stimuli were different locations of a dot on a card. If Ss could visualize a line dividing the card into two regions corresponding to the two categories, classification would be relatively easy. Most pattern spaces, however, are more difficult to picture geometrically.

In considering alternatives to the likelihood formulation of the discriminant function, we have strayed somewhat from the topic of this chapter—probability models. We return to this topic in the next section by considering a probability model which has the advantage of making a rather simple process assumption about information integration.

Summation of Cue Validities

A very simple type of process model would be to assume that Ss learn the cue validities or conditional probabilities of the features of a pattern and use the sum of the validities to make their decision. This is the type of recognition procedure used by the Pandemonium system (Selfridge & Neisser, 1960) which was developed to identify 10 handprinted characters (page 73). The recognition procedure consists of (1) input, (2) clean-up, (3) feature inspection, (4) comparison with a learned feature distribution, (5) computation of probabilities, and (6) decision. Recognition is based on the outcome of 28 feature tests such as the relative length of different edges, maximum intersections with a horizontal line, and number of horizontal and vertical strokes. During the learning phase, samples of the 10 letters are presented to the machine and tested for the presence of various features. The results of the feature tests are compiled in a table showing how many times each feature outcome occurred for each of the letters. During the recognition phase, features of an unknown letter are identified and used in determining the conditional probabilities of the different letters, given the results of the feature tests. For example, if the unknown letter had one horizontal stroke, the probability of an **A,** in view of one horizontal stroke, would be determined, as would the conditional probabilities for the other nine letters. The conditional probabilities of the letters are determined for each of the 28 feature tests and the 28 probabilities are summed giving a total score for each letter. The final decision is made by choosing the letter with the highest total.

A model very similar to the Pandemonium has been proposed by Beach (1964a,b) to account for how people make inferences from probabilistically valid cues. According to the model, a pattern which is very similar to a previously presented pattern is classified into the category containing the similar pattern. This type of a decision rule is based upon a "distance" formulation, the topic of the next chapter. If a pattern is not very similar to any of the category patterns, Ss must use the probabilistic cues of a pattern to infer the most likely category. Let $X = (x_1, x_2, \ldots, x_d)$ be a pattern in which x_m stands for a particular value of the mth cue. Then the validity of a particular cue value (x_m) with respect to Category k will be $P(\text{Category } k | x_m)$, that is the probability of Category k given the cue value, x_m. According to Beach's model, we calculate the average cue validity for each category and assign the pattern to the category with the highest average cue validity. The expected value is given by

$$E(k) = \sum_{m=1}^{d} \frac{p(k \mid x_m)}{d} \tag{3}$$

The pattern is assigned to the category having the highest expected value.

One of the attractive aspects of the integration rule expressed in Eq. (3) is that it appears to be a reasonable process model. The additive combination rule is much simpler than a normative decision rule such as a likelihood ratio formed from two multivariate distributions. A general theory of information integration developed by N. H. Anderson (1971) suggests that Ss often do combine information in an additive manner to form a response. The theory assumes that the total effect of two or more informational stimuli is the weighted sum of their scale values. A S's response can often be predicted from the equation $R = \Sigma w_i s_i$ where each piece of information is represented by two parameters: a scale value s along some dimension of judgment and a weight w representing the psychological importance of that dimension. Anderson has successfully applied the additive integration rule to personality impressions, decision making, psychophysical judgment, illusions, learning, and attitude change.

The relevance of Anderson's model to the classification problem is that the scale values would represent the cue validities and the weights could represent the saliency of the different cues or features. A dramatic illustration of how feature saliency can interact with cue validity is contained in a 1954 Ph.D. thesis by R. E. Goodnow (discussed in Bruner, Goodnow, & Austin, 1956, pp. 182–230). Subjects in Goodnow's experiment were required to classify schematic faces into two categories. The cue validity of the features was determined by giving Ss feedback after each classification. Under these conditions, Goodnow found large differences in cue preference. Height of the forehead was eventually treated as a virtually certain cue regardless of whether its validity was 100 : 0 or 67 : 33. Length of the nose, however, even when it had a 100 : 0 value, was used for making the objectively proper inference only 80% of the time. Since feature saliency can be an important factor in influencing Ss' judgments, it may be necessary to weight the various features differentially whenever they differ considerably in saliency.

We have discussed several different approaches to the classification problem in this chapter, and the reader may be interested in relating these models to more general theories of judgment. An excellent summary of alternative approaches to the study of information processing in judgment was recently prepared by Slovic and Lichtenstein (1971). The models presented in this chapter are related to the alternative approaches described in their paper. The likelihood ratio formulation corresponds to the Bayesian approach, the discriminant function corresponds to the correlational paradigm, and the cue validity summation model corresponds to integration theory. A particularly interesting aspect of the Slovic and Lichtenstein paper is their comparative analysis of these different models.

One point should be emphasized about these models and the structural models in Chapter III. I have tried to distinguish between feature models which represent patterns in terms of a feature vector and a more complex grammar of the form $G(P, A, R, C, T)$ specifying the primitives (P), attributes (A), relations (R), composition rules (C), and transformations (T). A feature vector specifies only the primitives and their values (attributes). It therefore lacks some descriptive power, but has the advantage of predictive power because many mathmatical models use a feature vector representation. The probability models considered in this chapter are examples.

Recently, a number of investigators working in the field of artificial intelligence have begun to investigate ways of combining the statistical and grammatical approaches. Kanal and Chandrasekaran (1972) have argued that real-world patterns do not usually correspond exactly to a structural model. Statistical decisions are therefore required not only to identify the primitives of a pattern, but to decide how the primitives are put together in order to classify a pattern. Their conclusion was that a hybrid model utilizing both grammatical and statistical techniques is more relevant for practical problems than the pure grammatical and statistical models.

An example discussed by Fu (1972) is particularly interesting because it illustrates how the two types of approaches can be combined. The problem is to decide whether a distorted version of a triangle is an equilateral triangle or a right triangle. The primitives are straight lines of different orientations which are combined according to different production rules. The production rules are probabilistic, since one primitive may be joined to any one of several primitives depending on the probability of each production. The stochastic grammar consists of a separate set of production rules with their associated probabilities for both an equilateral triangle and a right triangle. The classification of a distorted triangle as either a right triangle or an equilateral triangle requires (1) identifying the production rules which generated the distorted triangle, (2) finding the probability associated with each production rule for both the equilateral and right triangles, and (3) using these probabilities to form a likelihood ratio as a basis for classification.

The advantage of a stochastic grammar is that it may be possible to apply probability models to structured patterns that are difficult to represent as a feature vector. Although this is an exciting possibility, there is one problem with the preceding example, which may be a fundamental problem for the general application of stochastic grammars to visual patterns. Fu (1972) considered lines differing from a vertical line by approximately $0°$, $15°$, $30°$, and $45°$ to be separate primitives. Every time a line is joined to one of these lines would therefore require a separate production rule with an associated probability. As a result, the number of production rules can multiply rapidly, even for the generation of a simple pattern such as a triangle. An alternative approach would be to use some type of distance metric since it may be possible to treat orientation as a continuous dimension with differences in orientation related to distance along that dimension. I will try to make this clearer in the next chapter which shows how distance models can form the basis for a classification theory.

Summary

Many theorists have used probability models to account for how patterns are assigned to categories and hence recognized. Predictions derived from stimulus sampling theory state the probability that Ss will classify a pattern into a given category. The probability of selecting a category or response is a weighted average of the reinforcement probabilities for the constituent elements of a stimulus compound. The mixed model of stimulus sampling theory states that stimuli are learned as entire patterns but transfer to unlearned or novel patterns is determined by pattern components. In one version of the mixed model, transfer was successfully predicted from the probability of a subject selecting a particular component as the basis for responding. In contrast to stimulus sampling theory, statistical decision theory is based on a deterministic decision rule: Namely, Ss should always choose the most probable category. In a comparison of the two theories, results from several studies gave slightly greater support to a deterministic response rule and this rule has been used in most classification models.

The linear discriminant function can be used to obtain useful information such as whether Ss' classifications can be predicted from a linear combination of feature values, which features are emphasized in making a decision, and how consistent Ss are in making classifications. However, the linear discriminant function is too general to serve as a process model, since a variety of different strategies will result in linearly separable classifications. Three examples are (1) the use of a likelihood ratio in which the probabilities are calculated from multivariate normal distributions with equal covariance matrices, (2) a minimum distance classifier in which the test pattern is classified into the category with the closest prototype, and (3) an adaptive learning model in which the weights are adjusted after a misclassification.

A probability model with a simple integration rule is the additive model in which the cue validities or conditional probabilities of a pattern are summed for each category. This model has the advantage that an additive model of information integration has been shown successful in predicting Ss' responses across a variety of tasks. In addition, the features of a pattern can be differentially weighted if they differ greatly in saliency. The use of stochastic grammars as a pattern recognition model combines probability and structural models by assigning probabilities to production rules rather than to pattern components.

IX | Distance Models

A second general class of models are distance models. We will begin by considering the general properties of distance models and then will use them to formulate a prototype and several alternative decision rules. An important problem is to define the circumstances under which we can expect to maximize differences in the predictions of distance models and probability models. Imagine a category of 10 faces consisting of 8 faces with a short nose, 1 face with a medium nose, and 1 face with a long nose. The issue is whether people would more likely consider a face with a medium nose as a member of this category than a face with a long nose. According to a probability model, no distinction is made between the two faces since the probability of a medium nose equals the probability of a long nose. According to a distance model, however, a face with a medium nose would more likely belong to that category than a face with a long nose, since the average distance between that feature and the other patterns is less in the former case. In other words, the concept of stimulus generalization is incorporated into a distance model by representing the features on an interval scale rather than a nominal scale (Stevens, 1951).

A statement of how distance measures may be incorporated into a theory of pattern recognition was offered by Sebestyen (1962). Sebestyen proposed that the similarity of a pattern X to a category should be measured by the closeness of X to every one of the patterns known to be contained in the category. Let us denote the patterns in Category 1 by X_{1i}, $i = 1$, $N1$, and the patterns in category two by X_{2i}, $i = 1$, $N2$. The S's task is to classify new patterns, X_j. Similarity is taken to be the mean-square distance between X_j and the categories $\{X_1\}$ and $\{X_2\}$. "Distance" does not necessarily imply Euclidean distance but may mean closeness in some other metric. However, in order to be a metric, distance (d) must satisfy the usual conditions of distance measures:

$$d_{ij} = d_{ji}, \qquad d_{ij} \leqslant d_{ik} + d_{kj};$$
$$d_{ij} \geqslant 0, \qquad d_{ij} = 0 \qquad \text{iff} \quad i = j. \tag{1}$$

The first equation states the distance between two points is symmetrical—the distance between points i and j is the same as the distance between points j and i. The second expression is the triangle inequality and states that the distance between points i and j cannot be greater than the sum of the distances d_{ik} and d_{kj} where k is any third point. The third expression states that distances cannot be negative and the fourth equation states that the distance between two points is zero only when the two points are the same.

Sebestyen defines a similarity measure in which the metric d—the method of measuring distance between two points—is left unspecified.

$$S(X_j, \{X_1\}) = 1/N1 \sum_{i=1}^{N1} d^2(X_j, X_{1i}) \tag{2}$$

Equation (2) states that the similarity between pattern X_j and Category 1 is the average distance between X_j and the members of $\{X_1\}$. A possible classification rule is to compare the average distance of a test pattern to each category and classify the test pattern into the category that results in the least average distance.

In order to apply such a rule, it is necessary to compute the distance between pairs of patterns. A method of converting psychological similarity into distance measures was devised by Shepard (1962) and modified later by Kruskal (1964). Shepard proposed that distance and similarity should be monotonically related in such a way that the greater the similarity of two stimuli the smaller should be the distance between them in some multidimensional space. The exact form of the function relating distance and similarity is not specified "a priori," but is found empirically for each set of stimuli.

The Shepard–Kruskal scaling program was designed to represent N patterns in a multidimensional space based upon $N(N\text{-}1)/2$ initial similarity measurements. The solution is based upon the two constraints of (1) a monotonic function relating distance to similarity and (2) a representation in a space of minimum dimensionality. The basic idea is that the initial similarity measurements, which are only qualitative (based on an ordinal scale) are transformed into quantitative measurements (based on a ratio scale) by taking advantage of all the constraints inherent in the data. A stress factor, based on a goodness-of-fit test of the data to the function relating distances to similarity, is used to measure how adequately the stimuli can be represented in a space of given dimension.

Distances in the Shepard–Kruskal program are represented by the Minkowski r-metric:

$$d_{ij} = \left(\sum_{m=1}^{d} |x_{im} - x_{jm}|^r \right)^{1/r} \tag{3}$$

where d is the distance between stimuli i and j, m is the subscript for an orthogonal axis of the space, and x_{im} is a projection of stimulus i on axis m.

The stress factor can also be used to find that value of r which best fits the data. The two most popular spatial models are the city block model with $r = 1$ and the Euclidean model with $r = 2$ (Torgerson, 1958). The city block model with $r = 1$ seems applicable when the stimuli differ with respect to obvious and compelling dimensions such as brightness and size (Attneave, 1950). In this case, a S's ratings might behave as if they were the sum of the differences on the separate dimensions. The Euclidean metric, on the other hand, is more applicable when the separate dimensions are not obvious and the subject is more likely to judge the overall distance directly. Garner (1970) has shown that the integrality of stimulus dimensions is an important determinant of performance. The essence of integrality is whether the stimulus dimensions can be redefined into an effectively new dimension. Integral stimulus dimensions give rise to the Euclidean metric, facilitate the speed of classification when the dimensions are correlated, and interfere with classification on a single dimension when the dimensions are uncorrelated.

Classification and Attention

When Ss are able to analyze a pattern into its component dimensions, predicting how they will classify a pattern or even rate its similarity to another pattern becomes more difficult. Shepard (1964) in his article on attention and the metric structure of the stimulus, distinguished between "analyzable" and "unanalyzable" stimuli. Unanalyzable stimuli are viewed as unitary, homogeneous wholes as when S reports two different shades of red. Analyzable stimuli are usually described in terms of their perceptually distinct components or properties. The stimuli used in Shepard's experiment were of this type since Ss immediately noticed that the figures differed in both size and inclination. The purpose of the experiment was to determine how these dimensions combined to determine overall similarity, where similarity was defined in terms of direct subjective judgments and confusion errors during identification learning. The results indicated that, when the stimuli vary along perceptually distinct dimensions, the psychological metric changes as Ss shift their attention to one dimension or the other. However, for any one state of attention, the similarity judgments could be represented by a Minkowski metric somewhere between the Euclidean and city block varieties.

Support for the distinction between "analyzable" and "unanalyzable" stimuli also comes from Shepard's earlier studies on the relation between identification learning and classification learning. Shepard, Hovland, and Jenkins (1961) investigated the difficulty of learning various ways to assign stimuli to one of two classes. Sets of eight stimuli were always used in which each stimulus had one of two possible values on each of three different dimensions. In one set, each stimulus was large or small, black or white, and triangular or circular. In order to test for the effect of stimulus generalization on learning the class assignments, Shepard used the number of confusion errors made between pairs of stimuli during identification learning in which Ss had to learn a different response to each stimulus. According to the principle of stimulus generalization, the difficulty of learning a particular classification should be determined by the degree to which similar (confusable) stimuli are assigned to the same category. The predictions were inaccurate, however, because they did not take into account the fact that Ss could abstract the relevant from the irrelevant dimensions of the stimuli. The Ss used the relevant dimensions to form conceptual rules, and their performance was related to the simplicity of the rules used to describe the classifications.

In order to retest the stimulus generalization hypothesis using unanalyzable stimuli, Shepard and Chang (1963) used Munsell colors of the same red hue differing in brightness and saturation. Problems consisted of six different classifications of the eight stimuli into two equal subsets. The task was to learn which four colors belonged to each subset. Unlike the previous study, predictions based on confusion errors in identification learning were successful in predicting the difficulty in learning the various classifications. The results therefore supported the hypothesis that when stimuli are not analyzed into components, errors during classification learning should be largely accounted for by pairwise confusions in an identification task.

The results of the two studies by Shepard suggest that the analyzability of the stimulus dimensions is an important variable, but this should not be interpreted as implying that obvious dimensions necessarily prevent us from predicting the difficulty of learning various classifications from pattern similarities. Indeed, there were other characteristics of the 1961 stimuli which might have contributed to the failure of the predictions. First, there were only two values on a dimension in contrast to the colors which had a number of brightness and saturation values. Tighe and Tighe (1968) found that pretraining with four values per dimension led to faster reversal learning, but that pretraining with two values per dimension had no effect. They suggested that when only two values specified a dimension, the stimuli were most likely responded to in terms of their absolute properties rather than as continuous variations along a dimension. The stimulus generalization hypothesis might lead to successful predictions for analyzable stimuli if the stimuli had more than two values per dimension and simple conceptual rules could not be used in classifying the stimuli.

An experiment meeting these conditions was conducted by Brown and Dansereau (1970). The experiment represented an initial attempt to compare Ss' similarity judgments of Markov histoform patterns with their judgments as to whether two stimuli belonged to the same or different categories. The results suggested that somewhat different features were used in making classification responses and similarity judgments, again indicating the difficulty of relating the two types of judgments for analyzable stimuli.

Saliency and Validity

We have seen that when patterns are composed of a number of obvious dimensions or features, Ss may shift their attention from one feature to another, making it difficult to obtain consistent similarity or classification judgments. What determines which features are emphasized, and are the same features emphasized in similarity and classification judgments? One hypothesis is that Ss may be influenced primarily by feature saliency in making similarity judgments and feature validity in making categorization judgments. According to this interpretation, highly salient features would dominate similarity judgments but would not be emphasized in a categorization task if they did not provide useful information which would enable Ss to discriminate among the various categories. The example shown in Figure 9.1 can serve as an illustration. Patterns in Figure 9.1 differ on two dimensions. Let us assume that Dimension 2 is the more salient so that the judged similarity of two patterns is primarily determined by how much they differ along the second dimension. However, Dimension 2 is not very informative as in which category a pattern should be classified, so that Ss would have to shift their emphasis to Dimension 1 when making classification judgments. An ideal solution to the problem of feature emphasis would be (1) to calculate how saliency influences the differential weighting of features, (2) to investigate how these weights become modified by feature validity, and (3) to compare the derived validity weights for each subject with a set of normative weights.

A recent scaling program developed by Carroll and Chang (1970b) was designed to solve the first problem—how saliency influences the differential weighting of features. It is assumed that the relative saliency of the features may differ for each individual, so the different saliencies are represented for each subject by a set of perceptual weights. The model consists basically of a group stimulus space based on the similarity ratings of all Ss and a set of individual subject stimulus spaces derived from the group space by weighting each dimension by the perceptual weights of a particular subject. Mathematically, each subject space is a linear transformation of the group space. What this means is that the stimulus values on a dimension emphasized by S are multiplied by a high

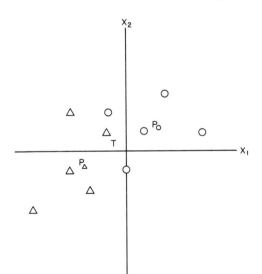

Figure 9.1. Two categories of patterns represented in a two-dimensional space. (△) Category 1 patterns; (○) Category 2 patterns; (P△) Category 1 Prototype; (P○) Category 2 prototype; T: test pattern.

weight and stimulus values on a dimension receiving little emphasis are multiplied by a low weight. To make the discussion less abstract, Figures 9.2 and 9.3 show a concrete example (Carroll Chang, 1970a). Figure 9.2 shows the group stimulus space in which colors differ on two dimensions. The stimulus space of a color deficient S can be represented as a transformation of the group space, with a low weight being given to the red/green dimension, indicating that this dimension had little influence on his similarity judgments (Figure 9.3). Since the transformation can only stretch or shrink the values along a dimension and not in-

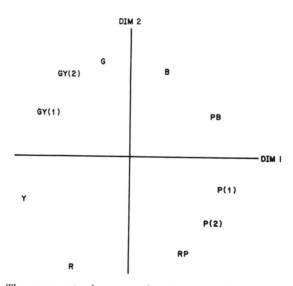

Figure 9.2.   The group stimulus space showing a two-dimensional representation for colors. [From Carroll and Chang (1970a).]

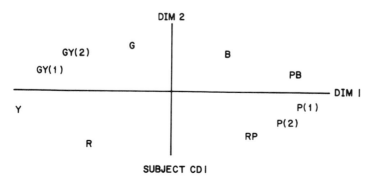

Figure 9.3.   A linear transformation of the group stimulus space showing the perceptual space for one subject. [From Carroll and Chang (1970a).]

terchange the position of stimuli, the derived space may not correspond exactly to the actual space for that individual, but the degree of correspondence can be measured and has generally been found quite adequate.

An important property of a dimension in a classification experiment is the validity of the dimension. The basic idea is that some features are more relevant than others in distinguishing between categories, so Ss should weight or emphasize these features more in making their decisions. Dimension 1 should receive greater emphasis for the categories shown in Figure 9.1 since the two categories are primarily separated along this dimension. But how much should each dimension be weighted? One approach is to find a set of weights which not only clusters patterns belonging to the same class but separates patterns belonging to different classes. The problem, mathematically, is to find the linear transformation that maximizes between set (class) distances while holding constant the sum of mean-square between-set and within-set distances (Sebestyen, 1962, pp. 37–43). Equation (4) shows that the distance between two patterns depends both upon how much the patterns differ on each dimension and the importance of the dimension.

$$d_{ij} = \left(\sum_{m=1}^{d} w_m{}^r |x_{im} - x_{jm}|^r \right)^{1/r} \tag{4}$$

where d_{ij} is the distance between stimuli i and j, m is the subscript for each orthogonal axis of the space, x_{im} is a projection of stimulus i on axis m ($m = 1, \ldots, d$ for d dimensions), and w_m is the weight for the mth dimension.

In the next section we compare this model with several alternative models to determine which can best predict how Ss classify patterns.

Categorization Models

Our concern in this section is with the type of strategies Ss use to classify patterns into categories. We will reexamine the issue of whether distance models can be used to predict how Ss classify patterns and we will compare distance models with probability models to see which model makes the best predictions. A more detailed description of the models and experiments is given elsewhere (Reed, 1972). The purpose of the study was to try to answer the question: "Given two classes of patterns defined by sets of exemplars, what kind of decision processes do Ss use to classify new patterns?" Subjects were always given two categories consisting of five schematic faces which differed in forehead height, eye separation, nose length, and mouth height. Each feature could take on one of three values (Figure 7.2, page 145). Exemplar faces were randomly assigned to a category under the constraint that the two categories could be separated by a linear discriminant function. The selection procedure usually meant that the categories occupied two regions in a multidimensional space, but there was no simple conceptual rule which distinguished between the patterns belonging to each category. An example of two categories is shown in Figure 9.4.

Two procedures were used to present the exemplar patterns. In one condition, Ss were simply shown the two categories on a sheet of paper as is illustrated in Figure 9.4. The Ss in this condition had access to the exemplar patterns throughout the experiment and could simply look at the category patterns before deciding how to classify a test pattern. In the second condition, Ss were shown the patterns sequentially in a paired-associates task and they had to learn which five patterns belonged to each category. In both conditions, the main part of the experiment required Ss to classify a series of test patterns into one of the two categories. One possible way to classify a test pattern is to use feature probabilities. A *cue validity* model similar to the one proposed by Beach (page 168) was used to test this hypothesis. Four versions of the cue validity model were tested in which the decision was determined by either the single most valid cue, the two most valid cues, the three most valid cues, or all four cues (features).

In addition to the cue validity model, a number of different distance models were tested. Figure 9.1 shows a two-dimensional spatial repre-

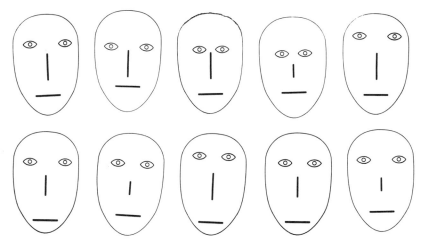

Figure 9.4. Two perceptual categories. The upper five faces are exemplars from one category and the lower five faces are exemplars from another category. [From Reed (1972).]

sentation of a categorization problem. The problem is to decide to which category the test pattern should be assigned. In order to test for a number of possible strategies, several classification models were formulated. The first is the *proximity algorithm,* based on the subset of patterns that are closest to the test pattern. The test pattern is classified into the category which has the largest number of patterns in this subset. The size of the subset can itself be a variable, but the simplest case occurs when S bases his decision upon the single category pattern which is most similar to the test pattern. The second classification model is an *average distance* model in which all the category patterns are used to make a decision. The average distance is found between the test pattern and the patterns in each category. The test pattern is then placed in the category which results in the smallest average distance. A third decision rule is a *prototype* model in which a prototype is constructed for each category to represent its central tendency and the test pattern is classified into the category with the nearest prototype. The final two models are variations of the average distance and prototype models in which the features are differentially weighted according to their validity in discriminating between the two categories. The weights are calculated by using the class-separating transformation discussed at the end of the previous section.

Four experiments were conducted in order to determine which model would best predict Ss' classifications. The results indicated that the weighted feature average distance and prototype models were the most successful models in three of the four problems. Both models made near optimal predictions when they were based on psychologically scaled distances. Additional converging operations suggested that the formation of a prototype was the predominant strategy used. It was always found that a significantly higher percentage of Ss correctly classified the prototype pattern than an equidistant control pattern (see the discussion of schema theory in Chapter II). In addition, many more Ss reported using a prototype rule than an average distance rule, particularly when they had to learn the patterns belonging to each category. Table 9.1 shows the percentage of Ss who reported using the different strategies to classify new patterns after they had learned the category patterns.

Perhaps the most important characteristic distinguishing the various strategies is the information processing demands placed upon the Ss. In the learning task, Ss had to remember information about the category patterns in order to classify new patterns. In order to use the average distance rule or the proximity rule, Ss would have to remember the five faces belonging to each category—a difficult task, as evidenced by the few Ss who reported using these strategies. The strategy placing the least memory demands upon Ss is the prototype rule in which Ss only have to

TABLE 9.1

PERCENTAGE OF SUBJECTS WHO REPORTED USING DIFFERENT CLASSIFICATION
STRATEGIES AFTER LEARNING THE CATEGORY PATTERNS[a]

Strategy	Percentage
(1) *Prototype* I formed an abstract image of what a face in category one should look like and an abstract image of what a face in category two should look like. I then compared the projected face with the two abstract images and chose the category which gave the closest match.	58%
(2) *Proximity Algorithm* I compared the projected face with all the faces in the two categories looking for a single face which best matched the projected face. I then chose the category in which that face appeared.	10%
(3) *Cue Validity* I looked at each feature on the projected face and compared how many times it exactly matched a feature in each of the two categories. I then chose the category which gave the highest number of matches.	28%
(4) *Average Distance* I compared the projected face with each of the five faces in category one and with each of the five faces in category two. I then chose the category in which the faces were more like the projected face, basing my decision on all faces in the two categories.	4%

[a] From Reed (1972).

store the two prototypes. The finding that the weighted feature models led to better predictions suggests that Ss were emphasizing the more relevant dimensions. There was some indication, however, that Ss did not differently emphasize the relevant dimensions to the extent predicted by the normative weights (Reed, 1972). This is not surprising in view of the conservatism often found in decision tasks (Edwards, 1968).

Although we have examined many theoretical approaches to the problem of pattern recognition, we have said little about applications. An example illustrating the application of a distance model is the problem of identifying a face by using the assistance of a computer (Goldstein, Harmon, & Lesk, 1972). A panel of 10 observers independently evaluated 21 features for each of 255 different human faces. The photographs were all white males, with no eyeglasses, scars, or deformities. The average value of the observers' ratings were given to the computer as the "official" description of each face. The problem given to the investigators was to develop an efficient decision-making technique which would enable the computer to match a S's description of a photograph with the description of the correct face stored in the computer's memory. Although this is a matching task rather than a classification task, it is analogous to the prototype classification rule since 10 different descriptions of each face were reduced to a single description (prototype) by using the average values of each feature.

The subject is given a photograph of one member of the population and he describes the face by choosing one feature at a time and rating the value of that feature. Either the subject or the computer can select the order in which the features are described, but they use different criteria in trying to find the most discriminable features. The subject has a photograph of a particular face, but does not know what other faces are in the population. He therefore chooses extreme features whose value is near an extreme of that feature's range—long hair or a short nose. The computer knows which faces are in the population, but does not know the particular face shown to the subject. It therefore chooses discriminable features on the basis of the population characteristics. The most discriminable features are those features having values uniformly distributed over the population, since a feature would not be very useful if all the faces had the same value for that feature. The differential emphasis of the different features is somewhat similar to the weighted feature models, but is more clearly related to the probability models since the distribution of values is the determining factor.

Figure 9.5 illustrates an interactive display between man and computer. The subject chooses the first four features on the basis of their extreme values. He then lets the computer choose the next six features and he also rates the value of these features. After every feature description, the computer ranks each member of the population according to a similarity measure. The similarity measure represents the similarity of the S's description to the official description of each member of the population and is calculated from the city block distance metric. The summary in the lower right corner of Figure 9.5 shows the order in which the features were selected, the rating assigned by the subject, the average official rating, and the rank of the correct face (No. 76) according to the similarity measure. The correct face was ranked first after four features, although the relative similarity measure (listed beneath each feature test in Figure 9.5) continued to decline for the other faces as more features were added.

Fifteen Ss participated in an experiment designed to test the feature selection aspects of the program. In one mode the subject selected every feature; in a second mode the computer selected every feature, and in a third mode the subject selected every feature until he decided there were no more outstanding ones and then used computer selection. The computer selection procedure resulted in the worst performance suggesting that knowledge of the population statistics is not as effective as

```
FEATURE
      EYEBROW WT.
THIN        MEDIUM        BUSHY
   1     2     3     4     5
=1
    93   244   183   223   159
  1.00  1.00  1.00  1.00  0.82

FEATURE
      EAR LENGTH
SHORT       MEDIUM        LONG
   1     2     3     4     5
=1
    72   244   175    93    43
  1.00  1.00  0.82  0.67  0.66

FEATURE
      LIP OVERLAP
UPPER       NEITHER       LOWER
   1           2           3
=1
    72   226   114   122    76
  1.00  0.73  0.66  0.61  0.60

FEATURE
      HAIR TEXTURE
STRAIGHT   WAVY          CURLY
   1     2     3     4     5
=4
    76   122    32   244    52
  1.00  0.74  0.56  0.55  0.50


FEATURE

          AUTOMATIC FEATURE SELECTION
******EYE SHADE
LIGHT       MEDIUM        DARK
   1     2     3     4     5
=3
    76    52    72   221   191
  1.00  0.56  0.45  0.38  0.36


******EYEBROW SEP.
SEPARATE    MEDIUM        MEETING
   1           2           3
=2
    76   147    52    84    72
  1.00  0.50  0.42  0.37  0.34
```

```
******EYE OPENING
NARROW      MEDIUM        WIDE
   1     2     3     4     5
=2
    76    72   226    26   191
  1.00  0.51  0.40  0.38  0.36


******UPPER LIP
THIN        MEDIUM        THICK
   1     2     3     4     5
=3
    76   191    72   221    52
  1.00  0.33  0.28  0.23  0.21


******HAIR SHADE
DARK   MED.  LT.    GRAY  WHT.
   1     2     3     4     5
=2
    76   221    72   226   191
  1.00  0.34  0.34  0.33  0.25


******LOWER LIP
THIN        MEDIUM        THICK
   1     2     3     4     5
=1
    76    72   221    84   191
  1.00  0.19  0.13  0.12  0.11

PLEASE TYPE TARGET NUMBER.
=76
```

ORDER	FEATURE	DESCRIPTION YOU	AVG.	RANK NO.	%
1	EYEBROW WT.	1	2.2	27	10.2
2	EAR LENGTH	1	2.3	8	2.7
3	LIP OVERLAP	1	1.2	5	1.6
4	HAIR TEXTURE	4	3.0	1	0.
5	EYE SHADE	3	2.7	1	0.
6	EYEBROW SEP.	2	1.3	1	0.
7	EYE OPENING	2	2.6	1	0.
8	UPPER LIP	3	2.9	1	0.
9	HAIR SHADE	2	1.5	1	0.
10	LOWER LIP	1	2.3	1	0.

Figure 9.5. Printout of an interactive dialogue between man and computer. [After Goldstein, Harmon, and Lesk (1972).]

knowledge of a target's outstanding features. Both subject selection mode and the mixed mode resulted in approximately equal performance, although Ss were more confident when using the mixed mode. In the mixed mode, the population was reduced to less than 4% over 99% of the time, and the target was correctly identified 70% of the time.

Additivity

The use of feature weights suggests a solution to one of the problems proposed by Shepard—that Ss abstract out the more relevant features when making classifications. By using weighted feature distance models, it is possible to weight each dimension to the extent that it is relevant to the classification problem. A second issue suggested by Shepard, Hovland, and Jenkins's results is also a problem for distance models. The success of distance models is limited by the extent to which Ss use conceptual rules based on the relationships and interactions between dimensions. An implicit assumption of all the models discussed in the previous section is that the features are independent and can be combined in an additive fashion. The principle of interdimensional additivity has been axiomatized for distance models by Beals, Krantz, and Tversky (1968). The hypothesis states that the perceived distance along each dimension contributes additively to overall dissimilarity [as expressed in Eq. (3)].

Tversky and Krantz (1969) used schematic faces to test for interdimensional additivity of three features. The overall shape was an ellipse which was either wide or long. The eyes were two circles which were either empty or filled. The mouth was a single line which was either straight or smiling. Subjects' dissimilarity judgments were used to test the hypothesis that the overall dissimilarity between faces can be decomposed into three additive components. The hypothesis was supported suggesting that the contribution of each dimension was independent of the values of the other dimensions. Tversky and Krantz concluded that for properly chosen dimensions an overall impression can be determined from a simple rule of combination of independent subimpressions.

A distinction must be made between similarity judgments between pairs of patterns and classification judgments when discussing the interaction of features. The nature of the classification problem may draw Ss' attention to a particular interaction that would ordinarily be unnoticed in judging pairs of patterns. For example, in one classification problem (Reed, 1972), it was noticed that the distance between the nose and the eyes was a perfectly valid cue for distinguishing between the two categories. This cue depended upon the interaction of two features: the length of the nose and the height of the eyes. Despite the limitation which additivity places upon distance models, the models did very well in predicting how Ss would classify fairly complex patterns. There are other types of patterns, however, which would be extremely difficult to represent in terms of a list of independent features and this places a limitation on the generality of the classification models considered in this and the previous chapter.

The advtantage of probability models and distance models is that they can be readily used as classification procedures to achieve the recognition of "noisy" patterns which do not exactly match past instances. Their disadvantage is that they are typically based upon an independent feature list, and hence fail to capture the structure of patterns. Structural models solve this last problem, but have the disadvantage that a structural description is usually written for a single pattern and not a class of patterns. Macleod (1971) has pointed out that the usefulness of class structural descriptions depends upon their ability to describe structure which is generally, but not necessarily always, present in class members. Objects may be treated as a member of a class if only minor corrections or additions are necessary to change a description of an object into a class structural description. Interpretation in terms of class structural descriptions should be capable of dealing with similarities rather than identities.

The ability to deal with similarities rather than identities is an asset that makes people very good at recognizing patterns. It seems that the type of model we should be looking for is a model which can combine a structural grammar with a distance metric. The grammar would be used to give a structural description to an ideal, most representative member of the class and the metric could be used to measure the similarity of a test pattern to the class prototypes. The metric could allow for differential weights to be assigned to different features or structural aspects which are of particular importance. When the patterns could be represented by an independent feature list, such a model would be equivalent to the weighted features prototype model discussed in the previous section. When important structural relationships exist among the features, a much more complicated metric would be required, for our current ideas about metrics are founded upon an orthogonal set of axes.

Our current ideas about how to construct such a metric are therefore quite limited. Townsend (1971a), in commenting upon the failure of alphabetic letters to yield a psychologically intuitive set of dimensions after multidimensional scaling recommended that it might be better to try to build up a psychophysics of simple visual elements from which to construct more complex patterns. Winston (1970), in representing scenes in terms of networks, claimed that for two scenes to be identical, the nodes of the networks must relate with each other in the same ways. However, given the failure to achieve a perfect match, there should be some way of ordering possible identifications so that one can be chosen as the best. Winston suggested that each kind of difference could be weighted according to its importance and the numbers combined to form a score for each comparison. He admitted, however, that the particular set of weights selected was chosen somewhat arbitrarily and that the weighting system needed further refinement. Our knowledge about metrics that can incorporate the structural aspects of a pattern is quite limited, and I view this as an important, but unresolved problem.

Summary

As an alternative to probability models, the models discussed in this chapter represent patterns as points in a multidimensional space making it possible to determine the distance between two patterns. If the patterns are composed of obvious features or dimensions, the judged similarity of two patterns will be determined by how much the patterns differ on each dimension and how much each dimension is emphasized. A scaling program developed by Carroll and Chang makes it possible to derive a set of perceptual weights for individuals indicating how much each dimension influenced a given person's similarity judgments. However, the features emphasized in judging the similarity of pairs of patterns may not be the same as the features utilized in classifying patterns into categories. In a classification task, the most important characteristic of a feature is how relevant it is in discriminating among the various categories. It is possible to calculate an ideal set of weights which would maximally separate the categories and in so doing represent the relevance of each dimension.

Several varieties of distance models were formulated in an attempt to predict how Ss would categorize patterns. Alternative models included classifying patterns on the basis of (1) the category pattern closest to the test pattern, (2) the average distance between the category patterns and the test pattern, and (3) the distance between category prototypes and the test pattern. Distance models were more successful than probability models in predicting Ss' classifications and the prototype model, in particular, was supported by the data. Weighted-feature models improved predictions suggesting that Ss were placing greater emphasis on the more relevant features. Distance models have also been used in a man–computer interactive system to compare the similarity of a S's description to descriptions stored in the computer. The S describes the features one at a time and has the option of choosing the most discriminable features himself or leaving the choice to the computer. Despite the success of the distance models, their usefulness is currently directly limited by the extent to which patterns can be represented in terms of independent features.

Part 5 | RESPONSE SELECTION

X | Set and Bias

Previous chapters have emphasized the role of the stimulus pattern in determining the response. We now turn to a discussion of factors other than the information contained in the stimulus that influence the response of the observer.

Additional information supplied by the experimenter or by the environment may greatly influence the S's decision. The effect of context on recognizing the letters of a word is well known to everyone who has tried to read nearly illegible handwriting. In addition, the frequency of a word can greatly determine whether it is correctly reported after a brief exposure—whether frequency is measured by how many times the word occurs in the environment or how many times it occurs during an experiment. The issue is basically how the observer selects a response criterion. At the beginning of Chapter VIII, we reviewed Bruner's (1957) requirements of a classification theory which included specifying the (1) features, (2) weights, (3) integration rule, and (4) response criterion. We considered the first three aspects of a theory in the previous two chapters and will consider the fourth aspect in this chapter.

The first section discusses the effect of set on performance. A *set* is usually some additional information about a stimulus such as the specification of a limited number of alternatives, the context of the stimulus, or the probability of presenting different stimuli. Giving the observer some additional information about a stimulus (such as that it will be one of four alternatives) usually results in improved performance, although it is not always obvious whether the set resulted in clearer perception or only made the correct response more likely. In order for set to influence perception, it must be given before the stimulus. Giving the set after the stimulus could only influence the response. We contrast the two techniques. In the second section we consider the argument that perception is improved when the observer is able to select a better coding strategy, as a result of the additional information supplied by the experimenter. A more efficient coding strategy can either increase the rate at which information in the perceptual array is transferred into verbal or visual memory or it can increase the probability of transferring the more important information. The final section considers how a set can result in a response bias. Observers are more accurate in "recognizing" common words than uncommon words and this is the result of their usually choosing a more common word when the perceptual evidence is consistent with several possibilities.

Effects of Set

Haber (1966), in a review of the effect of set on perception, examined two basic hypotheses that have been used to interpret set effects. The older interpretation and the one favored by the New Look theorists refers to a perceptual enhancement or "tuning" hypothesis in which selective attention results in a clearer perception of the stimulus or some attribute of the stimulus. The alternative hypothesis is that set does not operate on the perceptual system itself, but rather on either the responses or some aspects of the memory trace. There have been several formulations of this "response" hypothesis: (*a*) the set facilitates relevant responses by S, increasing the probability that S can identify the stimulus in his report; (*b*) the set causes S to report the emphasized attributes first, before memory of the stimulus fades; (*c*) the set modifies the organization of the memory trace so that the important attributes are remembered more accurately (Haber, 1966).

A common experimental procedure has been to compare the effects of a set given before the perception to the effects of a set given after the perception, but prior to the response. Lawrence and Coles (1954) employed this technique to distinguish between the stimulus or response locus of the set effect. According to their analysis, a perceptual tuning hypothesis has to predict that a set given before the stimulus, as compared to one given afterward, will provide greater facilitation of report. The Ss saw tachistoscopically presented pictures at various exposure intervals and were asked to identify them. The control group had no alternatives presented to it, whereas the two experimental groups each had a set of four alternatives for each stimulus. The experimenters found that alternatives given either before or after the stimulus facilitated recognition to an equal extent and that there was no interaction between the type of alernative and when it was presented in relation to the stimulus exposure. Both these results tended to support the hypothesis that the facilitative effect of alternatives operates on the memory trace or response aspects of the recognition process rather than perception itself.

An experiment by Lawrence and LaBerge (1956) also indicated that the selective effect of instructions operates primarily through memory and response factors. Cards from the Wisconsin Card Sorting Task differing in color, form, and number of objects were presented tachistoscopically to groups of Ss. Under *emphasis instruction*, in which Ss were asked to pay primary attention to one dimension only but report all three, the accuracy of report on the emphasized dimension was considerably greater than on the other two dimensions. Accuracy on the dominant dimension was not increased when Ss were not required to report the other two dimensions. Subjects receiving *ordered instructions* were asked to pay equal attention to and to record all three dimensions, but the order in which they were recorded was specified immediately after the stimulus exposure. Under ordered instructions the difference in accuracy between the first recorded dimension and the average of the other two was as large as the difference reported for emphasis instructions. Lawrence and LaBerge made the following conclusions:

(1) A constant amount of information is transmitted irrespective of instructions.
(2) The distribution of this information between dimensions depends upon the order in which they are reported.
(3) The effect of instructions is to determine which order of report occurs.

Harris and Haber (1963) have challenged Lawrence and LaBerge's suggestion that no assumption need be made about reorganization of memory or changes in response probabilities, but that only all memory for the stimulus is slowly fading. According to this interpretation, whatever is reported first will be more accurate than items reported later.

Harris and Haber used the same stimuli and procedure for inducing sets as Lawrence and LaBerge, but each S was tested under all set conditions, including a forced order of report on half the trials. Under forced order of report, Ss were told to report the attributes in a particular order, but to emphasize one of the attributes. The critical attribute was always reported more accurately than an incidental one, regardless of whether it was reported first, second, or third. The set effect was still obtained when controlling for order of report.

While the findings of Harris and Haber (1963) and Haber (1964) indicated that the set effect could not be accounted for by a fading memory and varying order of report, they did support an alternative explanation —the encoding process by which S translates the percept of a stimulus into memory. Subjects were trained to use one of two coding strategies— an Objects code based on the rules of English syntax (e.g., one red triangle, three blue stars) and a Dimensions code based on separating stimuli into their three dimensions (red, blue; triangle, star; one, three). The findings indicated that the facilitating effects of set were almost entirely accounted for by Ss using the Dimensions code. Those Ss who used the Objects code were not significantly more accurate on the emphasized as compared to the unemphasized dimensions. The results suggested that the set effect was due more to a change in the initial organization of the memory, produced by the strategy by which S encodes the stimulus rather than through the effects of a fading memory or through the changes in the probability of the correct response being available.

Although these studies emphasized the response nature of set, other experiments have shown perceptual effects under certain conditions. Long, Reid, and Henneman (1960) investigated the effect of set on the identification of letter patterns of varying levels of ambiguity. The experimenters used a differential set to limit the number of alternative responses. Set was found to play three roles in aiding the identification of ambiguous stimuli:

(1) Set causes greater perceptual accuracy by increasing the discrimination of potentially relevant elements or dimensions contained in the stimuli. Evidence for this role of set was the finding that under certain conditions a set both before and after the stimulus produced more identification than a set only after. However, this effect appeared only when a small number of alternatives were employed and stimulus patterns containing discriminable elements were used.

(2) Set also aided identification by making the residual elements of the ambiguous stimuli more interpretable. This was accomplished by

supplying otherwise unavailable responses and by eliminating possible competitors.

(3) Set increases the frequency of identification by reducing the number of possible responses. That this was not the only role of set was shown by increased identification after correction for increases in chance expectancy.

Long, Henneman, and Garvey (1960) used distorted spondaic words to determine if set was influenced by varying sense-modality. The words were presented through earphones and set was introduced by presenting groups of four words, one of which corresponded to the distorted stimulus word. Set was again seen as playing the three roles previously mentioned. Presentation both before and after the auditory stimulus produced more identifications than the presentation of restricted alternatives only after. This was true regardless of whether the presentation of alternatives was visual or auditory. However, when the same spondaic words were presented visually, the advantage of alternatives both before and after the stimulus disappeared. Although set significantly increased the number of identifications, presentation of alternatives both before and after the stimulus was not significantly better than presenting them only after.

While the previous two experiments varied set by employing different numbers of alternative responses, a third experiment (Reid, Henneman, & Long, 1960) determined whether set could be effectively increased by greater categorical restriction—giving the Ss more attributes of the category to which an ambiguous stimulus word belongs. Those Ss having the highest degree of set saw five successive descriptive or categorizing words. Thus, "Rams" might be described by sports–football–name–team–pro. The principal findings were that an increase in categorical restriction was accompanied by an increase of correct identification, but that presenting the categorizing terms before stimulation neither significantly improved identification, nor interacted with degree of categorical restriction.

Perhaps the most important determinant of our expectations outside the laboratory is the effect of context. We expect to see different objects if we are in the kitchen than if we are in the bedroom. Biederman (1972) has recently begun a series of studies to systematically explore the effects of context on the perception of real-world scenes. Figure 10.1 shows an example of a coherent and a jumbled photograph. The rearrangement was assumed to reduce the meaningfulness of the object's setting, independent of the complexity of the scene. One section was left in its original position and this section contained the cued object (a dog in

Figure 10.1.   Coherent scene and jumbled scene. Cued object would be the dog in the lower right section. [From Biederman (1972).]

this example). An arrow pointed to the object and occurred either before or immediately after a brief tachistoscopic exposure of the scene. The S's task was to indicate which object had been cued by pointing to one of four object pictures. The four alternatives were presented either before or after the exposure.

Performance was significantly better when the four alternatives and the cue occurred before the exposure, suggesting an improvement in perception. Performance was also significantly better for the coherent scenes, even when the subject knew where to look (when the cue preceded the scene) and what to look for (when the response alternatives preceded the scene). It is less clear how context affects performance and Biederman suggested two alternative explanations, one perceptual and the other responsive. The perceptual explanation states that context influences the manner in which objects are physically processed—in the initial segmentation, testing, and weighing of features. The response interpretation states that context has its effect at a later, inferential stage so that ambiguous stimuli are interpreted to be consistent with other aspects of the scene. Biederman did not choose either alternative, but suggested methods for testing the two alternative explanations in future experiments. Since context is essentially a set which occurs simultaneously with the tested object, a possible limitation of the perceptual explanation is that it assumes that other aspects of the scene are recognized before the tested object and then assist in the recognition of that object. This seems unlikely for brief exposures, particularly when the location of the tested object is cued in advance.

Encoding Strategies

The evidence has not been totally consistent in supporting either the perceptual or response interpretations of set and Haber (1966) finished his review article with the conclusion that both effects had been adequately demonstrated and it remained to show the conditions under which each will occur. One possibility is that some of the effects attributed to perception could actually be accounted for by an expanded version of Haber's encoding hypothesis. The hypothesis as formulated by Haber referred to the order in which Ss translated the perceptual attributes of the percept or sensory array into a more permanent verbal store. Encoding has been a central concept in information processing theories and many experimenters have investigated how different strategies can be used to encode information.

A particularly relevant experiment was conducted by Egeth and Smith

(1967). Their study was motivated by Lawrence and Coles's failure to obtain a perceptual facilitation when four alternatives were presented before the exposure of an object (p. 193). Egeth and Smith tested the possibility that a perceptual effect might occur if Ss were shown pictures of the alternatives rather than were told the names of the alternatives as in the Lawrence and Coles experiment. They hypothesized that showing pictures should facilitate the possibility of a perceptual effect and should be particularly helpful when the alternatives are physically similar. For example, if the four alternatives were "church," "school," "house," and "barn," Ss could examine the pictures to find a set of distinguishing features. The results indicated that presentation of the four alternatives both before and after a test picture resulted in greater accuracy than presenting the alternatives only after the test picture. The interaction between time of presentation and similarity also supported the hypothesis of perceptual selectivity—there was less difference in recognition accuracy due to the similarity of alternatives under the before–after condition than under the after condition. Egeth and Smith interpreted the results as being consistent with those of Harris and Haber. Dimensions are encoded in order of their importance and showing Ss pictures of the objects enables them to find the important dimensions.

Although a set can influence the order in which dimensions or features are processed, it can also influence encoding in other ways as was demonstrated by Aderman and Smith (1971) and Corcoran and Rouse (1970). Aderman and Smith were interested in a hypothesis proposed by E. Gibson and her associates that a spelling pattern can serve as a functional unit in the perception of tachistoscopically presented letter strings (Gibson, Pick, Osser, & Hammond, 1962). A spelling pattern is a group of letters which has an invariant pronunciation according to the rules of English, taking into consideration its context. For example, the letter string **GLURCK** contains three spelling patterns; **GL, UR**, and **CK**, but the letter string **CKURGL** contains only one spelling pattern (**UR**). The problem raised by Aderman and Smith concerned how Ss know to treat spelling patterns as units before they recognize the individual letters as units. Their experiment was designed to test the hypothesis that S's expectancy about what he will see determines the size of the units he will use. In order to assure that the effect was perceptual rather than an artifact of memory or response factors, the tachistoscopic exposure was immediately followed by a two-choice recognition test of one of the letters. If Ss are suddenly shown a letter string of spelling patterns (SP) after a series of unrelated letters (UL), they should process the string as unrelated letters and hence fail to achieve the higher recognition accuracy typically found for strings of SPs. Figure 10.2 shows the performance

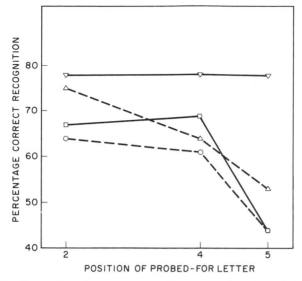

Figure 10.2. Proportion of correct recognitions as a function of the probed-for position, for four basic conditions: ($\triangledown$) Expect SP–present SP; ($\triangle$) Expect SP–present UL; ($\square$) Expect UL–present SP; ($\bigcirc$) Expect UL–present UL. [After Aderman and Smith (1971).]

of two groups of Ss who were expecting either SPs or ULs. When Ss were expecting unrelated letters, they were unable to use spelling patterns as functional units, resulting in a lower recognition accuracy—particularly for letters at the end of the string.

The study by Corcoran and Rouse (1970) was also concerned with the organization of Ss' encoding strategies. Again, the recognition of tachistoscopically presented words was the performance measure, but the experimenters' interest focused on the physical properties of the letters. If Ss were told in advance whether the word would be typed or handwritten, would their recognition accuracy be higher than if they did not have this prior knowledge? In the first experiment, typed and handwritten words were presented in either separate lists or mixed together so that Ss would not know what kind of material to expect. In Experiment II, two different samples of handwriting were used and in Experiment III, words typed in upper- and lowercase were used. The mixed condition resulted in poorer performance than the unmixed condition only in Experiment I. Corcoran and Rouse suggested that processes underlying the recognition of handwritten words were different than those underlying the perception of printed letters and that further studies using a variety of different handwritings and type fonts should reveal how great a physical difference is required before different recognition routines are used within the two classes.

The studies by Haber, Aderman and Smith, and Corcoran and Rouse, have in common the fact that Ss could utilize advance information to select encoding strategies which would enable them to better analyze and organize the information contained in the perceptual array. Certainly, there were differences in the way the strategies were used. In the first case, Ss encoded the most important attributes first; in the second case, Ss were able to use larger functional units; and in the third case, Ss were able to prepare for either writing or print. But in all three cases Ss were better able to transform the information in the perceptual array into a more permanent, encoded form. Was the improvement due to perception or response? Haber argues for response, while Aderman and Smith took a great amount of care to show their results were due to perception. Perhaps it is better to say that encoding links a response to perception. Insofar as advance information does not in any way affect the quality of the information in the perceptual array, but determines what encoding strategies Ss should select, the effect is basically a response effect. Insofar as recognition is the goal of perception, and recognition is dependent upon whether information in the perceptual array is encoded before being lost, the effect is basically a perceptual one. Improvement in performance resulting from giving information before the stimulus, as opposed to immediately after the stimulus, may depend upon whether Ss can use the information to modify their encoding strategy. Looking for particular discriminating features, changing the order in which dimensions are verbally coded, translating a word into spelling patterns rather than individual letters (hence, reducing the number of phonemes in the verbal code), and segmenting handwriting into its component letters are all encoding strategies that may be used immediately at the onset of the stimulus if advance information is available.

This view seems consistent with one of the models formulated by Broadbent (1967), although like Haber, Broadbent emphasizes response aspects. One type of response bias discussed by Broadbent is an observing response bias in which Ss may adjust their sense organs or central mechanism so as to maximize the effects of expected stimuli. It seems reasonable that an encoding strategy would fit into this category, being essentially a central adjustment. Broadbent states that predictions from this view are very similar to the view which regards set as purely perceptual with no response component. However, the view does emphasize that the perceptual effect depends upon the adjustment of the observer. Our argument that it is difficult to classify encoding as perception or response should not imply that the effects of set cannot have a perceptual or response effect. It may be difficult to find a pure perceptual effect, however, which would have to improve the quality of the perceptual array independently of the encoding strategy used by the observer.

The effects of set on response are well established. A special type of set which has a marked influence on word recognition is the frequency of occurence of the various words. It is clear that the greater recognition accuracy of the more frequent words is a response effect caused by a response bias in favor of the more common words. There is some debate as to how the response bias combines with sensory information to produce the final response but this also seems fairly well established. Some evidence on word recognition is presented in the next section, and a discussion of some theoretical models is contained in the following chapter.

Word Recognition and Response Bias

The fact that prior frequency of word usage affects visual and auditory thresholds has been sufficiently demonstrated by a number of investigators. Data from two experiments by Howes and Solomon (1951) showed that the visual duration threshold of a word was an approximately linear function of the logarithm of the relative frequency with which that word occurs in the Thorndike–Lorge word counts. Product–moment correlations between the two variables ranged from −.68 to −.75 in their main experiment. Howes and Solomon used 75 words and measured the recognition threshold by an ascending method of limits.

Solomon and Postman (1952) tried to test for the frequency effect under better experimental control by using pronounceable nonsense words. Frequency of usage was controlled by requiring Ss to read and pronounce the different words with frequencies ranging from 1 to 25. The design was used in order to have better control over the word frequency variable, as well as inherent differences among words in memorability and structural variations. Recognition thresholds were found to vary inversely with frequency of prior usage, but did not fit a linear logarithmic function.

These early findings were confirmed in an experiment by King-Ellison and Jenkins (1954). The investigators used a pack of 86 cards containing ten experimental words (five-letter paralogs). In each pack two of the paralogs appeared 25 times, two appeared 10 times, two appeared 5 times, two appeared twice and two appeared once. Every S was told that the paralogs were Turkish words and was asked to spell and pronounce the words in his deck. The correlations between the mean exposure time in tachistoscopic presentation and the logarithm of the frequency of presentation was found to be −.99, which confirmed the findings of other investigators.

The interpretation usually given for these word frequency effects is that a response bias is involved. Goldiamond and Hawkins (1958) conducted an experiment which was designed to determine to what extent the recognition thresholds could be obtained in the absence of a perceptual stimulus, and therefore be explained in response rather than perceptual terms. Subjects were first given a training session in which they saw nonsense syllables repeated at different frequencies. They were then told in a recognition session that these words would be flashed subliminally and they were to guess until accurate. A logarithmic relation was found between frequency of training and frequency of response in the recognition session.

Since no stimuli were actually present in the Goldiamond experiment, the results can be attributed to pure guessing by the Ss. In the experiments in which stimuli actually were present, Ss usually have partial information and the results might better be explained in terms of what Broadbent (1967) calls "sophisticated guessing." This view is supported by Postman and Rosenzweig (1957) and J. T. Spence (1963). According to Postman and Rosenzweig, the recognition of verbal stimuli is influenced to an important degree by the verbal habits of the perceiver. The speed with which a particular item is recognized depends on the frequency with which this item has been discriminated and used in the past. The effects of training are interpreted as reducing the number of alternatives in terms of which partially discriminated items can be completed. Each letter carries a smaller amount of information, and the stimulus pattern has become more redundant. Redundancy, in turn, facilitates perceptual recognition on the basis of reduced stimulus cues.

When words are presented rapidly at low illumination only a fragment of the stimulus is likely to be discriminated. Which of these possible words will be elicited by the fragment depends on the relative frequency with which the alternative verbal responses have been made in the past. This interpretation is confirmed by an examination of Ss' incorrect guesses, which tend to be high-frequency words. That the speed of recognition depends on the strength of verbal habits and not sheer frequency alone was demonstrated by Postman and Rosenzweig. Three-letter English words were used as stimuli to represent both words of different frequencies and trigrams or letter combinations of different frequencies. Thus, the three letter sequence "fin" is a meaningful word, but also forms a part of other words such as "finish" and "define." There was a significant inverse relationship between frequency of word usage and recognition threshold, but there was no relationship whatsoever between recognition thresholds and trigram frequency. The finding that word probability, and not letter probability, is primarily responsible for a differential bias was confirmed by Broadbent and Gregory (1971). Letter and word probabilty were experimentally varied by using a small fixed vocabulary

The influence of differential usage preferences on verbal identification was more directly studied by J. T. Spence (1963). The stimuli were presented in such a manner that S's partial perception could, to some degree, be controlled. These partial perceptions made two response alternatives equally appropriate, one a familiar word and the other a less familiar one. Four-letter words were used in which three letters were clearly visible and the fourth letter was either faintly typed or smudged. The following words composed one such list: B(A, U)NK, R(O, I)LL, DA(R, N)K, SE(L, R)F, CLU(B, E), BLU(E, R) L(I, O)ON, R(U, A)SH, MI(L, N)K, GO(A, U)T, DAT(E, A), and NOO(N, K). In two experiments, the frequency with which familiar responses occurred as guesses was significantly greater than the frequency of unfamiliar responses.

A somewhat different approach was used by Pollack, Rubenstein, and Decker (1959) to demonstrate that the relation between auditory thresholds and word frequency is due primarily to probability of responding. The experimenters determined recognition thresholds under two conditions, one in which the Ss had the complete set of words before them and one in which the words were unknown to the Ss. Results for 144 words revealed the usual relation of a lower auditory threshold for high-frequency words, but the relation completely disappeared when the message set was known. It would seem that when the subject had the words before him, the words all had equal probability of being used and the initial probabilities were irrelevant.

Similar findings have been reported by Pierce (1963) and Haber (1965). Pierce (1963) reported that frequency affected identification thresholds only when Ss did not have a list. Haber (1965) found that giving the S knowledge of the stimulus word immediately prior to its exposure increased the probability of S being able to perceive all of the letters of the word. Although there was a difference in probability of perceiving the letters in rare as compared to frequent words, this difference completely disappeared when S had prior knowledge of the word.

The effect of response bias on the word-frequency effect was recently reviewed by Broadbent (1967) in which he distinguished between four different types of response bias:

(1) Pure guessing
(2) Sophisticated guessing

(3) Observing response
(4) Criterion bias in decision.

The *pure guessing* model postulates that S perceives some of the stimuli correctly and guesses on the remaining trials. If his guesses are more frequently common words, he might by chance make some correct responses and increase his score on the common words. The model is unreasonable in that it would be very unlikely that a subject could pick a word out of his whole vocabulary and be correct by chance, unless of course a restricted vocabulary was used. More reasonable is the *sophisticated guessing* model in which S receives partial information and has to choose among a restricted set of alternatives. If he chooses at random out of this restricted set, but with a bias toward more probable words, he will, just as in the previous model, score some correct answers on common words by chance. The interpretation given by Postman and Rosenzweig (1957) and J. T. Spence (1963) would seem to be compatible with this model.

A third possible explanation is the *observing response* model, which states that S may adjust his sense organs so as to maximize the effects of stimuli which he expects, at the cost of being badly adjusted to detect improbable stimuli. Its prediction would be closely similar to the purely perceptual view with no response component except for the emphasis on the adjustment of the observer. A final interpretation (*criterion bias*), and the one favored by Broadbent, views the situation as analogous to a statistical decision, in which the stimulus provides evidence pointing to some word in S's vocabulary. The word frequency effect would then be obtained if S were biased in such a way as to accept a smaller amount of evidence before deciding in favor of a probable word rather than an improbable word.

Although Broadbent helped to clarify the various ways in which response bias could influence performance, his choice of a model has been criticized in two subsequent review articles (Catlin, 1969; Nakatani, 1970). Both writers argued for the sophisticated guessing model. Catlin made two major points. First, he argued that Broadbent's formulation of the sophisticated guessing model was inadequate because it depended upon an implausible assumption. A more adequate formulation of the sophisticated guessing theory correctly predicts the results obtained by Broadbent—that the ratio of "number of high frequency errors/number of low frequency errors" is independent of the frequency of the stimulus word. The second point made by Catlin was that Broadbent's theory does not predict that errors will tend to be similar to the stimulus word.

According to the theory, errors should be a random sampling of all words in the language, taking response bias into account. In order to understand why this is true, we have to take a closer look at Broadbent's model which was formulated as a choice model. We will do so in the next chapter.

Summary

Information about a stimulus can greatly influence what is reported during a recognition experiment. When the purpose of the information is to reduce the number of alternatives, the reduction may result in better perception or it may result in increased accuracy solely because there are fewer permissible responses. An experimental procedure for distinguishing between the two interpretations is to give the set either immediately before or immediately after the stimulus exposure. A greater improvement in performance due to giving a set before the stimulus is assumed to be the result of perceptual enhancement. The experimental findings have been mixed: Some experiments demonstrated equal facilitation regardless of when the set was given and other experiments found a greater improvement for a set given before stimulus presentation. The contextual effects of a visual scene have also not been definitely identified as facilitating perception or response, since context is essentially a set given simultaneously with the target stimulus.

One way in which a prior set can result in better performance is to enable Ss to utilize an optimal encoding strategy. The encoding strategy improves perception in that the observer is better able to translate information in the perceptual array into memory, but is response dependent in that the strategy is chosen by the observer. There are a variety of different strategies depending upon the demands of the task. Haber found that the order in which stimulus attributes are encoded is a function of their importance. Aderman and Smith found that pronounceable letter pairs are treated as units if Ss' previous experience during the task led them to expect such units. Corcoran and Rouse discovered that Ss apparently prepared themselves in different ways if they knew a word would be in print, as opposed to writing.

A group of experiments illustrating the importance of response bias includes those experiments that investigated the effects of word frequency on performance. Word frequency can be defined in terms of frequency of occurrence in print or frequency of occurrence during the experiment. In either case, performance (measured by percentage correct, duration threshold, or signal-to-noise ratio) is superior on high-frequency words. The interpretation of these findings supposes a response bias in favor of common words such that common words are reported whenever the observer is uncertain. Errors, however, tend to be perceptually similar to the correct stimulus indicating that Ss choose from a reduced set of alternatives consistent with whatever stimulus information is perceived.

XI | Recognition Models

We continue our discussion in this chapter of how pattern similarities and response biases jointly determine response selection, but we will do so at a more detailed level by examining some recognition models. In 1959, Luce proposed a choice model of recognition which postulated both similarity and bias parameters. Subsequent formulations have been influenced by his model, but have made additional process assumptions. One process assumption is that only a subset of stimuli similar to the presented stimulus is considered when choosing a response. Further process assumptions attempt to specify how the attributes of the stimulus determine its similarity to other stimuli. These assumptions are examined in the first two sections. In the final section, we critically evaluate the analysis-by-synthesis model which proposes that some knowledge of the possible alternative patterns guides the analysis of a pattern into its attributes.

Choice Models

The final topic of the previous chapter was Broadbent's (1967) formulation of four alternative response bias models and the criticism of his

207

criterion bias model for its failure to account for pattern similarities. Broadbent combined the idea of a criterion in signal detection theory with a special case of Luce's (1959) choice model to predict a confusion matrix, illustrated here for four stimuli (S_1, S_2, S_3, S_4) and their corresponding responses (R_1, R_2, R_3, R_4). For each stimulus, the probability of each response is specified in terms of two parameters. The parameter V specifies the degree of response bias associated with each of the alternative responses. Response bias is analogous to a criterion in statistical decision theory and a bias in favor of high-frequency words is analogous to having a lower criterion for responding with a high-frequency word. The parameter α is a perceptual parameter related to the probability of correctly perceiving each stimulus. Both the perceptual parameters and the response bias parameters may differ for each of the stimuli. The relative response strengths for each stimulus are given by the entries in Table 11.1.

A confusion matrix can be formed from Table 11.1 by converting the relative response strengths into response probabilities. This is done by dividing each strength by the sum of the row elements. The probability of giving a correct response to stimulus S_i is proportional to $\alpha_i V_i$ and is, therefore, a function of both perceptual and response bias parameters. The distribution of incorrect responses for each stimulus is determined only by the response bias parameters and is not a function of similarities existing among the stimuli. For example, the probability of an observer giving R_2, R_3, or R_4 as a response to stimulus S_1 would not be determined by the similarity between S_1 and each of the other three stimuli.

A model which does allow for the effects of stimulus similarity is the confusion-choice recognition model proposed by Nakatani (1972). The model postulates that the presentation of a stimulus may evoke from 0 to n acceptable responses (r_j), where n is the number of stimuli in the stimulus set. The sensory state of the observer specifies the subset of stimuli which is consistent with his observation. There are 2^n possible

TABLE 11.1

RELATIVE STRENGTHS OF FOUR RESPONSES IN THE PRESENCE OF EACH OF FOUR STIMULI[a]

Stimuli	Responses			
	1	2	3	4
1	$\alpha_1 V_1$	V_2	V_3	V_4
2	V_1	$\alpha_2 V_2$	V_3	V_4
3	V_1	V_2	$\alpha_3 V_3$	V_4
4	V_1	V_2	V_3	$\alpha_4 V_4$

[a] From Broadbent (1967).

sensory states since each of the n stimuli may or may not be a member of this subset. For $n = 4$, there would be 16 possible subsets ranging from $(0, 0, 0, 0)$ in which case none of the four stimuli are consistent with an observation to (r_1, r_2, r_3, r_4) in which case all of the stimuli are consistent with the observation. The following notation will be used to summarize Nakatani's formulation:

S_i Stimulus set $i = 1, \ldots, n$
R_j Response set $j = 1, \ldots, n$
r_j Acceptable response $j = 1, \ldots, n$
s_k Sensory state $k = 1, \ldots, m$ where $m = 2^n$

Figure 11.1 shows three levels of the model. There are two sets of *parameters* which are used to represent the perceptual and response aspects of recognition. The acceptance matrix specifies the probability of each response being evoked by a stimulus, which of course, is a function of the similarity between two stimuli. Similarity is determined by the distance between two stimuli in a multidimensional space. The per-

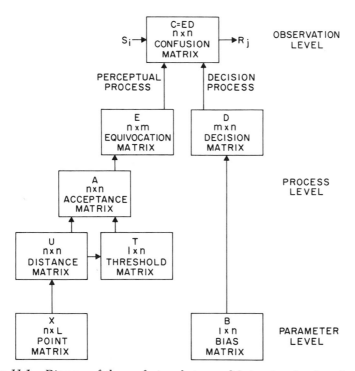

Figure 11.1. Diagram of the confusion-choice model showing the three levels and two processes with the associated matrices. [From Nakatani (1972).]

ceptual parameters are the dimensional coordinates of each stimulus, as listed in the point matrix for n stimuli and L dimensions. The bias matrix lists the response bias parameters, defined as the probability of giving each response in the absence of any sensory information.

The *process assumptions* are that the presentation of a stimulus results in one of the 2^n possible sensory states. The equivocation matrix specifies for each of the n stimuli the probability of evoking each one of the m possible sensory states. The probabilities are calculated from the product of the relevant acceptance probabilities. For example, if a_{1j} is the probability of S_1 evoking r_j, the probability of a sensory state consisting of only r_1 and r_4 would be given by

$$Pr(r_1 \text{ and } r_4 \mid S_1) = a_{11} \cdot (1 - a_{12}) \cdot (1 - a_{13}) \cdot a_{14} \quad (1)$$

The decision matrix specifies how observers should respond for each of the sensory states. The model assumes that response probabilities are determined by normalizing the response biases according to Luce's choice axiom (Luce, 1959). For example, if the bias parameters are $B_1 = 0.4$, $B_2 = 0.2$, $B_3 = 0.3$, and $B_4 = 0.1$, the model predicts that the probability of giving response R_1 would equal 0.8 if the sensory state consisted of r_1 and r_4.

$$Pr(R_1 \mid r_1 \text{ and } r_4) = B_1/(B_1 + B_4) = .4/(.4 + .1) = .8 \quad (2)$$

Finally, at the *observation level* there is the confusion matrix specifying the probability of giving response j to stimulus i. The predicted confusion matrix is found from the product of the equivocation matrix and the decision matrix. The prediction is made by considering, for each stimulus, the probability of evoking each sensory state and the probability of giving a certain response for each sensory state. The former probabilities are determined by the perceptual parameters and the latter probabilities are determined by the bias parameters. These parameters are estimated so as to produce the best fit between the experimental confusion matrix and the predicted confusion matrix. Nakatani was successful in predicting the confusion matrices for both previously published data on color and tone recognition and specially constructed synthetic data.

A related theoretical formulation was developed by Townsend (1971a) in order to analyze confusion matrices generated by tachistoscopically presenting letters of the alphabet. Two of the models—the overlap activation model and the choice model—predicted the obtained confusion matrices about equally well and better than a third model, an all-or-none activation model. The overlap activation model may be thought of as a special case of the model proposed by Nakatani (1972). The sensory states of the model consist of either a single letter whenever a letter is correctly perceived or two letters; the correct letter and one other letter. The probability of an incorrect letter appearing in the sensory state depends upon its similarity to the correct letter. When two letters appear in the sensory state, the response probability is calculated from the ratio of the relevant response bias parameters, as in Nakatani's formulation. The two models are basically similar except that fewer sensory states are allowed in Townsend's formulation.

The choice model developed by Townsend follows the formulation given by Luce (1963). If ν_{ij} is the similarity between stimuli i and j and B_j is the bias parameter for response j, the probability of giving response j to stimulus i is given as follows:

$$c_{ij} = \frac{\nu_{ij}B_j}{\sum_{k=1}^{n} \nu_{ik}B_k} \tag{3}$$

The summation is over all n stimuli. The problem with the choice model is that it does not specify the underlying process assumptions, particularly with respect to the underlying sensory states. As was the case with the previous models, the choice model uses both similarity parameters and bias parameters to account for the data of a confusion matrix. But it is not clear how many acceptable responses occur on any one trial. The number of acceptable responses ranges from 0 to n in Nakatani's confusion-choice model and from 1 to 2 in the overlap activation model.

Another alternative formulation would be to modify Broadbent's criterion bias model to account for the effects of stimulus similarity. Such a proposal was made by M. Treisman (1971) who suggested that partial cues compatible with a limited number of words could be accounted for by a rise in the central distribution on the decision axis corresponding to each of those words. Errors would then be a function of both the lowered criteria for high-frequency words and a rise in the means of the distributions for those words which are similar to the presented word. Although Treisman did not elaborate further on this modification of Broadbent's model, we can speculate on how it might compare to the previous models. First, as with the previous models, there would be a bias parameter for each word—in this case a criterion parameter. The decision axis would indicate the amount of evidence for each word and the lower criteria for frequent words would indicate that less evidence is necessary for reporting that word. The mean of the distribution for each word would be a function of which word was presented. The greater the similarity of a word to the presented word, the greater its mean value on the decision axis. The degree of evidence for each word could be defined as the difference between its fixed criterion value and a value on the decision axis that is randomly determined according to the normal distribution. An acceptable response for that word would be represented in the sensory state whenever the amount of evidence exceeded the criterion.

Such a formulation would be very similar to the confusion-choice model unless the degree of evidence (amount of evidence exceeding the criterion) was retained for each acceptable response represented in the sensory state. If there were different degrees of evidence associated with each acceptable response, a normative decision rule could be used to select the response corresponding to the stimulus with the greatest amount of evidence. The confusion-choice model and this version of a modified criterion bias model make different process assumptions in that (1) the acceptable responses are listed as all-or-none in the former model, but have associated degrees of evidence in the latter model and (2) a response is probabilistically selected under the constraints of the biases associated with each acceptable response in the former model, whereas the acceptable response with the greatest amount of evidence determines the response in the latter model.

The advantage of the confusion-choice and modified response bias models over the overlap activation and choice models lies in the process assumptions. The choice model does not make clear process assumptions and the overlap activation model is perhaps overly restrictive in allowing only one or two mediation responses. All four models are alike, however, in that the bias parameters and similarity parameters serve the same purpose, perhaps making it difficult to evaluate the models on the basis of predictive accuracy.

Pattern Similarities

Ideally, a recognition model should be able not only to specify the similarities among the stimuli, but to give some basis for the similarities. Nakatani's confusion choice model included such a basis. The goal of the model is to locate the stimuli and the corresponding responses in a Euclidean space of minimum dimensionality and to estimate the bias probabilities in order to give an adequate account of a confusion matrix. The distances between the stimuli determine the probability of a response being included in the sensory state. Although the distances are fixed by the spatial representation, the judgment of a particular distance is assumed to be normally distributed about the true value as a result of noise. If the judged distance of a stimulus is less than a certain threshold, the response is included in the sensory state. The acceptance probabilities a_{ij} are therefore determined by both the distance matrix and the threshold matrix (see Figure 11.1). The free parameters of the model are the spatial coordinates for each stimulus and the bias probabilities. The stimulus coordinates should hopefully suggest the underlying dimensions which determine interstimulus similarities and reduce the number of parameters in the model.

The number of parameters can be even further reduced if a set of features can be physically identified and used to predict confusion errors. Rumelhart (1971) has recently taken this approach to extend his multicomponent theory discussed in Chapter V. The stimuli in Rumelhart's experiment were the first six letters of the alphabet, constructed from a set of seven straight line segments. Figure 11.2 shows the letters and the set of features. A trial consisted of a 2-msec exposure of one of the letters. Subjects indicated which letter they thought was presented and these data were used to construct a confusion matrix.

Rumelhart's theoretical analysis assumes that the observer's response is determined by the specific features detected during the exposure. According to the model, the probability of detecting a feature is a function of the length of the line segment. The probability of observing a short segment (f_6, f_7) is equal to $1 - \alpha$; the probability of observing a medium segment (f_2, f_4) is equal to $1 - \alpha^2$; and the probability of observing a long segment (f_1, f_3, f_5) is equal to $1 - \alpha^3$. The longer the segment, the greater its detection probability and the single sensory parameter α specifies the chance of detection.

The observed features will usually be consistent with only a few of the six letters. The candidate set (corresponding to Nakatani's sensory state) is the set of responses which are still considered to be possible response alternatives after the features have been observed. A response is a member of the candidate set if all the observed features are features of that stimulus and not more than c features are missing. The parameter c specifies how many missing features an observer is willing to tolerate before refusing to accept a stimulus as a possible candidate. Suppose the observer detects features f_1, f_2, and f_6, corresponding to the letter **F**. If the observer were unwilling to tolerate any missing features ($c = 0$),

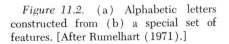

Figure 11.2. (a) Alphabetic letters constructed from (b) a special set of features. [After Rumelhart (1971).]

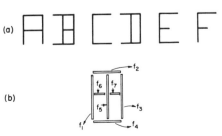

the letter **F** would be the only candidate. If he were willing to tolerate one missing feature, the letter **E** would also be a candidate, since only one feature (f_4) would be missing from the letter **E**. If he were to tolerate two missing features, the letter **A** would be added to the candidate set since the addition of two features (f_3, f_7) would complete this letter.

Assuming that the features are detected independently, we can calculate $P(F \mid S_i)$, the probability that a certain set of features (F) will be detected for a given stimulus (S_i). The value of $P(F \mid S_i)$ is equal to the product of the detection probabilities for each detected feature multiplied by ($1 -$ detection probability) for each nondetected feature of the stimulus. Both the sensory evidence $P(F \mid S_i)$ and the response bias B_i combine to determine which response is selected from the candidate set. The response is selected according to the Bayesian response rule:

$$P(R_i \mid F) = \begin{cases} B_i & \text{if no candidates;} \\[2mm] \dfrac{P(F \mid S_i)B_i}{\sum_k P(F \mid S_k)B_k} & \text{if } r_i \text{ is a candidate.} \end{cases} \quad (4)$$

The summation is over all responses in the candidate set. The bias parameter, as in the confusion-choice model, is equal to the response probability when there are no candidates.

The predicted confusion matrix is based on

$$P(R_i \mid S_j) = \sum_F P(R_i \mid F) \cdot P(F \mid S_j) \quad (5)$$

The summation is over all possible feature sets which can result from stimulus S_j.

How does Rumelhart's multicomponent model differ from the previous models? One difference is the Bayesian response rule which depends upon the sensory evidence $P(F \mid S_j)$ in addition to the response bias B_i. If our hypothetical subject had detected the features corresponding to the letter **F**, so that $F = (f_1, f_2, f_6)$, and could tolerate two missing features, his candidate set would consist of the letters **F**, **E**, and **A**. But the sensory evidence $P(F|S_i)$ would be greatest for the letter **F** since the missing features would lower the probability in the case of the letter **A** or **E**. In contrast, Nakatani's model postulates that only the bias parameters influence selection after the candidate set is determined.

The other possibility would be always to choose the response with the greatest amount of evidence as determined by $P(F \mid S_i)B_i$. This would correspond to the modified response bias model. One difficulty of such a model is that it raises the question of why postulate a candidate set if the response is always predetermined. Although it is true that only the response with the greatest amount of evidence could be selected, the size of the candidate set might determine the observer's confidence in the correctness of his decision or the time required to make that decision. For example, Halle and Stevens (1962) suggest that a preliminary analysis could be used to limit the number of attempted matches in an analysis-by-synthesis model (discussed in the next section). The size of the candidate set could determine the number of attempted matches, with the best match [as determined by $P(F \mid S_i)B_i$] being selected. The candidate set would, in this case, determine the number of attempted matches, but not which responses might be selected. The Bayesian response rule steers a middle course between the extremes of the confusion-choice model and the modified response bias model. The subject is free to select any response in the candidate set, but the sensory evidence influences which response is chosen.

Another interesting implication of the multicomponent model is that it suggests a perceptual basis for an asymmetrical confusion matrix. A confusion matrix is asymmetrical whenever $P(R_i \mid S_j)$ does not equal $P(R_j \mid S_i)$. In other words, the probability of reporting **E** when the letter **F** occurs may not equal the probability of reporting **F** when the letter **E** occurs. The other models can predict such a result on the basis of different response biases but, with the exception of Nakatani's model, they cannot predict a possible perceptual effect since they utilize only the overall similarity between two stimuli. The multicomponent theory can predict a perceptual effect on the basis of the number of missing features. If the S could not tolerate any missing features, the letter **E** could not enter the candidate set if **F** were presented. But he could report the letter **F** when **E** occurred and should do so whenever he detected only the three features composing the letter **F**.

The confusion choice model can account for perceptual asymmetries because it postulates that confusions depend upon a perceptual threshold, in addition to the distance between two stimuli. Perceptual asymmetries can result because the different stimuli have different thresholds. The process assumptions are not as clear in the confusion choice model as in Rumelhart's (1971) model, but this may give the former model greater generality. For example, we could postulate that the distance between two stimuli varies because on some occasions all the features of a stimulus are not detected as assumed by Rumelhart, or because all the features of a stimulus are detected, but are assigned different values on different occasions. The latter case would allow the extension of the model to include perceptual classification because the feature values of patterns in any stimulus class would vary for the different exemplars. The extension would be similar to the prototype model discussed in Chapter IX if we assumed that the scaled stimuli represent the category prototypes and any presentation of a stimulus is an exemplar pattern from one of the categories.

An advantage of the multicomponent model over the other models is its dependence upon fewer parameters. The perceptual aspects of the model are represented by a single parameter α, which specifies the detection probabilities for the three types of features. The reduction of parameters is, of course, dependent upon how effectively we can specify the features composing each stimulus and the degree to which the features of the stimulus set overlap to determine similarities. When these conditions are met, the multicomponent model would appear to be the best approach. When it is difficult to identify an overlapping set of features, the basic approach used by the confusion-choice model would appear to be necessary. A goodness-of-fit comparison of the models for the same sets of data and further tests of the psychological assumptions should help resolve the issue.

Analysis-by-Synthesis

An interesting aspect of Rumelhart's model is that it represents structural patterns as a feature vector, where each feature has one of two values: present or absent. The structural characteristics of a pattern are indirectly represented, since identical features (such as f_1, f_3, and f_5) are labeled differently when they are in different locations. Although the formulation demonstrates how a probability model can be applied to structural patterns, it has so far been applied to only a subset of specially constructed letters. But a probability formulation may be useful even when structural patterns are represented by a more complex grammar. One possibility recommended by T. Evans (1969) involves the application of probability and structural models at the separate stages of analysis and synthesis. Evans, an advocate of the structural approach, suggested that the use of probability measures might aid in assigning a description to a pattern. At each stage in the syntactic analysis of a pattern, a decision must be made as to whether a certain set of subpatterns can be regarded as the constituents of a pattern defined by a grammar rule. Evans suggested that the techniques developed in statistical pattern classification theory could be used in making such a decision.

This type of an approach has, in fact, been utilized in a program written by Mermelstein and Eden (1964) to recognize handwriting. The program searches for invariants of patterns by considering the movements that are used in executing handwriting. Strokes are specified in terms of

12 parameters which supply such information as the initial and final velocity values and the amount of displacement along the horizontal and vertical axes. The parameters are assumed to have multivariate normal distributions which are used to identify the various strokes. The handwritten words are analyzed by segmentation into strokes; the strokes are recognized by the statistical likelihood of their belonging to preselected classes; and the constraints inherent in letters and words are used to limit the output sequences generated. A threshold is established for the stroke-likelihood measure and all strokes exceeding the threshold are considered in the generation of letter sequences. Starting with the first choice of the first stroke, an exhaustive search accepts all legal sequences, and words are assigned likelihoods based on the sum of constituent stroke likelihoods.

The program shows how "analysis" and "synthesis" can interrelate. *Analysis* is the breaking down of a pattern into its component parts. *Synthesis* refers to putting these parts back together to make a whole. One way in which analysis and synthesis can interact is through analysis-by-synthesis in which some knowledge of the whole is used to aid in the recognition of the parts. This type of a model was proposed by Halle and Stevens (1962), whose aim was to find a recognition function that would relate acoustic signals to messages consisting of strings of phonemes. Halle and Stevens proposed a recognition model in which the mapping from the signal to the message space is accomplished largely through an active feedback process. Since analysis is achieved through matching to an active internal synthesis of comparison signals, the procedure is called "analysis-by-synthesis." The major problem confronting the proponents of such a model is how to achieve some economy in the matching procedure so as to avoid a large number of attempted matches. Halle and Stevens proposed that the need for a large dictionary can be overcome if it is possible to store only the generative rule for speech production. Analysis would then be accomplished by supplying the generative rules for all possible phoneme sequences, seeking a best match. A preliminary analysis would further limit the necessity of synthesizing a large number of comparison signals. The order of further synthesis could then be controlled by the outcome of the preliminary analysis and the previous synthesis of comparison signals.

There are two aspects of the analysis-by-synthesis model which should be differentiated. The first is the idea that a knowledge of the possible patterns influences how a pattern is analyzed. For example, Mermelstein and Eden's program used the constraints inherent in letters and words during the sequential identification of the various strokes. The second is the idea that if an exact match is not made between the input and one of the possible patterns, the system keeps reanalyzing and recycling until an exact match is achieved. In human perception, the first idea seems more likely than the second. Sutherland (1973) has pointed out that patterns are of importance to animals and man only insofar as they signify objects. Having a knowledge of possible structures is therefore important in recognition. Sutherland also suggested that more is involved in perceptual learning than learning critical features; such as learning what types of structures are in a given domain and eliminating impossible structures.

The second idea, that a failure to achieve a match results in a reanalysis and another attempted match, seems to characterize only a small part of human perception. Our ability to respond to similarity would seem to imply that two patterns can be compared directly for degree of similarity without having to transform one to match the other. In order to make the discussion more concrete, let us consider several examples.

Case 1. The first example is shown in Figure 11.3. If such a pattern were encountered on a printed page, we would expect the set of possible patterns to be the 26 letters of the alphabet. Contextual effects may further reduce the set of possible patterns to several, or even, a single letter. The reader's problem is to decide whether to change the left line to make an **A** or to change the right line to make an **H**. Which "change" he will make depends upon which letter seems the most similar if both alternatives are allowable by context, making the reanalysis unnecessary because the decision has already been made.

Case 2. The Wife : Mother-in-Law ambiguous figure is discussed by Hochberg (1970) to illustrate how our expectancies can influence our perception. Again, synthesis guides our analysis of the pattern since identification of some parts as being consistent with one interpretation determines how the other parts will be identified. Although our knowledge of possible structures guides our analysis of the pattern, it is likely that Ss are initially unaware that each part has two interpretations and so there is no need for a reanalysis during the initial synthesis. The alternative interpretation is probably not discovered until after some effort to reorganize the pattern.

Figure 11.3. An ambiguous letter.

Case 3. The final example is the ambiguous figure (pattern 1) shown on page 149. Synthesis is particularly important in this example because the way in which the parts are joined determines the structure of the pattern. One way in which the structure could be assigned a description is by two separate stages—a preliminary analysis followed by synthesis. If the preliminary analysis resulted in the identification of the primitives of the pattern, no further analysis would be necessary, since the pattern had been analyzed into its smallest units (see the discussion on page 48). If the preliminary analysis included composite lines as units, an attempted synthesis might reveal that it was necessary to split the composite lines into primitives. This case would correspond to the analysis-by-synthesis model in which an attempted synthesis revealed the need for a reanalysis. It might occur in the type of hierarchical model proposed by Vitz and Todd (1971) in which lines, angles, and areas are sequentially identified (see the discussion in Chapter III). A second possibility is that analysis and synthesis might proceed together with either primitives or composite lines being identified as units, depending on what was required for the synthesis. This possibility would correspond more to the sequential scanning model proposed by Hochberg (1970) and Noton (1970).

A question raised by the analysis-by-synthesis model concerns the temporal aspects of the matching process. Halle and Stevens (1962) suggest that a preliminary analysis could limit the number of attempted matches and their suggestion is supported by the models proposed by Nakatani and Rumelhart in which the final choice is made from a subset of patterns. Neither Nakatani nor Rumelhart elaborate on the temporal aspects of their models, but it seems that the most likely alternative would be to propose a two-stage process in which an initial parallel comparison eliminates very dissimilar patterns to establish the candidate set and a subsequent serial comparison of patterns in the candidate set results in the final choice. The parallel comparison is, of course, similar to Neisser's (1967) model and the serial comparison is similar to Sternberg's (1967) model (see Chapter IV). There are two ways in which the serial stage could be eliminated. The first is when only a single item enters the candidate set and the second is when many items enter the candidate set but all are inconsistent with the target (such as when S detects a curve while searching for the letter **Z**).

The search of the candidate set might proceed as proposed by Sternberg, although missing features and the possibility of not achieving an exact match would likely slow the serial comparison and make an exhaustive search necessary whenever an exact match was not obtained. A reanalysis of features as proposed by Halle and Stevens (1962) would further slow down the matching process and I think this is a disadvantage of their model, in addition to the problem raised earlier. That is, what controls the reanalysis unless it is the similarity of the analyzed pattern to the possible alternatives? And if one can judge the similarity, is a reanalysis necessary? I think not, and I believe that in most cases the initial analysis is used to compare the similarity of patterns and that a reanalysis is only necessary for those few cases when the perceiver is uncertain regarding the accuracy of his initial analysis.

Summary

Although it is well established that both stimulus similarity and response bias determine performance in a recognition task, recognition models differ in their specific process assumptions. One of the early models was a choice model proposed by Luce to predict a confusion matrix (the probability of giving response R_j to stimulus S_i for each stimulus and response) using similarity and bias parameters. Subsequent models have extended Luce's formulation to include more detailed process assumptions. Broadbent outlined the characteristics of four response bias models and developed one of the models by combining the idea of a criterion in signal detection theory with a special case of Luce's choice model. The model was a special case because it ignored similarity effects, a point which has been criticized by other investigators.

The two most complete recognition models are the confusion-choice model proposed by Nakatani and the extension of the multicomponent theory proposed by Rumelhart. Both models propose that the perceptual information is consistent only with some of the response alternatives on any trial so that only a subset of responses is considered. The acceptable responses are determined by the similarity of stimuli to the exposed stimulus, but the two models differ in their representation of similarity. Rumelhart's model is developed for the special case of six letters constructed from specified line segments. A single parameter is estimated to reflect the probability of detecting each line segment. Nakatani's model assumes that the stimuli can be represented in a multidimensional space and the perceptual parameters of the model are the spatial coordinates of each stimulus. Both models estimate response bias parameters, but once the acceptable responses are determined the confusion-choice model uses only the bias parameters to select a response, whereas the multicomponent model uses both perceptual and bias information to select a response.

Although neither investigator stated how the decision process operates in real time, the most likely possibility would seem to be an initial parallel comparison which would determine the acceptable responses followed by a serial comparison of the acceptable responses. The assumption is consistent with certain aspects of the analysis-by-synthesis model which proposes that a knowledge of possible patterns influences the analysis of a pattern's components. According to the model, a failure to achieve a match results in a reanalysis and another attempted match. As an alternative, it is suggested that a reanalysis is usually not necessary because the observer is capable of judging the similarity of his initial analysis to the acceptable responses.

XII | Overview

The purpose of this final chapter is to present a general overview of the previous 11 chapters. Figure 12.1 is a general conceptual framework which may be useful in relating the major points of the book. The framework is based on my attempt to integrate the previous material, but is greatly influenced by the theories of E. Gibson, Sutherland, and Posner.

Pattern recognition begins with *feature extraction* in which various parts of a pattern are identified. Chapter II presented various feature theories and the assumption that patterns are represented in terms of features was maintained throughout the book. Although features are a necessary part of a pattern-recognition theory, they are not sufficient for a complete theory because *relations* are also important for many types of patterns. Relations such as "parallel," "join," and "symmetry" usually involve features and so are identified at a later stage in the flow chart. The structural characteristics of patterns were examined in Chapter III. The identification of features and relations occurs during the stimulus examination stage in which the physical characteristics of the pattern are

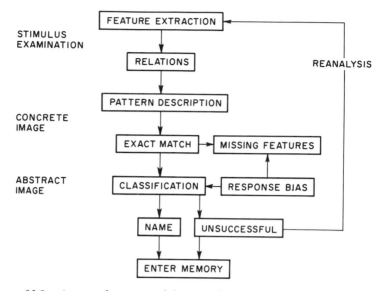

Figure 12.1. A general conceptual framework showing different stages of pattern recognition.

identified. Stimulus examination can continue until the end of iconic storage (Chapter V) and may be influenced by previous information (Chapter X).

The features and relations are combined to form a *pattern description.* The pattern description corresponds to a concrete image if it completely describes the pattern. It is then matched to descriptions of patterns that have been previously stored in memory. The matching process can involve either a structured visual image or a verbal description of the pattern. This distinction was made in Chapter VI. It does not involve a name because if the pattern has a name, the name is associated with one of the descriptions stored in memory and is retrieved only after a match is obtained. Chapter IV discussed various temporal aspects of the matching process, such as whether the attributes of a pattern can be matched in parallel. The matching process is fastest whenever an *exact match* is possible. An exact match is possible in most experiments because only a single exemplar of each pattern is used.

In some cases, *missing features* may prevent the occurrence of an exact match even when a single exemplar of each pattern is used. Features can be missing either from the perceptual pattern or from the description stored in memory. The first case occurs whenever recognition is difficult and a pattern is not always accurately perceived. The recognition models discussed in Chapter XI were formulated to account for this kind of data. The second case occurs when features of a stored description are forgotten. The multicomponent models presented in Chapter VII describe process assumptions for this case. It seems reasonable to assume that the match between a complete description and an incomplete description would involve the same decision process for both situations, but I do not know of any direct evidence which supports this hypothesis. It is likely, however, that the matching process is slower whenever there are missing features.

Another example of a situation which results in slower matching is when many exemplars represent a pattern and an exact match is not possible. In this case, *classification* is necessary. The longer time taken to make a name match (Aa) than a physical match (AA) illustrates that an exact match is faster than a match which follows classification. Recent experimental results obtained by Dave Bartram (personal communication) offer another example. A series of pictures (cats, dogs, cars, churches, chairs, etc.) were projected on a screen and Ss were required to name each picture as quickly as possible. The same category names were repeated over trials in a random order, but in one condition the same exemplar always occurred (i.e., the same cat) whereas in a second condition, different exemplars (different cats) occurred. Naming latencies declined over trials for both conditions, but showed a greater decline when the same exemplars always occurred and an exact match was possible.

We considered alternative classification models in Chapters VIII and IX. The main distinction was between probability models and distance models. My preference is the prototype model combined with a weighted-features, distance metric as a measure of similarity to the prototypes. The prototype model is consistent with the evidence reported in the final section of Chapter II and the differential weighting of features is consistent with the evidence which suggests that Ss differentially emphasize the more informative features. A prototype model simplifies the matching process because it is a simpler decision rule than most of the alternative rules considered in Chapters VIII and IX. It also provides some continuity in the matching process because Ss would normally match patterns to the stored prototypes unless they were expecting specific exemplars (such as letters of a certain type font) in which case they would match patterns to the descriptions of the particular exemplars. Whenever an exact match is not possible, *response bias* can influence the choice of a response. In Chapter X we saw how response bias results in greater accuracy for more frequently occurring words and in Chapter XI we saw how response bias can be incorporated into recognition models.

When a match is obtained between a pattern description and a stored description it may affect several possible *memory* codes.

(1) The pattern description may be entered into memory as a visual image or verbal code. The pattern description would differ from the stored description whenever an exact match was not obtained.

(2) The stored description (of a particular exemplar used in the experiment or a category prototype) may be activated and associated information stored, such as the time of activation. When the pattern is classified into a category, the category prototype may be modified if the new member changes the central tendency of the category.

(3) If the stored description is associated with a name, the name may be activated.

When an attempted match is *unsuccessful* (for example, a novel pattern), the pattern description can be entered into memory as a new pattern. An associated name may also be stored if a name was given to the pattern. An alternative procedure is to return to the stimulus examination stage and form a new pattern description for another attempted match. This procedure is part of the analysis-by-synthesis model discussed in Chapter XI. Although *reanalysis* is sometimes used in pattern recognition, I consider it to be the exception, rather than the rule.

Some of the issues raised in this book have been speculative ones, but they illustrate what we do not know, but would like to know—particularly the possibility of combining various theories into a more comprehensive theory. I hope that I have been able to accomplish two objectives in writing this book. First, I hope that I have been able to convey to the reader my feeling that the information-processing approach has, in a relatively short time, contributed much to our understanding of human pattern recognition. And second, I hope I have been able to convey some idea of problems which remain to be explored in order to further our understanding.

References

Aderman, D. & Smith, E. E. Expectancy as a determinant of functional units in perceptual recognition. *Cognitive Psychology,* 1971, **2**, 117–129.

Aiken, E. G. Auditory discrimination learning: Prototype storage and distinctive feature detection mechanisms. *Perception and Psychophysics,* 1969, **6**, 95–96.

Aiken, L. S. & Brown, D. R. A feature utilization analysis of the perception of pattern class structure. *Perception and Psychophysics,* 1971, **9**, 270–283.

Anderson, N. H. Integration theory and attitude change. *Psychological Review,* 1971, **78**, 171–206.

Anderson, T. W. *Introduction to multivariate statistical analysis.* New York: Wiley, 1958.

Ashby, R. C. *Design for a brain.* London: Chapman and Hall, 1952.

Asso, D. & Wyke, M. Visual discrimination and verbal comprehension of spatial relations by young children. *British Journal of Psychology,* 1970, **61**, 99–107.

Atkinson, R. C. & Shiffrin, R. M. Human memory: A proposed system and its control processes. In K. W. Spence & J. T. Spence (Eds.), *Advances in the psychology of learning and motivation,* Vol. 2. New York: Academic Press, 1968.

Atkinson, R. C. & Shiffrin, R. M. The control of short-term memory. *Scientific American,* 1971, **224**(2), 82–90.

Attneave, F. Dimensions of similarity. *American Journal of Psychology,* 1950, **63**, 516–556.

Attneave, F. Transfer of experience with a class schema to identification learning of patterns and shapes. *Journal of Experimental Psychology*, 1957, **54**, 81–88.

Bahrick, H. P. & Boucher, B. Retention of visual and verbal codes of the same stimuli. *Journal of Experimental Psychology*, 1968, **78**, 417–422.

Bahrick, H. P., Clark, S., & Bahrick, P. Generalization gradients as indicants of learning and retention of a recognition task. *Journal of Experimental Psychology*, 1967, **75**, 464–471.

Bamber, D. Reaction times and error rates for "same–different" judgments of multidimensional stimuli. *Perception and Psychophysics*, 1969, **6**, 169–174.

Bartlett, F. C. *Remembering, a study in experimental and social psychology.* London and New York: Cambridge Univ. Press, 1932.

Beach, L. R. Cue probabilism and inference behavior. *Psychological Monographs*, 1964, **78**(5), 1–20. (a)

Beach, L. R. Recognition, assimilation, and identification of objects. *Psychological Monographs*, 1964, **78**(6), 21–37. (b)

Beals, R., Krantz, D., & Tversky, A. Foundations of multidimensional scaling. *Psychological Review*, 1968, **75**, 127–142.

Biederman, I. Perceiving real-world scenes. *Science*, 1972, **177**, 77–79.

Biederman, I. & Checkosky, S. F. Processing redundant information. *Journal of Experimental Psychology*, 1970, **83**, 486–490.

Bower, G. H. A multicomponent theory of the memory trace. In K. W. Spence & J. T. Spence (Eds.), *The psychology of learning and motivation*, Vol. 1. New York: Academic Press, 1967.

Bower, G. H. A selective review of organizational factors in memory. In E. Tulving & W. Donaldson (Eds.). *Organization and memory.* New York: Academic Press, 1972.

Bradshaw, J. L. & Wallace, G. Models for the processing and identification of faces. *Perception and Psychophysics*, 1971, **9**, 443–448.

Brand, J. Classification without identification in visual search. *Quarterly Journal of Experimental Psychology*, 1971, **23**, 178–186.

Broadbent, D. E. Word frequency effect and response bias. *Psychological Review*, 1967, **74**, 1–15.

Broadbent, D. E. & Gregory, M. H. P. Effects of tachistoscopic perception from independent variation of word probability and of letter probability. *Acta Psychologica*, 1971, **35**, 1–14.

Brown, B. R. & Dansereau, D. F. Functional equivalence between same–different classifications and judged similarity of Markov patterns. *Perception and Psychophysics*, 1970, **7**, 307–310.

Bruner, J. On perceptual readiness. *Psychological Review*, 1957, **64**, 123–152.

Bruner, J. S., Goodnow, J. J., & Austin, G. A. *A study of thinking.* New York: Wiley, 1956.

Caldwell, E. C. & Hall, V. C. Distinctive-features versus prototype learning reexamined. *Journal of Experimental Psychology*, 1970, **83**, 7–12.

Carroll, J. D. & Chang, J. J. Reanalysis of some color data of Helm's by INDSCAL procedure for individual differences multidimensional scaling. *Proceedings of the APA, 78th Annual Convention*, 1970. (a)

Carroll, J. D. & Chang, J. J. Analysis of individual differences in multidimensional scaling via an N-way generalization of "Eckart–Young" decomposition. *Psychometrika*, 1970, **35**, 283–319. (b)

Catlin, J. On the word-frequency effect. *Psychological Review*, 1969, **76**, 504–506.

Chase, W. G. & Calfee, R. C. Modality and similarity effects in short-term memory. *Journal of Experimental Psychology,* 1969, **81**, 510–514.

Checkosky, S. Speeded classification of multidimensional stimuli. *Journal of Experimental Psychology,* 1971, **87**, 313–318.

Chomsky, N. *Syntactic structures.* The Hague: Mouton, 1957.

Chomsky, N. *Language and mind.* New York: Harcourt, 1968.

Clowes, M. B. Perception, picture processing, and computers. In N. L. Collins & D. Michie (Eds.), *Machine intelligence,* Vol. 1. Amsterdam: Elsevier, 1967.

Clowes, M. B. Transformational grammars and the organization of pictures. In A. Grasselli (Ed.), *Automatic interpretation and classification of images.* New York: Academic Press, 1969.

Cohen, G. Some evidence for parallel comparisons in a letter recognition task. *Quarterly Journal of Experimental Psychology,* 1969, **21**, 272–279.

Cohen, R. L. & Granstrom, K. The role of verbalizing in the memorizing of conventional figures. *Journal of Verbal Learning and Verbal Behavior,* 1968, **7**, 380–383. (a)

Cohen, R. L. & Granstrom, K. Interpolated task and mode of recall as variables in STM for visual figures. *Journal of Verbal Learning and Verbal Behavior,* 1968, **7**, 653–658. (b)

Cohen, R. L. & Granstrom, K. Reproduction and recognition in short-term visual memory. *Quarterly Journal of Experimental Psychology,* 1970, **22**, 450–457.

Corcoran, D. W. J. & Rouse, R. O. An aspect of perceptual organization involved in reading typed and handwritten words. *Quarterly Journal of Experimental Psychology,* 1970, **22**, 526–530.

Dallett, K. & Wilcox, S. Remembering pictures vs. remembering descriptions. *Psychonomic Science,* 1968, **11**, 139–140.

Dick, A. O. Processing time for naming and categorization of letters and numbers. *Perception and Psychophysics,* 1971, **9**, 350–352.

Deutsch, J. A. A theory of shape recognition. *British Journal of Psychology,* 1955, **46**, 30–37.

Dodwell, P. C. Shape recognition in rats. *British Journal of Psychology,* 1957, **48**, 221–229.

Dodwell, P. C. *Visual pattern recognition.* New York: Holt, 1970.

Dumas, J. Scanning memory for multidimensional stimuli with extended practice. *Perception and Psychophysics,* 1972, **11**, 209–212.

Edwards, W. Conservatism in human information processing. In B. Kleinmuntz (Ed.), *Formal representation of human judgment.* New York: Wiley, 1968.

Egeth, H. W. Parallel vs. serial processes in multidimensional stimulus discrimination. *Perception and Psychophysics,* 1966, **1**, 245–252.

Egeth, H. & Blecker, D. Differential effects of familiarity on judgments of sameness and difference. *Perception and Psychophysics,* 1971, **9**, 321-326.

Egeth, H. & Smith, E. E. Perceptual selectivity in a visual recognition task. *Journal of Experimental Psychology,* 1967, **74**, 543–549.

Elkind, D. Developmental studies in figurative perception. In L. P. Lipsitt & H. W. Reese (Eds.), *Advances in child development and behavior,* Vol. 4. New York: Academic Press, 1969.

Eriksen, C. W. Temporal luminance summation effects in backward and forward masking. *Perception and Psychophysics,* 1966, **1**, 87–92.

Eriksen, C. W. & Collins, J. F. Sensory traces versus the psychological moment in the temporal organization of form. *Journal of Experimental Psychology*, 1968, **77**, 376–382.

Eriksen, C. W. & Spencer, T. Rate of information processing in visual perception: Some results and methodological considerations. *Journal of Experimental Psychology Monograph*, 1969, **79**, 1–16.

Estes, W. K. & Hopkins, B. L. Acquisition and transfer in pattern-vs.-component discrimination learning. *Journal of Experimental Psychology*, 1961, **61**, 322–328.

Estes, W. K. & Taylor, H. A. A detection method and probabilistic models for assessing information processing from brief visual displays. *Proceedings of the National Academy of Sciences*, 1964, **52**, 446–454.

Estes, W. K. & Taylor, H. A. Visual detection in relation to display size and redundancy of critical elements. *Perception and Psychophysics*, 1966, **1**, 9–16.

Evans, S. H. A brief statement of schema theory. *Psychonomic Science*, 1967, **8(2)**, 87–88.

Evans, T. G. Descriptive pattern-analysis techniques: Potentialities and problems. In S. Watanabe (Ed.), *Methodologies of pattern recognition*. New York: Academic Press, 1969.

Fagan, J. F. Memory in the infant. *Journal of Experimental Child Psychology*, 1970, **9**, 217–226.

Fagan, J. F. Infant's recognition memory for faces. *Journal of Experimental Child Psychology*, 1972, **14**, 453–472.

Fellows, B. *The discrimination process and development*. Oxford: Pergamon Press, 1968.

Franks, J. J. & Bransford, J. D. Abstraction of visual patterns. *Journal of Experimental Psychology*, 1971, **90**, 65–74.

Friedman, M. P., Reed, S. K., & Carterette, E. C. Feature saliency and recognition memory for schematic faces. *Perception and Psychophysics*, 1971, **10**, 47–50.

Friedman, M. P., Trabasso, T., & Mosberg, L. Tests of a mixed model for paired-associates learning with overlapping stimuli, *Journal of Mathematical Psychology*, 1967, **4**, 316–334.

Frost, N. Contributions of visual and semantic codes to memory for pictures. Unpublished doctoral dissertation, University of Oregon, 1971.

Fu, K. S. On syntactic pattern recognition and stochastic languages. In S. Watanabe (Ed.), *Frontiers of pattern recognition*. Academic Press, 1972.

Garner, W. R. The stimulus in information processing. *American Psychologist*, 1970, **25**, 350–358.

Ghent, L. Perception of overlapping and embedded figures by children of different ages. *American Journal of Psychology*, 1956, **69**, 574–587.

Gibson, E. Perceptual learning. *Annual Review of Psychology*, 1963, **14**, 29–56.

Gibson, E. *Principles of perceptual learning and development*. New York: Appleton, 1969.

Gibson, E. J., Osser, H., Schiff, W., & Smith, J. An analysis of critical features of letters, tested by a confusion matrix. In *A basic research program on reading*. Cooperative Research Project No. 639, U.S. Office of Education, 1963.

Gibson, E. J., Pick, A., Osser, H., & Hammond, M. The role of grapheme–phoneme correspondence in the perception of words. *American Journal of Psychology*, 1962, **75**, 554–570.

Gibson, E., Schapiro, F., & Yonas, A. Confusion matrices for graphic patterns obtained with a latency measure. *The analysis of reading skill: A program of basic and applied research.* Final report, project No. 5-1213, Cornell University and USOE, 1968. Pp. 76–96.

Gibson, J. J. *The senses considered as perceptual systems.* Boston: Houghton-Mifflin, 1966.

Gibson, J. J. & Gibson, E. Perceptual learning: Differentiation or enrichment? *Psychological Review,* 1955, **62**, 32–41.

Glanzer, M. & Clark, W. H. The verbal-loop hypothesis: Conventional figures. *American Journal of Psychology,* 1964, **77**, 621–626.

Goldiamond, I. & Hawkins, W. F. Vexierversuch: The log relationship between word frequency and recognition in the absence of stimulus words. *Journal of Experimental Psychology,* 1958, **56**, 457–463.

Goldstein, A. G. & Chance, J. E. Visual recognition memory for complex configurations. *Perception and Psychophysics,* 1971, 9, 237–241.

Goldstein, A. G. & Mackenberg, E. Recognition of human faces from isolated facial features: A developmental study. *Psychonomic Science,* 1966, **6**, 149–150.

Goldstein, A. J., Harmon, L. D., & Lesk, A. B. Man–machine interaction in human-face identification. *The Bell System Technical Journal,* 1972, **51**, 399–427.

Gottschaldt, K. Gestalt factors in repetition. *Psychologische Forschung,* 1926, **8**, 261–318.

Gregg, L. W. & Simon, H. A. Process models and stochastic theories of simple concept formation. *Journal of Mathematical Psychology,* 1967, 4, 246–276.

Grill, D. P. Variables influencing the mode of processing of complex stimuli. *Perception and Psychophysics,* 1971, **10**, 51–57.

Guzmán, A. Decomposition of a visual scene into three-dimensional bodies. In A. Grasselli (Ed.), *Automatic interpretation and classification of images.* New York: Academic Press, 1969.

Haber, R. N. The effects of coding strategy on perceptual memory. *Journal of Experimental Psychology,* 1964, **68**, 357–362.

Haber, R. N. Effect of prior knowledge of the stimulus on word-recognition process. *Journal of Experimental Psychology,* 1965, **69**, 282–286.

Haber, R. N. Nature of the effect of set on perception. *Psychological Review,* 1966, **73**, 335–351.

Haber, R. N. Introduction. In R. N. Haber (Ed.), *Information-processing approaches to visual perception.* New York: Holt, 1969.

Haber, R. N. Where are the visions in visual perception? In S. J. Segal (Ed.), *Imagery: Current cognitive approaches.* New York: Academic Press, 1971.

Halle, M. & Stevens, K. Speech recognition: A model and program for research. *IRE Transactions on Information Theory,* 1962, **IT-8**, 155–159.

Harris, C. S. & Haber, R. N. Selective attention and coding in visual perception. *Journal of Experimental Psychology,* 1963, **65**, 328–333.

Hebb, D. O. *The organization of behavior.* New York: Wiley, 1949.

Hochberg, J. Attention, organization, and consciousness. In D. I. Mostofsky (Ed.), *Attention: Contemporary theory and analysis.* New York: Appleton, 1970.

Hochberg, J. & Brooks, V. The psychophysics of form: Reversible perspective drawings of spatial objects. *American Journal of Psychology,* 1960, **73**, 337–354.

Howes, D. H. & Solomon, R. L. Visual duration threshold as a function of word probability. *Journal of Experimental Psychology,* 1951, **41**, 401–410.

Hubel, D. H. & Wiesel, T. N. Receptive fields, binocular interaction and functional architecture in the cat's visual cortex. *Journal of Physiology,* 1962, **160**, 106–154.

Ingling, N. W. Categorization: A mechanism for rapid information processing. *Journal of Experimental Psychology,* 1972, **94,** 239–243.

Jackson, R. H. & Dick, A. O. Visual summation and its relation to processing and memory. *Perception and Psychophysics,* 1969, **6,** 13–15.

Jakobson, R., Fant, G. G. M., & Halle, M. Preliminaries to speech analysis. MIT. Acoustical Lab Technical Report, No. 13, 1952.

Jakobson, R., Fant, G. G. M., & Halle, M. *Preliminaries to speech analysis: The distinctive features and their correlates.* Cambridge, Massachusetts: MIT Press, 1961.

Jonides, J. & Gleitman, H. A conceptual category effect in visual search: O as letter or as digit. *Perception and Psychophysics,* 1972, **12,** 457–460.

Joula, J. F., Fischler, I., Wood, C. T., & Atkinson, R. C. Recognition time for information stored in long-term memory. *Perception and Psychophysics,* 1971, **10,** 8–14.

Kahneman, D. Methods, findings, and theory in studies of visual masking. *Psychological Bulletin,* 1968, **70,** 404–425.

Kanal, L. & Chandrasekaran, B. On linguistic, statistical and mixed models for pattern recognition. In S. Watanabe (Ed.), *Frontiers of pattern recognition.* New York: Academic Press, 1972.

Kaplan, G. A., Yonas, A., & Shurcliff, A. Visual and acoustic confusability in a visual search task. *Perception and Psychophysics,* 1966, **1,** 172–174.

Kaufman, L. & Richards, W. Spontaneous fixation tendencies for visual forms. *Perception and Psychophysics,* 1969, **5,** 85–88.

King-Ellison, P. & Jenkins, J. J. The durational threshold of visual recognition as a function of word frequency. *American Journal of Psychology,* 1954, **67,** 700–703.

Kinsbourne, M. & Warrington, E. K. The effect of an aftercoming random pattern on the perception of brief visual stimuli. *Quarterly Journal of Experimental Psychology,* 1962, **14,** 223–234.

Kruskal, J. B. Multidimensional scaling by optimizing goodness of fit to a nonmetric hypothesis. *Psychometrika,* 1964, **29,** 1–27.

Kubovy, M., Rapoport, A., & Tversky, A. Deterministic vs. probabilistic strategies in detection. *Perception and Psychophysics,* 1971, **9,** 427–429.

Laughery, K. R. Computer simulation of short-term memory: A component decay model. In G. H. Bower & J. T. Spence (Eds.), *The psychology of learning and motivation,* Vol. 3. New York: Academic Press, 1969.

Lawrence, D. H. & Coles, G. R. Accuracy of recognition with alternatives before and after the stimulus. *Journal of Experimental Psychology,* 1954, **47,** 208–214.

Lawrence, D. H. & LaBerge, D. L. Relationships between recognition accuracy and order of reporting stimulus dimensions. *Journal of Experimental Psychology,* 1956, **51,** 12–18.

Lee, W. Choosing among confusably distributed stimuli with specified likelihood ratios. *Perceptual and Motor Skills,* 1963, **16,** 445–467.

Lee, W. & Janke, M. Categorizing externally distributed stimulus samples for three continua. *Journal of Experimental Psychology,* 1964, **68,** 376–382.

Leeuwenberg, E. L. J. *Structural information of visual patterns.* The Hague: Mouton, 1968.

Lindsay, P. H. & Norman, D. A. *Human information processing.* New York: Academic Press, 1972.

Lindsay, R. K. & Lindsay, J. M. Reaction time and serial vs. parallel information processing. *Journal of Experimental Psychology,* 1966, **71,** 294–303.

Liss, P. Does backward masking by visual noise stop stimulus processing? *Perception and Psychophysics*, 1968, 4, 328–330.

Long, E. R., Henneman, R. H., & Garvey, W. D. An experimental analysis of set: The role of sense modality. *American Journal of Psychology*, 1960, 73, 563–567.

Long, E. R., Reid, L. S., & Henneman, R. H. An experimental analysis of set variables influencing the identification of ambiguous, visual stimulus objects. *American Journal of Psychology*, 1960, 73, 563–567.

Luce, R. D. *Individual choice behavior.* New York: Wiley, 1959.

Luce, R. D. Detection and recognition. In R. D. Luce, R. R. Bush, & E. Galanter (Eds.), *Handbook of mathematical psychology*, Vol. 1. New York: Wiley, 1963.

Luce, R. D. Learned versus optimizing behavior in simple situations. In M. W. Shelly & G. L. Bryan (Eds.), *Human judgments and optimality.* New York: Wiley, 1964.

Maccoby, E. E. What copying requires. *Ontario Journal of Educational Research*, 1968, 10, 163–170.

MacLeod, I. On finding structure in patterns. In S. Kaneff (Ed.), *Picture language machines.* New York: Academic Press, 1971.

Marcel, A. J. Some constraints on sequential and parallel processing, and the limits of attention. In A. F. Sanders (Ed.), Attention and performance III, *Acta Psychologica*, 1970, 33, 77–93.

McIntyre, C., Fox, R., & Neale, J. Effects of noise similarity and redundancy on the information processed from brief visual displays. *Perception and Psychophysics*, 1970, 7, 328–332.

Mermelstein, P. & Eden, M. Experiments on computer recognition of handwritten words. *Information and Control*, 1964, 7, 255–270.

Minsky, M. & Papert, S. *Perceptrons.* Cambridge, Massachusetts: MIT Press, 1969.

Moray, N. *Attention: Selective processes in vision and hearing.* London: Hutchinson, 1969.

Morin, R. E., Derosa, D. V., & Stultz, V. Recognition memory and reaction time. In A. F. Sanders (Ed.), Attention and performance, *Acta Psychologica*, 1967, 27, 298–305.

Nakatani, L. H. Comments on Broadbent's response bias model for stimulus recognition. *Psychological Review*, 1970, 77, 574–576.

Nakatani, L. H. Confusion-choice model for multidimensional psychophysics. *Journal of Mathematical Psychology*, 1972, 9, 104–127.

Narasimhan, R. A linguistic approach to pattern recognition. Report No. 121, Digital Computer Laboratory, Univ. of Illinois, 1962.

Narasimhan, R. On the description, generation, and recognition of classes of pictures. In A. Grasselli (Ed.), *Automatic interpretation and classification of images.* New York: Academic Press, 1969.

Narasimhan, R. & Reddy, V. S. N. A generative model for handprinted English letters and its computer implementation. *ICC Bulletin*, 1967, 6, 275–287.

Neisser, U. Decision time without reaction time: Experiments in visual scanning. *American Journal of Psychology*, 1963, 76, 376–385.

Neisser, U. *Cognitive psychology.* New York: Appleton, 1967.

Neisser, U. & Beller, H. K. Searching through word lists. *British Journal of Psychology*, 1965, 56, 349–358.

Neisser, U., Novick, R., & Lazar, R. Searching for ten targets simultaneously. *Perceptual and Motor Skills*, 1963, 17, 955–961.

Nickerson, R. S. Short-term memory for complex meaningful visual configurations: A demonstration of capacity. *Canadian Journal of Psychology,* 1965, **19,** 155–160.

Nickerson, R. S. Same–different reaction times with multi-attribute stimulus differences. *Perceptual and Motor Skills,* 1967, **24,** 543–554.

Nickerson, R. S. Binary-classification reaction time: A review of some studies of human information-processing capabilities. *Psychonomic Monograph Supplements,* 1972, **4,** No. 17, 275–318.

Nickerson, R. S. The use of binary-classification tasks in the study of human information processing. In S. Kornblum (Ed.), *Attention and performance IV.* New York: Academic Press, 1973.

Nilsson, N. J. *Learning machines.* New York: McGraw-Hill, 1965.

Norman, D. A. *Memory and attention.* New York: Wiley, 1969.

Norman, D. A. & Rumelhart, D. E. A system for perception and memory. In D. A. Norman (Ed.), *Models of human memory.* New York: Academic Press, 1970.

Noton, D. A theory of visual pattern perception. *IEEE Transactions on Systems Science and Cybernetics,* 1970, **6,** 349–357.

Odom, R. D. Effects of perceptual salience on the recall of relevant and incidental dimensional values: A developmental study. *Journal of Experimental Psychology,* 1972, **92,** 285–291.

Paivio, A. *Imagery and verbal processes.* New York: Holt, 1971.

Paivio, A. & Csapo, K. Concrete image and verbal memory codes. *Journal of Experimental Psychology,* 1969, **80,** 279–285.

Parks, T. E., Kroll, N. E., Salzberg, P. M., & Parkinson, S. R. Persistence of visual memory as indicated by decision time in a matching task. *Journal of Experimental Psychology,* 1972, **92,** 437–438.

Phillips, W. A. & Baddeley, A. D. Reaction time and short-term visual memory. *Psychonomic Science,* 1971, **22,** 73–74.

Pick, A. Improvement of visual and tactual form discrimination. *Journal of Experimental Psychology,* 1965, **69,** 331–339.

Pierce, J. Some resources of artifact in studies of tachistoscopic perception of words. *Journal of Experimental Psychology,* 1963, **66,** 363–370.

Pollack, I., Rubenstein, H., & Decker, L. Intelligibility of known and unknown message sets. *Journal of the Acoustical Society of America,* 1959, **31,** 273–279.

Posner, M. I. Abstraction and the process of recognition. In G. H. Bower & J. T. Spence (Eds.), *Psychology of learning and motivation,* Vol. 3. New York: Academic Press, 1969.

Posner, M. I., Boies, S. J., Eichelman, W. H., & Taylor, R. L. Retention of visual and name codes of single letters. *Journal of Experimental Psychology Monograph,* 1969, **79,** 1–13.

Posner, M. I., Goldsmith, R., & Welton, K. E. Perceived distance and the classification of distorted patterns. *Journal of Experimental Psychology,* 1967, **73,** 28–38.

Posner, M. I. & Keele, S. W. On the genesis of abstract ideas. *Journal of Experimental Psychology,* 1968, **77,** 353–363.

Posner, M. I. & Mitchell, R. F. Chronometric analysis of classification. *Psychological Review,* 1967, **74,** 392–409.

Postman, L. & Rosenzweig, M. R. Perceptual recognition of words. *Journal of Speech Disturbances,* 1957, **22,** 245–253.

Rabbitt, P. M. Learning to ignore irrelevant information. *American Journal of Psychology,* 1967, **80,** 1–13.

Reed, S. K. Structural models and the encoding of line patterns. Laboratory of Experimental Psychology, Univ. of Sussex, 1971.

Reed, S. K. Pattern recognition and categorization. *Cognitive Psychology*, 1972, 3, 382–407.

Reed, S. K. & Angaran, A. J. Structural models and embedded figure difficulty for normal and retarded children. *Perceptual and Motor Skills*, 1972, 35, 155–164.

Reid, L. S., Henneman, R. H., & Long, E. R. An experimental analysis of set: The effect of categorical restriction. *American Journal of Psychology*, 1960, 73, 568–572.

Rodwan, A. S. & Hake, H. W. The discriminant function as a model for perception. *American Journal of Psychology*, 1964, 77, 380–392.

Rosch, E. H. On the internal structure of perceptual and semantic categories. In T. M. Moore (Ed.), *Cognitive development and the acquisition of language*. New York: Academic Press, 1973.

Royer, F. Spatial orientational and figural information in free recall of visual figures. *Journal of Experimental Psychology*, 1971, 91, 326–332.

Rumelhart, D. E. A multicomponent theory of perception of briefly exposed visual displays. *Journal of Mathematical Psychology*, 1970, 7, 191–218.

Rumelhart, D. E. A multicomponent theory of confusion among briefly exposed alphabetic characters. Technical Report 22, University of California, San Diego, 1971.

Rumelhart, D. E., Lindsay, P. H., & Norman, D. A. A process model for long-term memory. In E. Tulving & W. Donaldson (Eds.), *Organization and memory*. New York: Academic Press, 1972.

Saltz, E. & Sigel, I. Concept overdiscrimination in children. *Journal of Experimental Psychology*, 1967, 73, 1–8.

Sanders, A. F. Short term memory for spatial positions. *Nederlands Tijdshrift voor de Psychologie*, 1968, 23, 1–15.

Sanders, A. F., & Schroots, J. J. F. Cognitive categories and memory span III. Effects of similarity on recall. *The Quarterly Journal of Experimental Psychology*, 1969, 21, 21–28.

Sebestyen, G. S. *Decision-making processes in pattern recognition*. New York: Macmillan, 1962.

Selfridge, O. G. Pandemonium: A paradigm for learning. In *The mechanization of thought processes*. London: Her Majesty's Stationery Office, 1959.

Selfridge, O. & Neisser, U. Pattern recognition by machine. *Scientific American*, 1960, 203, 60–68.

Shaffer, W. O. & Shiffrin, R. M. Rehearsal and storage of visual information. *Journal of Experimental Psychology*, 1972, 92, 292–296.

Shepard, R. N. The analysis of proximities: Multidimensional scaling with an unknown distance function. I. *Psychometrika*, 1962, 27, 125–140; II. *Psychometrika*, 1962, 27, 219–246.

Shepard, R. N. Attention and the metric structure of the stimulus space. *Journal of Mathematical Psychology*, 1964, 1, 54–87.

Shepard, R. N. Recognition memory for words, sentences, and pictures. *Journal of Verbal Learning and Verbal Behavior*, 1967, 6, 156–163.

Shepard, R. N., & Chang, J. Stimulus generalization in the learning of classifications. *Journal of Experimental Psychology*, 1963, 65, 94–102.

Shepard, R. N., & Chipman, S. Second-order isomorphism and internal representations: Shapes of states. *Cognitive Psychology*, 1970, 1, 1–17.

Shepard, R. N., Hovland, C. J., & Jenkins, H. M. Learning and memorization of classifications. *Psychological Monographs*, 1961, **75**, No. 13 (Whole No. 517).

Shepard, R. N. & Metzler, J. Mental rotation of three dimensional objects. *Science*, 1971, **171**, 701–703.

Shriffrin, R. M. & Atkinson, R. C. Storage and retrieval processes in long-term memory. *Psychological Review*, 1969, **76**, 179–193.

Shiffrin, R. M. & Gardner, G. T. Visual processing capacity and attentional control. *Journal of Experimental Psychology*, 1972, **93**, 72–82.

Slovic, P. & Lichtenstein, S. Comparison of Bayesian and regression approaches to the study of information processing in judgment. *Organizational behavior and human performance*, 1971, **6**, 649–744.

Smith, E. E. Choice reaction time: An analysis of major theoretical positions. *Psychological Bulletin*, 1968, **69**, 77–110.

Smith, E. E. & Nielsen, G. D. Representations and retrieval processes in short-term memory: Recognition and recall of faces. *Journal of Experimental Psychology*, 1970, **85**, 397–405.

Solomon, R. L. & Postman, L. Frequency of usage as a determinant of recognition threshold of words. *Journal of Experimental Psychology*, 1952, **43**, 195–201.

Spence, J. T. Contribution of response bias to recognition thresholds. *Journal of Abnormal and Social Psychology*, 1963, **66**, 339–344.

Sperling, G. The information available in brief visual presentations. *Psychological Monographs*, 1960, **74**, No. 11 (Whole No. 498).

Sperling, G. A model for visual memory tasks. *Human Factors*, 1963, **5**, 19–31.

Sperling, G. Successive approximations to a model for short-term memory. *Acta Psychologica*, 1967, **27**, 285–292.

Sperling, G., Budiansky, J., Spivak, J., & Johnson, M. Extremely rapid visual search: The maximum rate of scanning letters for the presence of a numeral. *Science*, 1971, **174**, 307–311.

Sperling, G. & Speelman, R. G. Acoustic similarity and auditory short-term memory: Experiments and a model. In D. A. Norman (Ed.), *Models of human memory*. New York: Academic Press, 1970.

Standing, L., Conezio, J., & Haber, R. N. Perception and memory for pictures: Single-trial learning of 2560 visual stimuli. *Psychonomic Science*, 1970, **19**, 73–74.

Sternberg, S. High-speed scanning in human memory. *Science*, 1966, **153**, 652–654.

Sternberg, S. Two operations in character recognition: Some evidence from reaction time measurements. *Perception and Psychophysics*, 1967, **2**, 45–53. (a)

Sternberg, S. Retrieval of contextual information from memory. *Psychonomic Science*, 1967, **8**, 55–56. (b)

Sternberg, S. Memory-scanning: Mental processes revealed by reaction-time experiments. *American Scientist*, 1969, **57**, 421–457.

Stevens, S. S. Mathematics, measurement, and psychophysics. In S. S. Stevens (Ed.), *Handbook of experimental psychology*. New York: Wiley, 1951.

Sutherland, N. S. Visual discrimination of orientation and shape by the octopus. *Nature*, 1957, **179**, 11.

Sutherland, N. S. Stimulus analyzing mechanisms. *Proceedings of a symposium on the mechanization of thought processes*. London: Her Majesty's Stationery Office, 1959.

Sutherland, N. S. Outlines of a theory of visual pattern recognition in animals and man. *Proceedings of the Royal Society*, 1968, **171**, 297–317.

Sutherland, N. S. Object recognition. In E. C. Carterette & M. P. Friedman (Eds.), *Handbook of perception*, Vol. 3. New York: Academic Press, 1973.

Thompson, J. H. What happens to the stimulus in backward masking? *Journal of Experimental Psychology*, 1966, **71**, 580–586.

Tighe, T. J. & Tighe, L. S. Perceptual learning in the discrimination processes of children: An analysis of five variables in perceptual pretraining. *Journal of Experimental Psychology*, 1968, **77**, 125–134.

Torgerson, W. S. *Theory and methods of scaling*. New York: Wiley, 1958.

Townsend, J. T. Theoretical analysis of an alphabetic confusion matrix. *Perception and Psychophysics*, 1971, **9**, 40–50. (a)

Townsend, J. T. A note on the identifiability of parallel and serial processes. *Perception and Psychophysics*, 1971, **10**, 161–163. (b)

Trabasso, T. & Bower, G. H. *Attention in learning: Theory and research*. New York: Wiley, 1968.

Treisman, M. On the word frequency effect: Comments on the papers by J. Catlin and L. H. Nakatani, *Psychological Review*, 1971, **78**, 420–425.

Tulving, E. & Donaldson, W. (Eds.) *Organization and memory*. New York: Academic Press, 1972.

Tversky, A. & Krantz, D. H. Similarity of schematic faces: A test of interdimensional additivity. *Perception and Psychophysics*, 1969, **5**, 124–128.

Tversky, B. Pictorial and verbal encoding in a short-term memory task. *Perception and Psychophysics*, 1969, **6**, 225–233.

Uttley, A. M. Conditional probability machines and conditioned reflexes. In C. E. Shannon & J. McCarthy (Eds.), *Automatic studies*. Princeton, New Jersey: Princeton Univ. Press, 1956, 253–275.

Vitz, P. C. & Todd, T. C. A model of the perception of simple geometric figures. *Psychological Review*, 1971, **78**, 207–228.

Vurpillot, E. The development of scanning strategies and their relation to visual differentiation. *Journal of Experimental Child Psychology*, 1968, **6**, 622–650.

Wickelgren, W. A. Acoustic similarity and intrusion errors in short-term memory. *Journal of Experimental Psychology*, 1965, **70**, 102–108.

Winston, P. H. Learning structural descriptions from examples. Report MAC TR-76, Massachusetts Institute of Technology, 1970.

Werner, H. Studies on contour: I. Quantitative analyses. *American Journal of Psychology*, 1935, **47**, 40–64.

Wolford, G. L., Wessel, D. L., & Estes, W. K. Further evidence concerning scanning and sampling assumptions of visual detection models. *Perception and Psychophysics*, 1968, **3**, 439–444.

Yonas, A. The acquisition of information processing strategies in a time-dependent task. Unpublished doctoral dissertation, Cornell Univ., 1969.

Zusne, L. *Visual perception of form*. New York: Academic Press, 1970.

Index

A

Abstract image, 4, 12, 13, 26–32, 132, 166, 178, 182, 183, 225
Aderman, D., 198, 199, 205
Aiken, E. G., 20, 25
Aiken, L. S., 164, 165
Analysis, 49, 50, 216–220 see also *Analysis-by-synthesis*
Analysis-by-synthesis, 7, 215–220
Anderson, N. H., 169
Anderson, T. W., 166
Angaran, A. J., 36, 51
Artificial intelligence, 39–44, 168, 170, 179, 183–187, 216, 217
Ashby, R. C., 17
Asso, D., 37–39
Atkinson, R. C., 2, 3, 60, 70, 71, 122, 123
Attention, see, Capacity, perceptual; Features, learning; Rehearsal, visual
Attneave, F., 27–29, 31, 33, 175
Austin, G., 169

B

Baddeley, A., 119
Bahrick, H. P., 133–136
Bahrick, P., 133, 134
Bamber, D., 60
Bartlett, F. C., 26
Bartram, D., 225
Beach, L. R., 168
Beals, R., 186
Beller, H., 80, 81, 83
Bias, see Response bias
Biederman, I., 61, 62, 195–197
Blecker, D., 65
Boies, S., 116, 117
Boucher, B., 134–136
Bower, G. H., 139, 140, 144, 145, 148, 152
Bradshaw, J. L., 62, 63
Brand, J., 82–84
Bransford, J. D., 28, 29, 33, 132